Economic
Development of
Korea

Economic
Development of
Korea

Chuk Kyo Kim
Hanyang University, South Korea

World Scientific

NEW JERSEY · LONDON · SINGAPORE · BEIJING · SHANGHAI · HONG KONG · TAIPEI · CHENNAI · TOKYO

Published by

World Scientific Publishing Co. Pte. Ltd.

5 Toh Tuck Link, Singapore 596224

USA office: 27 Warren Street, Suite 401-402, Hackensack, NJ 07601

UK office: 57 Shelton Street, Covent Garden, London WC2H 9HE

Library of Congress Cataloging-in-Publication Data
Names: Kim, Chuk Kyo, author.
Title: Economic development of Korea / Chuk Kyo Kim.
Description: New Jersey : World Scientific, [2019]
Identifiers: LCCN 2018045372 | ISBN 9789813274907
Subjects: LCSH: Economic development--Korea (South)--History. | Korea (South)--
    Economic conditions. | Korea (South)--Economic policy.
Classification: LCC HC467.756 .K549 2019 | DDC 338.95195--dc23
LC record available at https://lccn.loc.gov/2018045372

British Library Cataloguing-in-Publication Data
A catalogue record for this book is available from the British Library.

For any available supplementary material, please visit
https://www.worldscientific.com/worldscibooks/10.1142/11117#t=suppl

Desk Editor: Lum Pui Yee

Typeset by Stallion Press
Email: enquiries@stallionpress.com

Printed in Singapore

Contents

About the Author

Chuk Kyo Kim is a Professor Emeritus of Economics at the College of Economics and Finance, Hanyang University. He was Senior Fellow and Research Director at the Korea Development Institute (1971–1979), Vice President of the Korea International Economic Institute (1979–1981), and the founding president of the Korea Institute for International Economic Policy (1989–1992). He participated in the formulation of Korea's five-year development plans and worked in the capacity of advisor for several agencies of Korean government, including the Economic Planning Board, Ministry of Finance, Ministry of Trade, Industry, and Energy, Ministry of Science and Technology, and the Ministry of Finance and Economy until the early 1990s.

He served as President of the Korea International Economic Association in 1986. He also co-authored the book *Public Finances during the Korean Modernization Process* published by the Harvard University Press in 1986. Over the years, Dr. Kim has worked as a consultant for various international organizations (the ADB, UNDP, UNIDO, UNSFIR) as well as for KOICA and shared his expertise with several developing nations, from China, Indonesia, Malaysia, Vietnam, to Sri Lanka, Costa Rica, Uzbekistan, and Paraguay. He has published numerous papers and books on Korea's economic development.

Acknowledgments

I am indebted to many of my former colleagues and associates at the Korea Development Institute (KDI), Korea International Economic Institute (the present Korea Institute for Industrial Economics and Trade, KIET), and Korea Institute for International Economic Policy (KIEP), who provided invaluable assistance in writing some of the chapters included in this book. I cannot acknowledge all of them individually but would like to express my deep gratitude particularly to Dr. Chul Hong, Prof. Jae Won Kim, Prof. Chan Hyun Son, Prof. Joon Sung Park, Dr. Kyu Ho Hwang, and Dr. Hyunjoo Ryou of the Bank of Korea for their contributions.

I would also like to take this opportunity to express my gratitude to international organizations including the Asian Development Bank, UNDP, UNIDO, and KOICA for giving me opportunities to work for developing countries, which greatly enriched my knowledge on development policy issue. I am grateful to the numerous government officials and staff of central bank in China, Costa Rica, Indonesia, Malaysia, Sri Lanka, Paraguay, Vietnam, and Uzbekistan for their support and cooperation while I was working as a consultant for their governments.

I am indebted to Prof. Hong Yul Han, Prof. Hyoung Soo Zang, Dr. Choong Kyu Choi, and Dr. Jong Wook Won for reading earlier drafts of this book and making useful comments which greatly contributed to improving the quality of this book. Ms. Suna Park at the Institute of Economic Research of Hanyang University helped me greatly by gathering and tabulating data. My special thanks go to editorial staff of KIEP for their competent and efficient works.

Introduction

This book is a revised and updated version of the author's earlier work on the same subject, the second edition of which was published in Korean in 2016. Although much has been written on the development of the Korean economy, few publications have analyzed the development of the Korean economy from a historical perspective covering the post-crisis period and are, at the same time, not heavy and readable.

The purpose of this book is to provide a systematic and policy-focused analysis of Korea's development performance from a historical perspective. Although this book draws on the Korean edition, it has been revised, improved, and updated to reflect recent developments in the Korean economy. It analyzes how Korea advanced from the least developed to the developed country stage within a relatively short period, what the underlying factors were, and what lessons can be drawn from the Korean experience. The book covers a wide range of issues including the role of government, capital accumulation, growth and structural change, industrial development and concentration, economic liberalization, human resource and technology development, social development, and income distribution.

This book consists of 14 chapters. A brief historical overview of the development process is presented in the first chapter, followed by a discussion on the role of the government in the second chapter in terms of policy responses to changing economic circumstances.

Since Korea's rapid growth is due largely to capital accumulation, Chapter 3 deals with the accumulation process in terms of savings and investment rates, the role of financial institutions, and the efficiency of investment in growth process.

The growth and structural change of the economy is analyzed in Chapter 4, in which sources of growth are examined through quantitative as well as qualitative analysis. Since the quantitative analysis based on growth accounting is too simple to explain the complex long-term growth process, it is complemented by qualitative analysis based on the major institutional and policy factors considered critical for the successful implementation of development policy.

Chapter 5 is devoted to a discussion of industrial development policy and analyzes how it evolved over time, what the industrial incentive system looked like at different stages of industrial development, and its impact on industrial growth and structural transformation. The growth strategy of transforming industries from import substituting into export-oriented industries is also examined in the context of nondurable consumer goods, durable consumer goods and intermediate goods, and capital goods.

The Korean model of industrialization is often described as one centered on large-scale enterprises (LSEs), for the development policy greatly favored large firms while discriminating against small and medium-sized enterprises (SMEs). Accordingly, Chapter 6 investigates the impact of industrial policy on SMEs development, and the policy response that attempted to remedy the unbalanced growth between LSEs and SMEs. SME development policy and the problems faced by SMEs are also critically reviewed with some policy suggestions.

Although Korea's development policy was very successful in terms of growth and structural transformation, it was accompanied by a number of undesirable side effects, one of which was the concentration of economic power in the hands of big business groups known as *chaebols*. The chaebol concentration is analyzed in Chapter 7 in terms of size of chaebols in the economy, their business diversification and corporate ownership, followed by a discussion on government policy aiming to control the chaebols.

Chapter 8 discusses liberalization policy, first providing a historical overview on the subject, followed by a discussion of major features, sequence of the liberalization process, and its economic consequence. One important consequence associated with liberalization policy was the 1997 financial crisis, which had a far-reaching impact on the Korean economy.

Chapter 9 is thus devoted to a discussion of the causes of the crisis and the government's policy response. The causes of the crisis are examined in terms of structural weaknesses of the economy and underlying institutional problems which played no less an important role in bringing about the financial crisis. The IMF intervention and government policy response are further examined in terms of sectoral reforms accompanied by discussion of achievements and limitations.

Education and human resource development is discussed in Chapter 10, in which Korea's rapid educational expansion is reviewed in terms of education level, educational spending and attainment, followed by a discussion of educational contribution to economic growth. Chapter 11 is devoted to a discussion of the role of science and technology policy in industrial development and analyzes in detail the policy measures that promoted industrial innovation at different stages of industrial development, followed by a discussion of their achievements and constraints.

The 1997 financial crisis and its impact on poverty and distribution led the government to shift the policy from growth to income distribution and welfare. Chapter 12 is thus devoted to discussion of social development and income distribution. It begins with a review on the evolution of social development policy over the past half century, followed by discussion of the growing income inequality following the financial crisis and the policy response to correct it. While Korea's overall income distribution is acceptable by international comparison, it is evident that the polarization of income distribution has deepened due to the growing income gap between the rich and poor.

Chapter 13 is devoted to a discussion on the potential growth rate, which has been falling steadily since the early 1990s. This trend is examined in terms of factor inputs and productivity growth, followed by a discussion on policy directions for enhancing potential growth. It has been pointed out that Korea's potential growth rate is likely to decline further, largely due to the rapidly aging population and related structural problems. Therefore, suggested measures include comprehensive structural reforms aimed at increasing labor supply and stimulating investment, upgrading human capital formation and enhancing the efficiency of R&D, and promoting new growth industries including the service sector. The characteristics of the Korean development model and the lessons it conveys are briefly summarized in the Chapter 14.

Chapter 1

A Historical Overview

1.1 Post-War Reconstruction and Foreign Aid (1950s)

Korea was divided into South and North following its liberation from Japanese colonial rule in 1945. As most mining and manufacturing industries were located in the northern part of the Korean Peninsula, the division of the country made the South (the Republic of Korea) an agriculture-based, resource-poor country. The Korean War, which broke out in 1950 and lasted for 3 years, caused tremendous human and physical damages. Out of population of 20 million, over a million South Korean civilians died or went missing. Almost half of the nation's manufacturing capacity, railroad network, and electricity generation capacity were destroyed, not to mention the destruction of urban housing, roads, and other infrastructure.

The total damages were estimated higher than the GNP in 1953.[1] Thus, the Korean government gave top priority to the reconstruction of infrastructure and factories destroyed during the war. Korea relied heavily on foreign assistance to rehabilitate the economy. From 1945 to 1960, the total foreign aid to Korea amounted to USD 2,935.7 million, out of which USD 2,356.3 million was contributed by the United States, accounting for 80 percent of total aid received (Table 1.1). The rest was provided by the United Nations. The foreign aid accounted, on average, for as much as 8.2 percent of GNP and financed 74.2 percent of imports during this period.

---

[1]For a detailed explanation, see Kim (2012, pp. 10–11).

1

Table 1.1   Foreign Aid Received, 1945–1960 (Unit: USD million)

	US	UN	Total
1945–1952	611.0	241.4	852.4
1953–1960	1,745.3	338.0	2,083.3
1945–1960	2,356.3	579.4	2,935.7

Sources: Lee (2002, p. 341) for 1945–1952; Krueger (1979, p. 67) for 1953–1960.

Table 1.2   Foreign Aid and the National Economy, 1951–1960 (Unit: percent)

	1953	1954	1955	1956	1957	1958	1959	1960	1953–1960 Average
Aid/Import	58.3	73.9	69.3	76.1	86.6	84.9	73.1	71.4	74.2
Import/GNP	12.9	7.3	9.8	13.1	12.0	10.7	10.1	12.6	11.1
Aid/GNP	7.5	5.4	6.8	10.0	10.4	9.1	7.4	9.0	8.2
Counterpart Fund/Gov't Rev.	11.9	29.9[a]	46.5[b]	—	52.9	51.5	41.6	34.6	38.4

Notes: [a] 15 months from April 1954 to June 1955.
[b] 18 months from July 1955 to December 1956.
Sources: Krueger (1979, p. 67); Bahl *et al.* (1986, p. 227).

The counterpart fund generated by the sales of aid goods was the important source of government revenue, accounting for 38.4 percent of total government revenue during the period of 1953–1960 (Table 1.2). It was also the major source of financing investment due to the low national savings rate. As shown in Table 1.3, the national savings rate averaged 4.2 percent during the period 1953–1960, financing only 34.1 percent of investment with the rest financed by foreign savings which averaged 8.1 percent.

The US aid was provided under the International Cooperation Agency (ICA) program and Public Law 480. The former consisted of project, non-project, and technical assistance, while the latter was to provide agricultural surplus, mainly for supporting defense

Table 1.3 Savings and Investment Rates, 1953–1960 (Unit: percent)

	Investment Rate	National Savings Rate	Foreign Savings Rate[a]
1953	15.4	8.8	6.6
1954	11.9	6.5	5.4
1955	12.3	5.2	7.1
1956	8.9	−2.9	10.8
1957	15.4	5.5	9.9
1958	12.9	4.8	8.1
1959	11.2	4.2	7.0
1960	10.9	0.8	10.1
1953–1960	12.3	4.2	8.1

Note: [a]Investment Rate–National Savings Rate.
Source: The Bank of Korea.

expenditures. Project assistance under the ICA program was directed to support investment activities in the form of providing machines and equipment, while the non-project assistance provided raw materials and consumer goods, which were sold to the private sector to raise government revenues. Technical assistance was used for the overseas training of local officials and for foreign advisers.

There was considerable policy conflict between the Korean government and the US aid agency regarding the use of aid funds. The Korean government wanted to rebuild the manufacturing industry to facilitate growth and demanded more project assistance. The US aid agency, however, insisted on providing non-project assistance to control inflation, for it was primarily concerned with stabilization rather than growth. The aid conflict was negotiated and coordinated by the Combined Economic Board (CEB),[2] which was jointly chaired by the representatives of the US aid mission in Korea and the Korean government. The US aid was mostly provided in the form

---

[2]The CEB was established in 1952 to deal with policy coordination between the US aid mission and the Korean government in accordance with the "Agreement on Economic Coordination between the Korean government and the United Command," which was signed in May 1952.

of non-project assistance.[3] Between 1954 and 1961, for example, 74.7 percent of aid funds were allocated to non-project assistance.[4] Thus, the US government, as a principal donor, had a great influence on Korea's post-war economic policy and even intervened in the budgeting process of the Korean government.

In 1953, the government launched a 3-year comprehensive reconstruction plan (1954–1956) supported by USD 628 million of aid funds. Approximately 70 percent of the funds were allocated to imports of raw materials and consumer goods, while the rest was allocated to facility investment (Lee, 2002, p. 285). The investment was focused on repairing roads, transportation, communications and harbors, and on some key industries such as the cement and fertilizer industries.

The Korean economy made significant recovery thanks to the reconstruction plan. Most industrial production reached or surpassed pre-war levels by 1956, but inflation was a persistent problem due to monetary expansion. Despite the large inflow of foreign aid, the budgetary deficit continued due to low tax revenues until the mid-1950s, so that the government had to rely on borrowings from the central bank and issuing bonds. The banking sector was another source of monetary expansion, because commercial banks had to rely heavily on the central bank for their credit lending due to low financial savings. The result was a rapid increase in money supply accompanied by a high inflation rate. As shown in Table 1.4, the money supply (M2) and consumer price increased by 78.8 percent and 45.2 percent per year between 1953 and 1956, respectively.

The US aid mission was greatly concerned about galloping inflation and requested the Korean government to adopt a financial stabilization program, which was implemented from 1957. Government

---

[3]The US government has contributed more than USD 6 billion in economic assistance to Korea from 1945 to 1980, and most of the aid was contributed before 1965 in the form of grants. Thereafter, the amount of economic assistance has declined rapidly, and a larger part has taken the form of loans (Mason *et al.*, 1980, p. xxx).

[4]For details on aid conflicts, see Song (1994, pp. 155–159); Haggard (1990, pp. 54–60).

Table 1.4   Major Economic Indicators, 1953–1960 (Unit: percent)

	GNP Growth	CPI Increase	M2 Growth[a]	Tax Revenue/ GNP	Fiscal Balance/ GNP[b]
1953	—	52.5	137.5	5.5	−1.5
1954	5.1	37.1	81.6	6.5	−3.5
1955	4.5	68.3	60.9	6.2	−1.7
1956	−1.4	23.0	35.1	7.1	0.0
1957	7.6	23.1	14.7	7.5	2.3
1958	5.5	−3.5	32.0	8.9	−2.7
1959	3.8	3.2	9.3	12.0	0.8
1960	1.1	8.0	0.4	12.0	2.9

Notes: [a]Year-end basis; [b]Consolidated general government account.

Sources: National Accounts 2009, The Bank of Korea; Bahl *et al.* (1986, p. 57, 260).

expenditures were strictly controlled, and borrowings from the central bank and the issuance of national bonds for industrial reconstruction were suspended. Tax reform was also carried out to increase revenues. The fiscal reform led to a substantial reduction in the budgetary deficit. As shown in Table 1.4, tax revenue as a share of GNP increased rapidly since 1957 so that the fiscal deficit was almost eliminated during 1957–1960, leading to a substantial reduction in money supply and price increases after 1957.

The government adopted a multiple exchange rate system throughout the 1950s to reduce import costs while stimulating exports. Despite the high inflation rate, the government kept the official exchange rate overvalued to reduce import costs of raw materials and equipment and to acquire more dollar redemption for won advances.[5] The excessive demand for imports was controlled through quantitative restrictions and high tariffs. Notwithstanding the higher exchange rate, exports did not witness a significant increase because most of them originated

---

[5]The won advances were provided to UN forces for their local currency expenditures and were repaid in dollars. Since the foreign exchange receipts through won advances were an important source of foreign exchange earnings, the overvaluation of the exchange rate was favored by the Korean government.

in primary products which were not sensitive to the exchange rate. The size of Korean exports at the time was also extremely small and amounted to a little over USD 30 million in 1960, approximately one-tenth of imports. Thus, most of the imports were financed by foreign aid.

The industrial policy was inward-looking, protecting domestic industries through high tariffs and quantitative restrictions. Prior to 1950, a uniform tariff rate of 10 percent was imposed on all imports except those financed by foreign assistance. A new law was enacted in 1950 to protect domestic industries. High tariffs were imposed on those items which were domestically produced, and duties on food grains and non-competitive equipment and raw material imports were exempted. The simple average of all tariff rates was around 40 percent.[6]

Imports were further controlled through a trade program that was announced semi-annually by the government, and controls were applied only to Korea's normal trade transactions excluding aid-financed imports. Since aid-financed imports constituted more than two-thirds of total imports, overall imports were not much affected by the restrictive import policy and fluctuated depending on the foreign aid inflows.

The industrial policy was characterized by the import substitution of nondurable consumer goods such as textiles, processed foods, and chemicals. Some import substitution also took place in such intermediate goods as fertilizer, cement, and plate glass, reflecting the growing domestic demand for them. The manufacturing sector as a whole enjoyed relatively rapid growth of 12.8 percent per annum between 1953 and 1960. The GDP growth rate was, however, moderate and averaged 3.9 percent due to the sluggish growth of agriculture (2.4 percent), which was the dominant sector of the economy in the 1950s.

Although by 1960 the Korean economy fully recovered from the war, it confronted a number of macroeconomic and structural problems. Economic growth began to slow down due to the falling

---

[6]Frank, Jr., *et al.* (1975, p. 36).

aid. Furthermore, the US aid policy began to shift from grants to loans from 1958, aggravating balance of payments difficulties. As the US aid declined rapidly after 1957, economic growth continued on a downturn and unemployment and inflation began to rise in the early 1960s. Political repression accompanied by economic stagnation gave rise to the student revolution in April 1960, which led to the collapse of the Rhee Syngman government.

1.2 Outward-Oriented Industrial Development (1960s)

Korea's modern economic growth started with the political change when the military government led by President Park Chung Hee came to power in 1961. At the time, Korea was one of poorest countries in the world. The country's per capita GNP was less than USD 100, with almost half the population living below the absolute poverty line. The greatest concern of the President Park was naturally the eradication of poverty through high economic growth.

To achieve high economic growth, the government adopted the unbalanced growth strategy, setting industrialization as the primary goal of development policy and launched in 1962 its first five-year development plan (1962–1966) with the annual target growth rate of 7.1 percent. The original plan was very ambitious, placing great emphasis on the import substitution of intermediate and capital goods, which resulted in inflation and a serious foreign exchange crisis in 1963. The situation was exacerbated by aid cut of US government which was not sympathetic to the military government.

Therefore, the government had to revise the plan, shifting the development strategy from import substitution to export promotion. An outward-oriented industrialization policy was adopted to over-come small domestic market under the national slogan of "nation-building through exports." Based on this development strategy, the government directed all the relevant policy measures toward supporting export activities.

A variety of fiscal, financial, and administrative incentives was devised to support exports, including the unitary floating exchange rate system. The most powerful incentive was the heavily subsidized export credit provided at a preferential interest rate far below the commercial lending rate. In 1964, for example, the interest rate on export credit was 8 percent, while the rate on commercial lending was 16 percent. The intensive support for exports continued in the second half of 1960s by reducing the interest rate to 6 percent and successive devaluation of exchange rate to reflect relative price changes.

These policy efforts led to the phenomenal expansion of commodity exports, which grew at an average annual rate of 40 percent between 1962 and 1971. As the balance of payments improved in the mid-1960s, the government joined the GATT in 1967 and made efforts to liberalize trade, shifting its import policy from a positive to a negative system. The efforts for import liberalization could not, however, continue further due to worsening balance of payments difficulties (Table 1.5).

It is important to note that while promoting exports, the Korean government began at the same time to encourage import substitution in heavy and chemical industries (HCIs) such as machinery,

Table 1.5   Major Economic Indicators, 1961–1970 (Unit: percent)

	GNP Growth	CPI Increase	M2 Growth[a]	Current Account/ GNP	Tax Revenue/ GNP	Fiscal Balance/ GNP[b]
1961	5.6	8.2	59.4	1.4	9.6	−0.2
1962	2.2	6.6	25.2	−2.5	10.8	−3.5
1963	9.1	20.2	7.6	−5.0	8.9	0.1
1964	9.6	29.5	15.3	−1.0	7.2	0.3
1965	5.8	13.5	51.9	0.0	8.6	1.1
1966	12.7	11.3	51.5	−2.6	10.8	−5.3
1967	6.6	10.9	61.3	−4.2	12.1	−2.8
1968	11.3	10.8	72.0	−8.0	14.4	−1.2
1969	13.8	12.4	54.7	−7.9	15.1	−4.1
1970	7.6	16.0	24.9	−7.5	15.4	−1.6

Notes: [a]Year-end basis; [b]Consolidated general government account.

Sources: National Accounts 2009, The Bank of Korea; Bahl *et al.* (1986, p. 57, 260).

shipbuilding, electronics, steel, and petrochemicals in the second five-year plan (1967–1971). The special laws were enacted to promote them by stipulating various supports.

The dramatic export growth coupled with support for HCIs led to investment boom generating inflationary pressure. Therefore, the government took various measures to mobilize domestic savings to meet the rapidly growing investment demand. A number of important fiscal measures were taken to increase tax revenue and to increase the efficiency of tax administration. In 1966, the Office of Tax Administration was established to improve the efficiency of tax administration, and tax reform was further undertaken in 1967 to make the tax structure more supportive of economic development. Thus, the tax revenue share of GNP increased from 9.6 percent in 1961 to 15.4 percent in 1970. Despite the swift increase in tax revenues, the public sector continued to show a fiscal deficit in the 1960s due to rapidly rising government expenditures for economic development.

An interest rate reform was also undertaken in 1965 to boost financial savings. The interest rate on 1-year savings deposits doubled from 15 percent to 30 percent, and the rate on commercial loans increased from 16 percent to 26 percent. The high interest rate policy brought about a dramatic increase in financial savings while discouraging unproductive investment, which greatly contributed to finance private investment. Thanks to rapid export growth and investment boom, the Korean economy began to take off from the early 1960s, growing at an average annual rate of 8.4 percent between 1961 and 1970 (Table 1.5).

Great efforts were made to promote technical manpower development with emphasis placed on adequate supply of skilled workers to support export industries. The Vocational Training Act was enacted in 1967 to facilitate skill formation. Technical high schools were expanded together with opening of evening classes. Many public and private vocational training institutions were established, and in-plant training programs were also introduced; they became the major supply sources of skilled workers in the 1960s. In addition to skill formation, the government established the Korea Institute of

Science and Technology (KIST) in 1966 to foster local technological capability building.

Although the development policy in the 1960s was very successful in terms of exports and growth, inflation and balance of payments problems continued to plague the Korean economy. Exports had a dramatic growth, but imports also grew rapidly reflecting booming investment, making it impossible to reduce the trade deficit due to the extremely low initial base of exports. As a result, current account deficit as a ratio of GNP jumped from 2.6 percent in 1966 to 7.5 percent in 1970. Money supply continued to increase swiftly on the back of expansionary fiscal and monetary policy, generating inflationary pressure.

Despite some negative problems indicated above, the 1960s were a turning point for Korea's economic development, since the economy grew rapidly, supported by high investment and export growth. Not only did exports expand at a rapid pace, but they also grew over a wide range of manufacturing industries, and thus became an engine of growth. The investment rate rose significantly to facilitate growth and exports. Manpower development in the form of skill formation was institutionalized to support industrial development. In short, one can say that the institutional and industrial basis for self-sustaining growth was created in the 1960s.

1.3   Industrial Upgrading and a Big Push for Rural Development (1970s)

Entering the 1970s, Korea faced serious challenges on both the external and internal front. Protectionism against labor-intensive products rose in developed countries as the world economy slid into recession in the early 1970s. As for security, there were several signs of US forces withdrawing from Asia, which worried Korean policymakers. The tension between North and South Korea heightened when North Korean commandos attempted to assassinate President Park in 1968, and this had a great impact on the political and military situation in Korea. There was little doubt that such shifting circumstances led the Korean government to make greater efforts to achieve self-reliance and self-defense.

One of the responses to these changes was the amendment of the Constitution in 1972, which removed all the restrictions to President Park's re-election. He wanted to complete Korea's modernization task he had initiated a decade ago, and presumably he believed he was the only one equipped for this task.

Another policy reaction was setting the promotion of the HCI as the government's top policy goal. The rising protectionism in labor-intensive industries prompted Korean policymakers to steer the structure of exports toward capital and technology-intensive industries. Security concerns also played an important role in the HCI drive due to growing tensions between North and South Korea. Until the early 1970s, North Korea was ahead of South Korea in industrial development, particularly when it came to heavy industries. Thus, President Park felt a strong need to develop the defense industry.

For these reasons, the government began to intensify its support for HCIs, which were already designated as strategic industries to be promoted. A series of preferential financial and tax incentives were devised to facilitate investment in HCIs. The tariff structure was streamlined to increase protection for HCIs, and non-tariff barriers were tightened and extended to cover most HCIs. Preferential credits were made available to finance investment in HCIs by creating the National Investment Fund (NIF) in 1974. Technical and engineering education was strengthened to enhance the competitiveness of HCIs and a number of state-funded research institutes were set up to stimulate R&D activities.

It was clearly an extremely risky decision for the Korean government to venture into HCIs, considering Korea's weak financial system and low technology level at the time. International financial institutions such as the World Bank were very critical of Korea's ambitious HCI promotion plan. Despite the criticism at home and abroad, the Korean government pushed ahead with the plan in the belief that HCIs would become the nation's leading export industries in the future, for Korea's comparative advantage was expected to move toward capital and technology-intensive products.

The HCI drive was greatly successful in boosting investment in the HCI sector, leading to the rapid growth of the manufacturing sector and its structure change. Manufacturing sector grew 16.2 percent per annum from 1971 to 1980, much higher than the GDP growth of 9.1 percent during the same period. The share of HCIs in manufacturing output thus rose from 39.7 percent in 1970 to 58.3 percent in 1980. The HCI drive had, however, entailed several unwanted side effects as it overheated the economy, thereby generating strong inflationary pressure which, coupled with the overvalued exchange rate, seriously eroded industrial competitiveness resulting in balance of payments difficulties (Table 1.6).

There was also a significant policy change in the 1970s with regard to development of the agricultural sector. The unbalanced growth strategy based on industrialization brought about a relative decline in the agricultural sector, resulting in great food shortage and income disparity between urban and rural households. This led policymakers to readjust the development strategy toward more balanced development between agriculture and industry, because the decline of the agricultural sector could become a major bottleneck for further growth and social stability. Thus, from the third five-year plan (1972–1976), great efforts were made to develop the agricultural sector.

A dual price policy was introduced to stimulate grain production. The government paid more than the market price to purchase rice and barley, and sold them at lower prices. This dual price policy had multiple effects, because it not only increased farm household income but also contributed to enhancing self-sufficiency in food grains. As a result, farm household income rose at a much faster pace than urban household income, resulting in the substantial improvement of farm household income relative to urban household income (Table 1.7). The dual price policy also made it possible for Korea to achieve self-sufficiency in rice in 1976, by stimulating the production of a new variety of rice called "*Tongil* (unification)," which yielded on average 25–30 percent more than traditional varieties.

Another notable policy effort in the field of rural development was the New Village (*Saemaul*) Movement, which was launched in 1970 and became a national movement in 1973. The movement was originally initiated to improve the living conditions of rural areas. However, the emphasis shifted toward income-generating activities

Table 1.6   Major Economic Indicators, 1971–1980 (Unit: percent)

	GDP Growth[a]	CPI Increase	M2 Growth[a]	Wage Increase (Non-Agriculture)	Exchange Rate (Won/Dollar)	Current Account/GDP	Fiscal Balance/GDP[b]	Tax Revenue/GDP
1971	10.4	13.5	29.3	15.4	347.7	−8.9	−2.2	14.4
1972	6.5	11.7	33.6	17.5	392.9	−3.5	−4.6	12.4
1973	14.8	3.2	36.1	11.5	398.3	−2.3	−1.6	12.0
1974	9.4	24.3	21.5	31.9	404.5	−10.5	−3.9	13.1
1975	7.3	25.2	25.2	29.5	484.0	−8.9	−4.5	14.9
1976	13.5	15.3	35.1	35.5	484.0	−1.1	−2.8	16.2
1977	11.8	10.1	40.1	32.1	484.0	0.0	−2.6	16.1
1978	10.3	14.5	35.4	35.0	484.0	−2.0	−2.5	16.6
1979	8.4	18.3	29.7	28.3	484.0	−6.6	−1.4	16.9
1980	−1.9	28.7	44.5	23.4	607.4	−8.3	−3.0	17.0

Notes: [a]Year-end basis; [b]Consolidated central government account.

Sources: National Accounts 2009, The Bank of Korea; The 60-Year History of the Korean Economy-I (2010, appendix tables 2-6, 2-7, 2-9, 2-11, 2-14).

Table 1.7   Comparison of Urban and Farm Household Income, 1965–1978
(Unit: percent)

	Farm Household Income as % of Urban Household Income	Off-Farm Household Income as % of Farm Household Income
1965	99.7	20.8
1966	80.6	22.1
1967	60.1	22.2
1968	62.6	23.5
1969	65.3	23.3
1970	67.1	24.1
1971	78.9	18.1
1972	83.0	17.7
1973	87.4	18.8
1974	104.6	19.7
1975	101.6	18.1
1976	100.4	24.3
1977	102.0	27.7
1978	98.3	28.0

Source: Moon (1980, p. 151).

as it became popular among villagers. Farmers were encouraged to carry out productive activities such as the cultivation of cash crops, raising livestock, repairing river dikes, and so forth. The government supplied technical and financial assistance to the rural community.

The Saemaul Factory Program was launched in 1973 to increase non-farm income so as to catch up with urban household income. To attract industries to rural areas, the government provided tax and financial incentives to firms investing in or relocating their factories to rural areas. As a result, the share of non-farm income in farm household income increased rapidly since the mid-1970s, resulting in the near disappearance of the income disparity between urban and rural household income in the late 1970s (Table 1.7).

The active agricultural development policy and the New Village Movement thus enabled the swift growth of farm household income and the significant improvement of living conditions in rural areas, which considerably bridged the economic and social disparity between urban and rural areas during the 1970s. It is also remarkable that Korea achieved self-sufficiency in rice, the staple food of the Korean people, after decades of failure.

To summarize, great progress was made in industrial as well as agricultural development in the 1970s. The HCI drive fueled unprecedented high economic growth accompanied by a rapid structural transformation toward capital and technology-intensive industries, which enabled the Korean economy to enjoy continuous high income and export growth in the subsequent decades. In conclusion, the 1970s can be described as the period that laid the economic foundation upon which Korea could emerge as a new industrial power, accompanied by remarkable achievements in the agricultural sector.

1.4 Market Opening and Liberalization (1980s)

Although the HCI drive was very successful in terms of economic growth, it had unwanted side effects such as a soaring inflation, structural imbalances within the manufacturing sector, and balance of payments difficulties. The booming economy due to massive investments in the HCIs led to a rapid increase in wages, generating strong inflationary pressure. The rapid wage increase coupled with overvalued exchanged rate seriously eroded the competitiveness of Korea's labor-intensive industries. The excessive support for the HCIs, on the other hand, brought about an overinvestment in many industries while distracting investment from export-oriented light industries. As a result, the balance of payments problem became very serious following the second oil shock in 1979 (see Table 1.6).

The new government inaugurated in September 1980 initiated wide-ranging policy reforms to cope with these structural problems. The basic philosophy was that the Korean economy should rely more on market forces for its resource allocation than on government intervention, because it was simply too large and complex to be managed by a handful of policymakers in the government. Thus, development policy shifted toward greater reliance on market forces for resource allocation by opening the market and promoting competition.

As a first step, the government began to stabilize the economy through tight fiscal and monetary policy measures because price stabilization was essential for the market mechanism to work. The overall expansion of money supply was strictly controlled and the government expenditures were cut back sharply. As a result, the government budget deficit as a percentage of GDP fell from 4.3 percent in 1981 to virtually zero percent in 1986. The wage increase was also controlled through incomes policy. Furthermore, the government enacted the Fair Trade and Anti-Monopoly Act in 1981 to prohibit cartel arrangements, price fixing, and other monopolistic practices, which had been the important sources of inflation in the past. Along with the stabilization policy, the government moved to rehabilitate the floating exchange rate regime that had been suspended since 1974. The exchange rate was devalued by 20 percent in early 1980 and came under a managed floating system in the subsequent years.

Trade and industrial policy was also reformed in line with overall policy direction. The government began to overhaul the industrial incentive system, replacing the industry-specific support with functional support focused on technology and manpower development. Thus, the government eliminated most of the incentives given to HCIs, while intensifying its support for industrial innovation and R&D activities. The preferential credit support system was totally abolished in 1982 as the government eliminated preferential interest rate for policy loans. As an effort to liberalize the financial sector, the government began to privatize the commercial banks in 1981, reducing its intervention in the operation of banking institutions.

The comprehensive import liberalization was launched in 1984, aiming for 95 percent of import liberalization by 1988. This was designed to induce foreign competition so as to strengthen industrial competitiveness. Tariff reform was also carried out in 1984 to reduce protection for domestic industries. The foreign investment and technology import were significantly liberalized with an introduction of the negative system in 1984. Technology licensing was fully liberalized when the approval system switched to a report system in the same year.

As a result of these comprehensive policy efforts, the Korean economy performed extremely well, growing at 8.7 percent per year between 1981 and 1990. One of the most significant achievements during the 1980s was a successful control of inflation from which the Korean economy had been suffering for a long period. As shown in Table 1.8, the consumer price, which increased at two-digit level during the 1970s, dropped drastically from the 21.4 percent increase in 1981 to a 3.4 percent increase in 1983 and remained extremely stable thereafter. The balance of payments also improved significantly during this period. The trade balance showed a surplus in 1985 for the first time in Korea's history. The budget deficit, which had been a critical source of inflation in the past, shrunk drastically, turning into a surplus in 1987.

The outstanding performance of the Korean economy, however, began to subside due to the political democratization movement in the late 1980s, which led to huge labor disputes and a steep rise in wages. Nominal wages increased rapidly from 1988, far exceeding the productivity growth, which caused a rapid rise in the unit labor cost. As a result, the balance of payments surplus precipitously disappeared, turning into deficit again in 1990. In short, although the Korean economy paid a high price for political democratization, the 1980s were remembered by most Koreans as a period of growth with stability accompanied by political advancements toward a more democratic government.

1.5 Globalization, Financial Crisis, and Structural Reform (1990s)

The political democratization movement in the late 1980s led to the birth of Kim Young Sam government in 1992. Influenced by global movement toward liberalization, the government announced globalization to be the national policy goal. The policymakers in the new government believed that many of Korea's structural problems including weak industrial competitiveness and inefficient financial sector basically lay in the heavy government intervention in the economy, hence the government control over the private sector should be removed as much as possible to facilitate growth and resolve structural problems.

Table 1.8 Major Economic Indicators, 1981–1990 (Unit: percent)

	GDP Growth	CPI Increase	M2 Growth[a]	Wage Increase (Non-Agriculture)	Current Account/GDP	Fiscal Balance/GDP[b]	Real Effective Exchange Rate (2000 = 100)[c]
1981	7.4	21.4	36.1	20.7	−6.4	−4.3	98.6
1982	8.3	7.2	37.0	15.8	−3.3	−4.0	92.6
1983	12.2	3.4	22.9	11.0	−1.8	−1.5	89.8
1984	9.9	2.3	19.0	8.7	−1.4	−1.2	92.8
1985	7.5	2.5	18.1	9.2	−0.8	−0.8	96.0
1986	12.2	2.8	29.5	8.2	4.2	−0.1	114.7
1987	12.3	3.1	30.2	10.1	7.2	0.2	113.6
1988	11.7	7.1	29.8	15.5	7.7	1.2	93.0
1989	6.8	5.7	25.8	21.1	2.3	0.0	82.0
1990	9.3	8.6	25.3	18.8	−0.8	−0.8	82.6

Notes: [a]Year-end basis; [b]Consolidated central government account; [c]Based on unit labor cost.

Sources: National Accounts 2009, The Bank of Korea; The 60-Year History of the Korean Economy-I (2010, appendix tables 2-6, 2-7, 2-9, 2-11, 2-14).

Reflecting the rise of pro-market ideology in the early 1990s and the consequent loss of legitimacy of centralized coordination, the government abolished the five-year development planning system by dismantling the Economic Planning Board and launched the so-called five-year new economy plan (1993–1997) which was designed to facilitate market-led development through liberalization and deregulation, and wide-ranging reform measures were undertaken to this end.

The government further dismantled the selective industrial policy which, among others, monitored investment activities of chaebols. Since chaebols were no longer controlled by the government, they were able to pursue their business expansionism. They diversified their business into non-banking financial institutions such as insurance, securities, and short-term financing corporations. They expanded their investment through debt financing and cross-debt guarantee practices among their affiliate companies. The result was overinvestment and overdiversification by the chaebols, which was typically exemplified by Samsung's entry into the already overcrowded automobile industry in 1994. The lack of investment coordination also led to overinvestment in many other industries including semiconductors, petrochemicals, and shipbuilding.

The misallocation of credit was further facilitated by a weak regulatory system. The loan classification standards were not very stringent. Accounting and disclosure standards were also below international standards, and market value accounting was not widely practiced. The weak regulatory control was compounded by fragmented supervision system. The supervision of the financial sector was split between the Bank of Korea and the Ministry of Finance, so that it was not possible to carry out an effective oversight on financial institutions. Due to the weak prudential control and lack of unified supervisory framework, financial liberalization resulted in rather rapid expansion of private sector credit, leading to huge corporate indebtedness.

The formerly closely tied relationship between the government and financial institutions also underwent a considerable change. The government actively promoted the financial liberalization from the early 1990s and significantly relaxed its control over the financial sector. The five-year financial liberalization plan was launched in 1993 to accomplish interest rate deregulation, abolition of policy loans, reduction of entry barriers, granting of more managerial autonomy, and capital account liberalization.

As a consequence of the financial deregulation, financial institutions became considerably independent in their business operation. Their management practices and patterns, however, did not change much because they had little experience in commercially oriented lending practices. Although most financial institutions were officially privatized, credit lending continued to concentrate on the chaebols because they believed that the government would not allow the chaebols to go bankrupt.

The capital market opening also failed to improve efficiency of the financial sector. Since 1994, the government accelerated the capital market liberalization to prepare for joining the OECD. As the decision to join the OECD was highly politically motivated, the capital market liberalization was not accompanied by a strong regulatory framework, and thereby stimulated the financial institutions to rely on the cheaper foreign borrowings since the domestic interest rate was much higher than the international rate. The merchant banks which engaged in most financial transactions borrowed and lent recklessly, leading to a rapid increase in foreign liabilities. In consequence, the rapid pace of liberalization and the market opening raised the vulnerability of the Korean financial institutions which lacked proper credit assessment and risk management tools.

The exchange rate policy also contributed to encouraging excessive foreign borrowing. The Korean currency was effectively tied to the US dollar with very little variation, resulting in its overvaluation. As shown in Table 1.9, the real effective exchange rate dropped considerably between 1992 and 1996. Moreover, the government intervened in the foreign exchange market in order to maintain the overvalued currency because devaluation could trigger inflation and increase the debt service burden of the private sector. The intervention was further intensified as the Southeast Asian crises started to press upon the Korean won, resulting in the rapid depletion of foreign exchange reserves.

Table 1.9   Major Economic Indicators, 1991–2000 (Unit: percent)

	GDP Growth	CPI Increase	Wage Increase (Non-Agriculture)	Unemployment Rate	Current Account/ GDP	Fiscal Balance/ GDP[b]	Real Effective Exchange Rate[a] (2000 = 100)
1991	9.7	9.3	17.5	2.4	-2.7	-1.8	77.0
1992	5.8	6.2	15.2	2.5	-1.2	0.7	81.9
1993	6.3	4.8	12.2	2.9	0.2	0.3	85.2
1994	8.8	6.3	12.7	2.5	-1.2	0.4	83.5
1995	8.9	4.5	11.2	2.1	-1.7	0.3	75.0
1996	7.2	4.9	11.9	2.0	-4.5	-0.2	69.1
1997	5.8	4.4	7.0	2.6	-1.6	-1.4	77.8
1998	-5.7	7.1	-2.5	7.0	11.7	-3.9	111.2
1999	10.7	0.8	8.2	6.3	5.5	-2.5	107.1
2000	8.8	2.3	8.0	4.1	2.4	1.1	100.0

Notes: [a]Based on Unit labor cost; [b]Consolidated central government account.

Sources: National Accounts 2009, The Bank of Korea; The 60-Year History of the Korean Economy (2010, appendix tables 2-6, 2-7, 2-9, 2-11, 2-14).

As briefly mentioned above, the liberalization and deregulation policy turned out to aggravate the structural problems of the Korean economy. The policy was successful in the sense that it greatly stimulated investment and growth. Investment rate was as high as around 37–38 percent during 1991–1996 accompanied by GDP growth of 7.8 percent during the same period. The problem was that high growth brought about wage hikes and inflation, deteriorating balance of payments difficulties. The result was a rapid growth of external debt, short-term liabilities in particular, which far exceeded Korea's foreign exchange reserves, leading to financial crisis in November 1997.

After the crisis, the government undertook wide-ranging structural reforms that greatly contributed to regaining the stability of the economy. Although the crisis was overcome relatively quickly thanks to the support from the IMF, it had significant social and economic impacts. As shown in Table 1.9, the unemployment rate rose sharply, as more than 10,000 firms went bankrupt. For the first time in Korea, nominal wages fell, resulting in the marked reduction of real wages. Massive unemployment and wage reduction broadened the income gap between the rich and the poor, deteriorating income distribution.

Another important consequence was a significant slowdown of economic growth after a short recovery in 1999 and 2000. The chaebols, the driving force of economic growth, were deeply affected by the crisis and the ensuing structural reforms. The financial institutions pursued a conservative lending policy, leading to weak private sector investment. Furthermore, social development became the primary concern of the government, reflecting the policy shift from growth to equity. Thus, the overall economic conditions were not conducive to investment, and so the economic growth continued to remain sluggish until very recently.

Entering the 2000s, the government pursued the innovation-driven development strategy because the 1997 crisis revealed that the inputs-driven, chaebols-dependent growth strategy was no longer sustainable due to falling potential growth rate which was expected to accelerate in the future. Thus, President Kim Dae Jung, who took office in 1988, searched for new sources of growth while carrying out drastic reforms in government, labor, business, and finance. The Kim government greatly supported small high-tech venture firms and ICT industries as new sources of growth. The innovation-driven growth strategy continued under the Roh Moo Hyun government in the name of next-generation growth engines, and similar programs were also launched under the Lee Myung Bak as well as Park Kuen Hye government. Unfortunately, they were not very successful due to sluggish investment and productivity growth, and institutional inefficiency, which are discussed in detail in Chapter 13.

Chapter 2

Role of Government

2.1 Two Competing Views

There are two competing views on interpreting the role of government in Korea's development process, the neoclassical view versus the revisionist view. The former is based on the market model, contending that the market played a major role in resource allocation while the government played a minor role, primarily providing a relatively stable macroeconomic environment. The government intervened in the product and factor markets, but policy distortion was limited because inter-industry differences in incentives were small, so that resources were allocated largely in line with the static comparative advantage. In other words, as price distortion was minimized, the outward-oriented development policy led the economy to specialize in accordance with its comparative advantage, resulting in rapid export and income growth. The policy was reversed in the 1970s due to the heavy and chemical industry (HCI) drive, but this did not last long and soon returned to the earlier outward-oriented policy, which enabled the Korean economy to enjoy sustained high growth. According to this view, the export promotion policy was the key to successful industrialization, while the import substitution policy was discredited from the viewpoint of allocative efficiency.

The revisionist view proposed by A. H. Amsden, R. Wade, and others is based on the institutional model. It argues that market failures were pervasive in the economy, leading the government to intervene in resource allocation by governing the market and getting the prices wrong in order to facilitate the growth of industrial sectors, which would not have developed under the working of comparative advantage. Basically, they consider industrialization from the dynamic view of the market, where economies of scale and technical change, rather than allocative efficiency, takes central place. In other words, unlike the neoclassical view, the import substitution policy constitutes an important vehicle of industrialization.

According to Amsden, even in labor-intensive sectors like cotton textiles, low wages are a necessary but not sufficient condition as a base upon which to compete against the higher productivity of countries with higher wages, because a low wage advantage cannot offset a higher productivity advantage. Therefore, government intervention was a necessary evil to spur development. In the 1960s, for example, despite low wages, the Korean textile industry was unable to compete against Japanese textile industry due to the productivity gap. Thus, the Korean government had to intervene to offset Japan's higher productivity with a wide range of subsidies (Amsden, 1989, p. 143).

According to the neoclassical view, with the accumulation of physical and human capital, the structure of exports shifts toward capital and skill-intensive industries. Therefore, the equal treatment of export and import substitution is essential to ensure efficient resource allocation and the exploitation of economies of scale which is particularly important in intermediate goods, producer goods, and consumer durables (Balassa, 1981, p. 21).

The transition from labor-intensive to capital and skill-intensive industries is not, however, smooth and straightforward as presumed by the neoclassical view, because the nature of competitiveness differs as it moves from an emphasis on cheap labor to skill and technology, where markets are imperfect. Therefore, government intervention is necessary to remedy market failures. The revisionist is of the view that a comparative advantage can be reshaped in the desired direction, arguing that "climbing the ladder of comparative advantage is a matter of creating competitiveness, usually with government assistance, rather than stepping into it" (Amsden, 1989, p. 243). Thus, the question is how and where to intervene and under what sort of incentive regime intervention is more likely to be successful (Moreira, 1995, p. 30).

The revisionist acknowledges that an outward-oriented policy is necessary and important, but government intervention should not be industry or market neutral as contended by the neoclassical view. Instead, it should be selective, supporting priority industries through incentives such as subsidies, trade restriction, and credit allocation. The incentives should be, however, provided in exchange for concrete performance in order to increase productive efficiency. According to this view, identifying priority industries is not so difficult because the objective of the development policy is primarily to catch up, so that developing countries as late comers can learn from the experience of developed countries. For example, Korea's HCI promotion policy was almost patterned after the Japanese industrial policy, which had been the backbone of Japan's successful industrialization.

2.2   The Changing Role of Government

As briefly explained above, both views hold some truth since Korea's development policy has elements from both sides. The neoclassical view was based largely on the development policy of the 1960s and 1980s, while the revisionist view focused on the HCI drive policy of the 1970s. It does not seem realistic to explain the role of government solely with one or the other model, because changes are inevitable when the economy faces either a different policy environment or enters a different stage of development. The role of government has changed considerably during the past half century and can be divided into four stages as follows:

(1) Laying the Groundwork for Development (1950s);
(2) State-led Development (1960s–1970s);
(3) Transition to Market-oriented Development (1980s);
(4) Toward Market-led Development (1990s).

2.2.1 *Laying the Groundwork for Development (1950s)*

Although the government in the 1950s was primarily concerned with the reconstruction of the war-torn economy, it undertook several important policies that had significant impacts on the development of the national economy. The first important policy action was the trade and industrial policy aimed at rebuilding the manufacturing sector, which was heavily destroyed during the Korean War. To promote the manufacturing industry, the government intervened extensively in resource allocation, placing trade, finance, and foreign exchange under government control. Commercial banks were nationalized, and lending rates were kept low to assist the business sector. The foreign exchange market was tightly controlled, and a multiple exchange rate system was adopted with the official exchange rate greatly overvalued. Industrial policy was inward-looking and focused on the easy import substitution of nondurable consumer goods.

Industrial and trade policy in the 1950s was often criticized for its negative impact on exports due to the overvalued exchange rate. Even if the exchange rate was realistically adjusted, it seems that given the initial conditions of the economy that had virtually no industrial base, exports would have hardly responded to relative price changes.[1] In other words, without the import substitution policy in the 1950s, Korea would have hardly been able to achieve such rapid export growth in the next decade, because the import substituting industries became export industries in the 1960s. This suggests that the import substitution policy in the 1950s played an important role in laying the groundwork for rapid export growth in the 1960s.

Another important policy that had a significant impact on the development of the economy was the disposal of Japanese-owned properties that were confiscated by the US military government in 1945. Japanese-owned properties constituted 14.3 percent of total farmland, and approximately 80–90 percent of the entire manufacturing industry at the time of liberation, indicating that

---

[1]For a critical view of the exchange rate policy in the 1950s, see Krueger (1997, p. 300); for a different viewpoint, Moreira (1995, p. 34).

Japan completely dominated the Korean economy before liberation (Lee, 2002, p. 87).

There was considerable debate regarding the ownership of the vested properties. While politicians preferred the state ownership of vested properties, the administration supported the idea of private ownership, leading to the enactment of the Vested Properties Disposal Act in 1949. Thus, most of the vested properties were sold to private individuals including former employees, businessmen, and skilled workers in the same line of business and technocrats. Since properties were sold at prices significantly below the market price in installment payments over 15 years, those who acquired the properties earned enormous capital gains, and many of them became successful businessmen and emerged as leaders in the Korean business community (Cho, 1994, p. 13). Most of the former Japanese properties were converted into private ownership by 1958. The privatization of vested properties made an economically important contribution to building the institutional basis for capitalistic market-oriented economic development in Korea.

The other two significant policies implemented during this period were the development of the educational system and land reform, which had far-reaching impacts on the social and economic development of Korea. Immediately after achieving independence, the Korean government placed a strong emphasis on education because Korea's most valuable resource was its people. Compulsory public education at the elementary level, initiated during the period of the US military government (1945–1948), was formally adopted by the newly established Korean government in 1949. This was followed by a spectacular increase in the secondary school system and higher education.

As a result, enrollment in the formal education system increased sharply at all levels. As shown in Table 2.1, the enrollment ratio of the entire population, defined as school enrollment as a percentage of the entire population, increased from 5.7 percent in 1945 to 13.3 percent in 1953 and 18.5 percent in 1960. The enrollment ratio in elementary school jumped from 59.6 percent in 1953 to 86.2 percent in 1960, and that of middle school and high school rose from 21.1 percent

Table 2.1 School Enrollment as Percentage of Corresponding Age Group, 1945–1975

Type of school	1945	1953	1955	1960	1965	1970	1975
Elementary school (ages 6–11)	—	59.6	77.4	86.2	91.6	102.8	107.6
Middle school (ages 12–14)	—	21.1	30.9	33.3	39.4	53.3	74.0
High school (ages 15–17)	—	12.4	17.8	19.9	27.0	29.3	40.5
College (ages 18–21)	—	3.1	5.0	6.4	6.9	9.3	8.6
% of total to the total population	5.7	13.3	17.2	18.5	22.0	25.3	28.8

Source: Mason *et al.* (1980, p. 352).

and 12.4 percent to 33.3 percent and 19.9 percent, respectively. The college enrollment ratio more than doubled during the same period. It is important to note that the expansion was more or less balanced across all levels of education. The swift advancement of education, influenced by Confucian principles that highly value education, undoubtedly laid an important foundation for rapid economic growth by accumulating human capital.

Land redistribution was initiated by the US military government in 1945 by selling former Japanese land to tenants, and land reform was carried out by the Korean government which promulgated the Farmland Reform Act in 1949. The farmland distributed by the US military government and the Korean government amounted to 577,000 hectares, and 573,000 hectares were privately sold by landowners to their tenants. Thus, a total of 1,150,000 hectares were distributed from 1945 to 1951, which accounted for 78.2 percent of the total farmland to be reformed (Ban *et al.*, 1980, p. 286).

Land reform brought about a dramatic change in the pattern of land ownership. As shown in Table 2.2, in 1945 only 13.8 percent of all Korean farmers owned land, while 51.6 percent of farmers owned no land at all. After the land reform, the situation was reversed, with 71.6 percent of farmers acquiring full ownership and tenant farmers accounting for only 5.2 percent of all farmers in 1964.

Land reform had a great impact on the social and economic development of Korea. An immediately visible impact was income

Table 2.2   Owner–Tenant Distribution of Farm Households (Unit: percent)

	1945	1964
Full owner	13.8	71.6
Owner–tenant	16.4	14.8
Tenant–owner	18.2	8.4
Tenant	48.9	5.2
Farm laborer and burnt field farmer	2.7	—
Total	100.0	100.0

Source: Ban *et al.* (1980, p. 286).

redistribution in favor of tenants, because after land reform rent payments fell from one quarter of income to around 2 percent according to the Farm Household Surveys. Thus, farm household income net of rents in the early 1960s was 30 percent or more above the 1930s level (Ban *et al.*, 1980, p. 301).

Land reform also facilitated the decline of the landlord class, which had formed the backbone of the Korean society for centuries and thereby laid the groundwork for an equitable distribution of income. It also contributed to human resource development, since many landlords, in anticipation of land reform, donated their land to educational institutions, which led to the founding of many private secondary schools, colleges, and universities in the 1950s (Lee, 1985, p. 8). Land redistribution did have a positive impact on agricultural productivity, since land reform improved incentives for tenant investment. Rice production witnessed considerable productivity growth following land reform. As shown in Table 2.3, rice yield per hectare increased significantly in the 1960s compared with the early 1950s.

The widespread expansion of education, industrial rebuilding based on the private ownership of property, and land reform made meaningful contributions to the economic and social development of Korea, as they provided an institutional and economic basis on which Korea was able to achieve growth with equity. Although President Rhee Syngman was blamed for corruption and political mismanagement, the contribution of his government to Korea's

Table 2.3   International Comparison of Paddy Rice Yields (Unit: kg per hectare)

Country	1952–1956	1961–1965	1970	1974
Korea	3,340	4,110	4,550	5,046
Japan	4,340	5,020	5,640	5,838
Taiwan	2,810	3,670	4,160	4,143
India	1,280	1,480	1,700	1,640
Thailand	1,350	1,760	1,970	1,703

Source: Mason *et al.* (1980, p. 227).

economic and social development should not be overlooked since his government laid the groundwork for development.

2.2.2   *State-Led Development (1960s–1970s)*

Moving into the 1960s, the government began to view the development issue from a more systematic and long-term development perspective, which was conceived but not implemented in the 1950s.[2] The military government launched a series of five year-development plans, the ultimate goal of which was to achieve self-sustained growth through industrialization.

The first five-year development plan (1962–1966) was formulated under the principle of "guided capitalism," whereby the state plays a dominant role in resource allocation while preserving private ownership of property.[3] In other words, the government assumed the role of a capitalistic developmental state, pursuing state-led development, which was reflected in the nature of the development plan. The development plan was target-oriented and had the characteristics of resource planning focused largely on investment planning. Decision-making was highly centralized and carried out by a small group of elite bureaucrats who intervened deeply in resource

---

[2]Under the Rhee Syngman government an attempt was made to formulate a three-year economic development plan (1960–1962) in 1959, but it was not implemented due to the fall of the Rhee government in 1960.

[3]For the meaning of guided capitalism, see Ahn (1962, pp. 36–37); Office of the Presidential Secretariat (1975, p. 18).

allocation. This policy continued throughout the entire period under the Park administration (1961–1979), although the policy focus slightly differed between the 1960s and the 1970s.

To facilitate industrialization, the government implemented industrial targeting policies, selecting strategic industries to be promoted. In the 1960s, an emphasis was placed on labor-intensive industries, while the priority shifted to promoting heavy and chemical industries in the 1970s. The government owned key industries such as oil, fertilizer, gas, steel, electricity, transport, and communications and invested in a wide range of other activities including finance, manufacturing, and service sectors. The share of public sector investment in total investment averaged approximately 35 percent over the period 1963–1979 (Sakong, 1993, p. 27). Consequently, the size of public enterprises grew rapidly, and their value added accounted for 7–9 percent of GDP and approximately 9–11 percent of non-agricultural GDP during the 1970s and 1980s (Table 2.4).

The government also intervened in the financial market to support industrialization. All the commercial banks that were privatized in the late 1950s were *de facto* renationalized to control the financial flow of banking institutions. The preferential policy loan system was introduced to support the strategic sectors of the economy and played a major role in financing investment, with its share in domestic credit being almost as high as 50 percent during the 1970s (Sakong, 1993, p. 35). Foreign capital inducement was promoted by providing government guarantees for loan repayment; this greatly facilitated the inflow of foreign loans. By controlling financial institutions, the

Table 2.4   Public Enterprise Sector and Its Share of GDP, 1963–1986 (Unit: percent)

	1963	1970	1973	1975	1977	1980	1984	1986
Value-added share of GDP	6.3	8.0	7.7	7.2	6.6	9.1	9.2	9.7
Value-added share of non-agricultural GDP	11.1	10.9	10.3	9.5	8.5	10.7	10.6	10.9

Source: Sakong (1993, p. 31).

government was not only able to channel financial resources into strategic sectors of the economy but could also discipline private firms to comply with government policies.

The government also played a vital role as a provider of manpower and technology for development. In the 1960s, emphasis was placed on science and technology infrastructure building and skill formation to support exports. Technical high schools were expanded to produce skilled workers, and the Vocational Training Act was enacted to facilitate skill formation. KIST, Korea's first modern technical research institute, was established to support industrial development. Local technological capability building continued in the 1970s, along with the strengthening of manpower development. The engineering colleges were greatly expanded, Korea Advanced Institute of Science (KAIS) was set up in 1971 to produce high-caliber manpower, and many specialized state-funded research institutes were established in the 1970s to carry out R&D activities for HCIs. Hundreds of Korean scientists and engineers working abroad were brought back to Korea to help assimilate and adapt the imported technology.

As mentioned above, the state became a prime mover in the development process, building the basis for self-sustained growth, which firmly took root during the 1960s–1970s. There were a number of positive signs for sustained growth. The growth rate continued to remain high, supported by booming investment and export growth. Exports increased rapidly with heavy and chemical industrial exports accounting for a growing share of total exports. Investment rates continued to rise quickly, enabling high economic growth. The domestic savings rate more than doubled, financing more than two-thirds of investment.

2.2.3   *Transition to Market-Oriented Development (1980s)*

The 1980s marked a transition period during which the government policy shifted from state-led to market-oriented development. Although the state-led development policy was a success in terms of growth and industrial advancement, it was accompanied by undesirable side effects that had to be remedied for sustained growth.

The new government led by President Chun Doo Hwan sought an alternative development policy to solve these problems.

The policymakers in the new government believed that given the growing complexity and size of the Korean economy, its management cannot be left to a small group of elite bureaucrats and therefore government intervention should be reduced while exposing the economy to market forces. The underlying philosophy was that market forces should play a more active role in resource allocation, while the government should pay more attention to social development, an issue that was neglected in the past. The background behind this policy shift was as follows.

First, inflation and balance of payments difficulties became very serious following the second oil shock in 1979, so macroeconomic stability was urgently needed to make the market mechanism work; second, government support and protection alone could not enhance industrial competitiveness, which was seriously eroded due to soaring inflation; third, the demand for social development such as health, housing, and social security was expected to grow rapidly with the rise of income, implying that social policy should be an important part of the overall development policy.

This policy change was reflected in the fifth five-year plan (1982–1986), the basic goal of which was to achieve stability, efficiency, and equity. The title of the plan was also changed from "economic development plan" to "economic and social development plan," to emphasize the importance of social development. The basic direction of the development plan was manifested further in the sixth five-year plan (1987–1991), which stressed social policy more strongly than in the fifth plan. As the government began to rely more on market forces for resource allocation, the nature of the development plan became more indicative and perspective-oriented rather than target-oriented, policies became more regulatory than developmental, and a series of measures were undertaken to this end in the early 1980s.

First, the policymaking process became gradually decentralized from the early 1980s, as private sector participation was greatly encouraged in the planning and policy formulation process. Many experts from businesses, trade unions, consumer organizations, and academia participated in the working committee of the development plan, a new practice, and a series of public policy forums were held to facilitate feedback and consensus building.[4]

Second, a liberalization policy was formulated to activate the market mechanism in the trade, financial, and foreign exchange markets and implemented gradually in order to minimize adjustment costs.

Third, industrial targeting policy was abolished as the industrial incentive system shifted from industry-specific support to functional support, and direct government assistance was provided only for structural adjustment for a limited period.

Fourth, competition policy was reinforced by enacting the Monopoly Regulation and Fair Trade Act to regulate the abuse of market power, business integration, and unfair trade practices. Previous efforts to introduce the law for promoting competition and fair trade had failed due to strong opposition from the business community, which resulted in the increasing concentration of economic power in the hands of large business groups.

As mentioned above, considerable efforts were made in the 1980s to liberalize the economy in trade, investment, and financial sector. It is, however, noted that a gradual and phased approach was taken to minimize social costs. As a result, not much progress was made except in import liberalization, because the liberalization policy was, in most cases, limited in scope and depth. Even in the case of import liberalization, a considerable number of products were banned from being imported from Japan.

Liberalization in the service sector was largely barred, and despite its privatization the bank operation was still under government control and interest rate liberalization was delayed. The government continued to intervene in the private sector, as the industrial rationalization program was carried out in many industries that were suffering from excess capacity and lack of international competitiveness. In other words, the Korean economy was making a

---

[4]For a more detailed discussion on the policymaking process in the 1980s, see Kim (2008a, pp. 41–53).

transition toward market-oriented development, in which the role of
the state shifted from a comprehensive to a limited developmental
state.[5]

2.2.4   *Toward Market-Led Development (1990s)*

As indicated above, economic liberalization in the 1980s was a partial
one in the sense that it was limited in depth and scope. Influenced by
global movement toward liberalization in the early 1990s, the Kim
Young Sam government thought that the liberalization policy should
be accelerated to facilitate market-led development. Pro-market
ideology prevailed among the policymakers who believed that liberalization and deregulation policy would lead to efficient resource
allocation, thereby sustaining high economic growth while resolving
many of the structural problems that plagued the Korean economy.
From this viewpoint, they abolished the five-year planning system
that had been the backbone of the state-led development policy,
and a wide-ranging reform was undertaken in the government, trade,
investment, and financial sector to facilitate market-led development.

Although the reform policy brought about high economic growth,
as mentioned in previous chapter, it failed to have a smooth transition
to market-led development because the structural problems of the
past were aggravated rather than resolved, leading to the financial
crisis in 1997. The reason behind the policy failure seemed mostly
attributable to the institutional deficiencies which prevented the
market economic order from functioning properly.

The financial market was liberalized, but this was not accompanied by stronger prudential regulation. This led to a rapid increase in
non-performing loans, thereby threatening the stability of the entire
financial system. Despite deregulation, bank operations were still
under government influence, as bank directors and executives were
appointed by the government. Thus, commercial banks continued to
serve as the main conduit of resource distribution in line with government policy directions. This *de facto* public role of commercial banks

---

[5]For a discussion on the limited developmental state, see Kim (1992, pp. 22–28).

hampered the development of a genuine banking industry based on profit-oriented, accountable, and transparent management principles. As a result, the moral hazards of "too big to fail" continued to play a major role in credit lending. Financial deregulation might have encouraged competition by lowering entry barriers, but it failed to resolve the moral hazard problem.

The opening of the capital market did not contribute to improving the efficiency of the financial sector either, since it was not supported by a strong regulatory framework. The market opening policy encouraged private businesses to rely on cheaper foreign borrowings, leading to a rapid increase in the foreign liabilities of merchant banks. Supervision over merchant banks was virtually non-existent to the extent that the government was not even aware of the huge mismatch in the maturity structures. The hasty pace of liberalization and market opening measures raised the vulnerability of Korean financial institutions that were not equipped with proper credit assessment and risk management tools. Premature capital market liberalization coupled with an overvalued exchange rate policy precipitated the situation.

Over several decades, Korea's major business groups employed a debt-financed expansion strategy via the highly aggressive use of leveraging. There was no adequate monitoring mechanism to impose management accountability and transparency, and the lack of an effective governance structure enabled the continuance of such high-risk business strategies. This management pattern and practice did not change, since they gained more freedom in their investment activities following the dismantling of selective industrial policy in the late 1980s. There was no longer an effective control and coordination mechanism that could keep a check on the investment behavior of chaebols. The result was excessive competition among chaebols, which led to overinvestment in many leading industries and a consequent decline in profitability.

The problems mentioned above are institutional problems that contributed to the failure of the liberalization policy. From late 1996, there were a number of warning signs: a series of corporate bankruptcies, a rising current account deficit, and serious non-performing loans of commercial and merchant banks. In response to the deepening crisis, the government attempted a few reform measures such as the prudential regulation of financial institutions and the labor reform bill but did not reach implementation, due to strong pressure from interest groups. These failed attempts further weakened international confidence in the Korean economy, resulting in the financial crisis. Korean policymakers did not realize the importance of the institutional aspects of the market economy. In other words, they did not realize that the functioning of the market economy requires far more than just dismantling regulations, cutting subsidies, and reducing protection.

Korea's rapid industrialization over the past several decades owed much to the authoritarian rule of strong political leadership. Since the early 1990s, the state retreated from directing the economy without preparing the institutional framework required for the functioning of the market economy. In other words, the disciplining mechanism of the past had disappeared without being replaced by a new one conducive to the working of market economy, and this was why the Korean economy failed to make a smooth transition from state-led to market-led development.

The 1997 financial crisis marked a turning point in Korea's structural reform. As noted above, the crisis was deeply rooted in institutional deficiencies, calling for fundamental reforms to remedy them. Korea's structural problems were so intertwined with politics and chaebols that attempts at internal reform alone would have hardly been successful unless supported by external shocks such as the IMF intervention. Therefore, one could argue that the external shock treatment was a necessary evil for the successful implementation of structural reforms.

After signing the IMF-supported assistance program, Korea swiftly implemented a wide range of reform measures, the goal of which was to build a sound and liberal market economic order. Sweeping reforms were undertaken in the finance, business, labor, and public sectors, and many of the structural problems that contributed to the crisis were resolved. The detailed discussion of structural reforms is given in Chapter 9.

Banks were recapitalized with public funds, and regulatory and supervisory oversight was considerably strengthened. Corporate governance and transparency improved as measures were taken to align business practices with international standards. Corporate debt levels were significantly reduced through equity financing and business restructuring, and consequently corporate debt/equity ratios dropped by a considerable degree. Capital market liberalization was accelerated to induce FDI, so that most business sectors, except radio and television broadcasting, were open to foreigners. The labor market was also reformed to enhance labor flexibility by legalizing layoffs for management reasons. Small government was pursued by reorganizing the government structure and privatizing state-owned enterprises.

Although the reforms made an essential contribution to restructuring the Korean economy toward market-led development, the outcome was unsatisfactory because the growth rate decelerated after a short recovery from the crisis, and many of the former informal institutions remained unchanged, impeding the working of the market economy. Government influence over financial institutions was overall not much changed, the corporate sector investment continued to remain weak due to various regulations, and the flexibility of the labor market did not improve due to powerful labor unions, implying that further efforts were required for the better working of a market economy including the formal as well as informal institutional reforms.

Chapter 3

Capital Accumulation

3.1 Savings and Investment Rates

One of the important features of Korea's development process is rapid capital accumulation. As shown in Table 3.1, investment as a ratio of GDP rose rapidly during the past 50 years, rising on average from around the 10 percent level in the 1950s to around 20 percent in the 1960s and 30 percent or more from the 1970s onwards up until the financial crisis in 1997, which enabled the Korean economy to sustain high economic growth during this period. Therefore, to understand the genuine sources of growth we must analyze the factors behind such rapid accumulation.

It is also remarkable that Korea witnessed the rapid rise of savings rate, much faster than investment rate. The national savings rate, which was on average around 4 percent in the 1950s, rose to 10.5 percent in the 1960s, 22.6 percent in the 1970s, and 32.3 percent in the 1980s (Table 3.1). As a result, investment was increasingly financed by domestic savings. As shown in Fig. 3.1, self-financing ratio of investment (Ratio 2), defined as national savings as a ratio of investment, increased rapidly from the 1960s, rising from 31.4 percent in the 1950s to 50.1 percent in 1960s and 76.5 percent in the 1970s. In the 1980s, investment was almost entirely financed by the domestic savings (Table 3.1).[1]

---

[1]The savings and investment rates are estimated based on the SNA system of 1968 which differs slightly from the SNA system of 1993. The Bank of Korea

Table 3.1   Savings and Investment Rates, 1953–2000 (Unit: percent)

	1953–1960	1961–1970	1971–1980	1981–1990	1991–2000
GDP Growth	3.9	8.5	9.1	8.7	6.6
Investment Rate (A)	12.3	19.8	29.5	32.6	34.7
National Savings Rate (B)	4.2	10.5	22.6	32.3	35.6
Foreign Savings Rate	7.9	9.1	6.9	0.4	−1.0
B/A	31.4	50.1	76.5	99.3	104.5

Note: The savings and investment rates are estimated based on the SNA system of 1968.

In contrast, the self-financing ratio of investment (Ratio 1), defined as gross savings as a ratio of investment, declined from the mid-1950s up until the end of 1960s, reflecting falling foreign aid and thereafter remained almost same as the Ratio 2 because of negligible foreign aid (grants). Since the 1993 SNA system does not distinguish between national and foreign savings, it is not appropriate to evaluate sources of investment when the foreign aid played an important role in capital formation, as experienced in the 1950s and 1960s.

As mentioned above, Korea relied heavily on foreign aid for financing investment in the 1950s and 1960s. Foreign direct investment (FDI) did not play any notable role until the early 1990s, because Korea was not an attractive investment destination due in part to its many FDI-related restrictions. As a result, FDI inflows were meager. As shown in Table 3.2, total FDI inflows amounted to USD 7,785

(BOK) compiled the National Accounts based on the 1968 SNA system until the early 1990s, but from 1995 the BOK started to compile the National Accounts based on the 1993 SNA system and revised time-series data on savings and investment rates. The 1993 SNA system has, however, some shortcomings as it defines gross savings as the difference between total consumption and Gross National Disposable Income (GNDI) which includes the current transfers from the rest of the world, leading to overestimating savings rate. As a result, as shown in Fig. 3.1, the self-financing ratio of investment (Ratio 1) is much high than the one (Ratio 2) based on the 1968 SNA system during the 1950s–1960s.

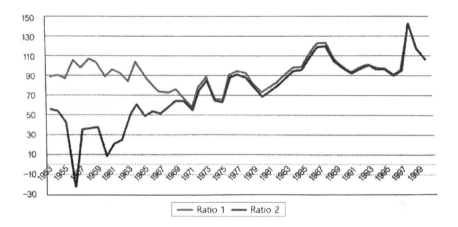

Figure 3.1   Self-Financing Ratio of Investment, 1953–2000 (Unit: percent)

Note: Ratio 1: Ratio of gross savings to investment. Ratio 2: Ratio of national savings to investment.

Source: National Accounts 2009, The Bank of Korea.

Table 3.2   Foreign Capital Inflows, 1962–1992 (Unit: USD million, percent)

	1962–1965	1966–1972	1973–1978	1979–1985	1986–1992
Loans	133 (15.1)	3,285 (76.8)	10,296 (91.8)	29,934 (85.7)	14,212 (46.7)
FDI	13 (1.5)	227 (5.3)	704 (6.3)	1,157 (3.3)	5,684 (18.7)
Bonds	—	—	219 (1.9)	3,823 (11.0)	1,0493 (34.6)
Grants	739 (83.4)	763 (17.8)	—	—	—
Total	886 (100.0)	4,275 (100.0)	11,219 (100.0)	34,914 (100.0)	30,289 (100.0)

Note: Figures in parentheses indicate composition ratios.

Source: Wonhyuk Lim (2011, p. xxxi).

million during the 30 years from 1962 to 1992, accounting for less than 10 percent of total foreign capital inflows during this period.

Therefore, the government had to rely on foreign loans to finance ambitious industrial development plan. To facilitate foreign borrowings, the government guaranteed repayment for foreign loans as early as 1962 since the Korean firms lacked the international credibility to raise capital in international capital markets. The big difference in domestic and foreign interest rates also encouraged

Korean firms to borrow from abroad. Thus, the inflow of foreign loans increased rapidly from the 1960s to the 1980s, accounting for 75.7 percent of total foreign capital inflows during the period 1962–1992. Although the heavy reliance on foreign loans led to extensive corporate indebtedness, foreign loans made an important contribution to rapid capital accumulation as they were mostly tied to investment projects.

3.2   Accumulation Process

3.2.1   *Investment, Growth, and Increase in Savings*

Capital accumulation involves three interdependent elements. The first one is the increase in savings to finance investment. The second is the creation of finance and credit mechanisms through which savings are channeled into investment. The third is how to ensure investment efficiency to facilitate the accumulation process.

During the reconstruction period of the 1950s, there was not much room for raising domestic savings, because the public sector was running huge fiscal deficits and households were too poor to generate savings. Thus, the domestic savings rate was extremely low, averaging 4.2 percent during the 1950s. However, it is notable that considerable accumulation took place in the business sector thanks to government policies.

Throughout the 1950s, the government maintained an overvalued exchange rate and low bank lending rate to support industrial development. The selective allocation of aid funds, coupled with the overvalued exchange rate, created enormous economic rents for those firms that had access to cheap bank loans and imports because the privileged firms had more or less monopolistic market. Though these rents were not entirely used for productive activities, a considerable amount was invested in the manufacturing sector, in particular the three so-called "white industries", namely the cotton spinning, sugar refinery, and flour mill industries, which grew rapidly in the 1950s. The low price of rice brought about by imports of the US agricultural surplus also supported the accumulation of the urban industrial sector, as it kept wages low.

Thus, the private sector displayed a relatively high savings rate of 6.9 percent in the 1953–1960. In other words, the three low prices for rice, bank loan interests, and the exchange rate were the major contributors to capital accumulation during the 1950s (Cho, 1994, p.15). However, the overall domestic savings rate remained on average at 4.2 percent during the same period, due to the negative public savings rate of 2.7 percent.

Another important potential source of accumulation was the land reform undertaken in 1949 and 1950. An extensive redistribution of land took place before and after the Korean War. Landowners were compensated with government bonds, but the government did not redeem them on time and most landowners were not permitted to use the bonds as collateral for business loans. This led to a drastic decline in bond prices, resulting in the collapse of landowners who had no income sources other than land. Thus, land reform failed to induce the capital of landowners into industrial development, and mostly benefited speculators and usury money lenders who procured the bonds at extremely low prices (Lee, 2002, p. 472).

The land reform had, however, a positive impact on income distribution, as it improved the income of former tenant farmers who became landowners. Widespread farm ownership was also conducive to the effective implementation of various agricultural development programs such as extension services, cooperative movements, and community development, leading to higher productivity growth. Rice production also witnessed considerable productivity gains from the 1960s. Therefore, it can be said that land reform laid the foundation for the growth and better distribution of income in the agricultural sector, with positive impacts on accumulation in the long run.

Entering the 1960s, great efforts were made to increase domestic savings to support the development plan. The tax system was reformed, and the interest rate was raised to mobilize domestic savings. Thus, the domestic savings rate more than doubled in the 1960s, rising from 4.2 percent to 10.5 percent. The private savings rate of 8.2 percent made the main contribution, while the government savings rate remained as low as 2.3 percent due to the expansionary fiscal policy.

Although financial and fiscal policy measures made an important contribution to raising the savings rate, the rising investment rate seemed to have played a critical role in pushing up the savings rate by boosting income. The Korean economy expanded swiftly from the mid-1960s due to an investment boom, resulting in a sharp increase in savings. During the 1965–1970, the GNP grew 10.4 percent per year and the domestic savings rate almost doubled, rising from 5.7 percent in 1965 to 10.8 percent in 1970. In a rapidly growing economy, investment, growth, and savings interact in a virtuous circle, because high levels of investment initially spur growth, leading to higher income, which in turn raises the savings rate as income grows faster than the consumption increase. Therefore, a high investment rate can be regarded as the major contributor to a rapidly rising savings rate, implying that in a growing economy savings follow investment, not the other way around.

It is also noted that the relatively low wage costs made a significant contribution to accumulation. There was a large migration of surplus rural labor into the urban industrial sector in the 1960s. Wages rose considerably due to the investment boom, but real wage growth lagged behind productivity growth, which caused the rate of return on capita[2] to climb steadily until the early 1970s, thereby contributing to capital accumulation (Fig. 3.2).

In other words, a larger surplus was generated with more inflow of labor into the urban industrial sector, implying that a Lewis type of accumulation took place in the 1960s. It is interesting that the rate of return on capital in Taiwan is almost as high as in Korea and is similar in movement. Korea and Taiwan displayed many similarities in terms of factor endowment and industrial development policy,[3] which led to high growth and high rates of return on capital for both countries in the 1960s and 1970s.

Despite the rising savings rate, it was impossible to satisfy the ever-increasing demand for investment, which was why half of

---

[2]Defined as $(V\text{-}W)/K$ where V, W, and K denote value added, labor compensation, and capital stock, all in real terms, respectively.

[3]For more details, see Kim (1984, pp. 131–137).

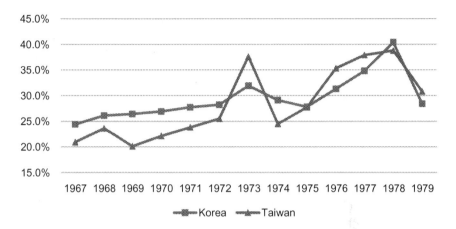

Figure 3.2   Rate of Return on Capital in Manufacturing, 1967–1979
Source: Kim *et al.* (1984, p. 186).

investment had to be financed by foreign savings in the 1960s. The heavy reliance on foreign savings continued on into the 1970s, as investment demand accelerated on the back of the HCI drive policy. The domestic savings rate more than doubled, rising from 10.5 percent in the 1960s to 22.6 percent in the 1970s. The increase in the savings rate was not enough to meet the booming investment demand, which led to an investment rate of 30 percent in the 1970s. Although the 1970s witnessed a decline in the reliance on foreign savings, they still financed more than one-third of total investment.

The investment rush in the HCI sector overheated the economy, causing a steep rise in wages. From 1972 to 1979, nominal wages in the manufacturing sector increased 28.8 percent per year, while labor productivity increased 11.3 percent, resulting in a 17.5 percent increase in labor costs (Table 3.3). Since labor costs grew faster than inflation, which averaged 15.3 percent of growth, profits were squeezed, posing a negative impact on capital accumulation. As shown in Table 3.4, the profit-to-sales ratio declined in the 1970s. Since the real wage rate increased faster than labor productivity growth, the rate of return on capital recorded negative growth during

Table 3.3 Growth of Wages, Labor Productivity, and Unit Labor Cost, 1967–1979 (Unit: percent)

	Nominal Wages (A)	Labor Productivity	Unit Labor Cost[a]	Consumer Price (B)	Real Wages (A–B)
1967–1971	21.9	18.7	3.7	13.2	8.7
1972–1979	28.8	11.3	18.4	15.3	13.5
1967–1979	26.4	12.0	12.9	14.6	11.8

Note: [a]Nominal wage/labor productivity.
Source: Kim *et al.* (1984, p. 187).

Table 3.4 Profit-to-Sales Ratio, 1961–2000 (Unit: percent)

	Current Profit-to-Sales Ratio	Operating Profit-to-Sales Ratio
1961–1970	6.6	11.0
1971–1980	3.5	8.1
1981–1990	2.5	7.2
1991–2000	1.3	7.1

Source: The Bank of Korea.

the 1973–1979.[4] Consequently, despite the rising investment rate, the growth rate of fixed capital formation fell considerably in the 1970s (Table 3.5).

The 1980s witnessed a critical change in the accumulation process as the government pursued a stabilization policy that had a significant impact on savings and investment rates. The investment rate, which rose rapidly until the end of the 1970s, fell from the early 1980s due to tight monetary and fiscal policy measures, and stabilized at around 30 to 32 percent until the mid-1980s. The domestic savings

---

[4]As shown in Fig. 3.1, the rate of return on capital declined in the early 1970s and suffered a sharp fall in 1979, so that despite the significant increase from 1975 to 1978 it displayed slightly negative growth between 1973 and 1979. It should be noted, however, that the rate of return on capital in Korean manufacturing was as high as around 30 percent on average in the 1960s and 1970s. This is the reason Korea could maintain an investment rate of over 30 percent for several decades.

Table 3.5   Growth Rate of Fixed Capital Formation (Unit: percent)

	GDP	Gross Fixed Capital Formation	Agriculture and Fishery	Mining and Manufacturing	SOC and Service
1953–1960	3.9	10.2	11.2	17.7	9.9
1961–1970	8.5	22.4	18.9	22.5	23.9
1971–1980	9.1	14.0	8.7	23.3	13.5
1981–1990	8.7	12.1	14.0	16.1	11.8
1991–2000	6.6	5.6	1.2	5.8	5.6
2001–2010	4.4	3.2	−4.3	6.3	2.2

Source: National Accounts 2009, 2014, The Bank of Korea.

rate, on the other hand, rose steadily owing to sustained income growth and the improved fiscal position of the public sector, so that investment was increasingly financed by domestic resources.

From the mid-1980s, the Korean economy regained its growth momentum thanks to the "three lows" brought by the Plaza Accord in 1985. The investment rate rose rapidly because the government lifted restrictions on industries, the entry into which was prohibited under the rationalization program. The problem was that the profit rates of the corporate sector began to fall continuously due to rapidly rising wage costs and high interest expenses on accumulated debts.

Despite falling profit rates, the investment boom continued into the 1990s because the Kim Young Sam government supported chaebols to stimulate the economy, leading to their excessive expansion. Since Korean firms and chaebols mostly financed their investment with bank loans, the debt-to-equity ratio worsened further, deteriorating profitability, which was already low. Profitability indicators such as return on assets and profit rates in the manufacturing sector continued to decline in the 1990s.

Although the investment rate in the years before the financial crisis was, on average, higher in the 1990s than in the 1980s, the overall efficiency of investment appeared to have declined in the 1990s because, as shown in Table 3.6, the incremental capital-output ratio (ICOR) rose to 5.0 in the 1991–1997 from 3.7 in the 1981–1990. This is consistent with the decline in profitability, which in turn led to the

Table 3.6   Trends of ICOR[a], 1953–1997

1953–1960	1961–1970	1971–1980	1981–1990	1991–1997
3.2	2.3	4.0	3.7	5.0

Note: [a]Investment rate/growth rate.

deceleration of capital accumulation. As shown in Table 3.5, fixed capital formation in real terms, which increased by two-digit levels until the 1980s, witnessed a sharp fall in the 1990s.

3.2.2   *Role of Financial Institutions*

Financial institutions played no less an important role in savings mobilization and investment promotion. The Korean government began to reform financial institutions from the early 1960s. The major objective was to mobilize financial resources and channel them into strategic sectors to be promoted. Before 1962, there were not many financial institutions through which financial resources could be mobilized, aside from several commercial banks. Thus, savers often utilized informal financial markets that were not helpful for investment financing. Therefore, various kinds of financial institutions and means of savings were developed to meet growing financial needs.

From 1961, the government began to diversify the banking sector by establishing specialized banks to provide financing for agriculture, small business, SMEs, housing, etc. A high interest rate policy was also implemented to increase financial savings. Thus, overall bank deposits as well as savings deposits witnessed phenomenal growth during the 1960s, which led to the dramatic rise in bank loans that enabled the rapid expansion of investment and output. Total bank loans as a ratio of GNP underwent a remarkable increase from 7.4 percent in 1964 to 26.1 percent in 1969.[5]

A development bank was created to finance long-term investment by providing subsidized credits. The Korea Development Bank (KDB), established in 1954, played a crucial role in financing

---

[5]For bank loans, see Nam and Kim (1997, p. 151).

Table 3.7   Ratio of Financial Savings to GNP, 1972–1993 (Unit: percent)

	Bank Savings	Non-Bank Savings	Stocks	Corporate Bonds
1972	21.7	6.9	1.0	0.2
1975	19.2	8.8	2.6	0.7
1978	21.4	12.0	3.9	2.8
1980	23.3	17.1	3.6	6.1
1983	25.2	31.4	3.8	7.1
1985	25.5	39.7	2.7	9.1
1988	27.8	57.7	10.4	9.0
1990	29.4	76.6	17.3	13.4
1993	34.6	104.4	14.5	16.8

Source: Summary of Financial Statistics, Ministry of Finance, various years.

long-term investment and provided 77.8 percent and 63.1 percent of total facility loans of financial institutions in the 1950s and 1960s. Even in the 1970s and 1980s, almost half the facility loans were provided by KDB (KDB, 2004, p.100, 119, 137).

Entering the 1970s, government policy was directed toward developing non-bank financial institutions (NBFIs) and the capital market to diversify financial assets and institutions for mobilizing domestic resources. This policy led to the birth of various NBFIs, and their assets and liabilities gained significantly in the 1970s. A number of institutions, such as investment finance companies and mutual savings and finance companies, were instrumental in attracting private savings from the unregulated money market into the regulated financial sector.

In the 1980s, the government pursued a financial liberalization policy, leading to a host of new NBFIs. Since NBFIs were less regulated than banks, while lending and deposit rates were higher than bank rates and market entry was easier, they grew rapidly in the 1980s and played an important role in mobilizing financial resources for investment. As shown in Table 3.7, the financial savings of NBFIs as a share of GNP increased dramatically since the early 1970s, while those of banking institutions did not gain much until the end of the 1980; thus, they became the most important source of financial savings, accounting for 76.6 percent of GNP in 1990.

Efforts were also made to activate the stock market, which was established in 1956. It did not play any major role in financing investment until the 1960s because it was dominated by the trading of government bonds and plagued by speculation and price manipulation. As noted earlier, Korean firms relied heavily on domestic and foreign loans, which led to high debt-to-equity ratios. Therefore, it was imperative to diversify financing sources to reduce their debt burden.

Thus, the government took a series of measures to foster a sound security market. In September 1968, the government enacted the Act on Fostering the Capital Market, aimed at encouraging major corporations to go public, and in the same year the Korea Investment Development Corporation was established to take charge of promoting the issuance market. The Corporate Tax Act was revised to provide tax benefits for corporations going public. In 1972, measures were taken to encourage public offerings by enacting the Public Offering Promotion Act, which empowered the government to designate corporations deemed eligible to go public.

Measures were further taken in 1975 to facilitate public offerings of large business groups, because despite government efforts, large-scale enterprises were mostly family-owned and remained closed to the public. The government set up criteria for public listings, and companies that met the criteria were required to go public within a certain period. Consequently, the number of listed firms and the amount of new equity issued jumped sharply in 1975–1978, reflecting the booming economy during this period.

Efforts to stimulate the security market continued in the 1980s. In 1983, measures to expand capital market function were taken to induce corporations in good credit standing to sell stocks and help stimulate security issuances at the market price. In 1986, measures were further taken to facilitate public offerings and to raise funds through the capital market. Encouraged by government policies and high economic growth, the stock market turned increasingly bullish from 1986. The amount of new equity issued as a share of GNP rose dramatically from 2.7 percent in 1985 to 17.3 percent in 1990 (Table 3.7).

Until the 1970s, the corporate bond market did not play any important role in raising funds for long-term investment because of the dominant role of government bonds. However, entering the 1980s, the situation changed as the government pursued a tight monetary and fiscal policy which led to the substantial reduction of public bond issuance. As economic growth picked up from the mid-1980s, the demand for investment increased rapidly, prompting the government to stimulate the corporate bond market. The government provided various incentives for corporate bond issues that greatly facilitated the growth of the bond market. Thus, the amount of corporate bonds issued began to rise swiftly, and the balance amounted to KRW 48.2 trillion, accounting for 16.8 percent of GNP in 1993 (Table 3.7).

As mentioned above, financial savings mobilized through the security market grew rapidly from the 1980s and became an increasingly important source of financing investment. As shown in Table 3.7, financial savings were significantly diversified and grew rapidly in the 1980s and 1990s. Thus, the total financial savings including those of banks and NTBFs, which had accounted for 50.1 percent of GNP in 1980, soared to 136.8 percent of GNP in 1990.

3.2.3 *Efficiency of Investment*

Another important issue related to capital accumulation is whether mobilized resources are efficiently utilized. This is because if resources are not productively invested, it could impede growth by imposing a negative impact on accumulation. This is particularly so for an economy in which the government intervenes extensively in resource allocation.

The Korean government intervened deeply in resource allocation from the 1950s to the 1980s. Despite extensive government intervention, it appeared that investment was, in general, efficient during this period, as reflected in the movement of the ICOR. As shown in Table 3.6, the ICOR remained at a relatively low level until the 1980s, although there was a slight increase in the 1970s due to excess capacity in heavy industries in the late 1970s.

The relatively low ICOR[6] was due first to the outward-oriented development policy emphasizing the allocation of resources in the manufacturing sector, in which Korea had or was likely to have a comparative advantage. As shown in Table 3.5, until the 1980s fixed capital formation in the mining and manufacturing sector grew much faster than that of other sectors of the economy. In the 1960s, investment was largely directed to labor-intensive light industries in which Korea had a comparative advantage. In the 1970s, many efforts were made to promote capital and technology-intensive HCIs with potential comparative advantages. There were some allocation problems due to the excessive investment in HCIs, but the problem could be overcome through the rationalization program in the 1980s.

Another important factor that contributed to the low ICOR was related to the availability of complementary factors of production such as skill and technology with which capital was to cooperate. The productivity of investment is affected by the industries or sectors in which resources are allocated, but more importantly, by skill and technology that determine productivity. Since these complementary factors of production are mostly deficient in the early stage of development, the Korean government made consistent policy efforts to increase the supply of these factors from as early as the 1960s.

In this regard, Korea was in a better situation compared to other developing countries because of its high primary school enrollment rate and industrious labor force, and for this reason the importance of Korea's initial conditions was often overstated in their contribution to growth and accumulation.[7] More important was the fact that these

---

[6]In the period of 1960–1970, the ICOR was 1.8 in Singapore, 2.1 in Korea, and 2.4 in Taiwan while it was 5.5 in Chile, 5.7 in India, and 9.1 in Uruguay. The former countries followed an outward-oriented strategy and the latter countries employed an inward-oriented strategy. See Balassa (1981, p. 16).

[7]Rodrik argues that by 1960 Korea had a skilled labor force relative to physical capital stock and income levels which made Korea ready for an economic take-off. His argument is based on Korea's high primary school enrollment ratio. The interpretation of this into a skilled labor force seems somewhat exaggerated. The skill formation of the Korean labor force began after the government launched its first five-year development plan in 1962. For Rodrik's argument see Rodrik (1995, p. 78), and for a detailed discussion on skill formation, see Chapter 11.

complementary factors were continuously upgraded and expanded through strenuous policy efforts, and thus played a vital role in enhancing the absorptive capacity of capital which in turn made the relatively high rate of return on capital possible.

In the 1960s, for example, the policy was focused on skill formation in terms of expanding technical high schools and vocational training. In the 1970s, technical manpower development and engineering education was strongly emphasized to support heavy and chemical industries, while in the 1980s the policy turned toward facilitating R&D activities and technology development of the private sector to enhance industrial competitiveness. In short, the outward-oriented industrialization policy supported by manpower and technology development was a major contributing factor to successful industrialization, which led to sustained growth and accumulation.

3.3 Characteristics of the Accumulation Process

We have explained the factors behind the rapid capital accumulation that enabled the Korean economy to sustain high growth over the last half century. Key features of Korea's accumulation process can be summarized as follows.

First, Korea relied heavily on foreign sources of investment for industrial development and relied on foreign loans rather than FDI. Foreign loans were encouraged by providing government guarantees for repayment, facilitating their inflow. Although the high growth policy based on foreign borrowings was in part responsible for the financial crisis in 1997, it also made an important contribution to Kore's successful industrialization in the sense that it was driven by Korean enterprises, not by foreign firms.

Second, the government played an important role in the accumulation process as it provided a favorable business environment for investment and growth. The government provided subsidized credits and other forms of subsidies based on performance criteria, which greatly facilitated private investment. On the other hand, the labor union movement was suppressed, making it possible to contain the increase in wages within productivity growth. This kind of policy continued until the mid-1980s and made it possible for the business sector to extract a large surplus that was invested rather than consumed, leading to sustained accumulation and growth.

Third, the savings rate increased much faster than the investment rate, financing an increasing share of investment. The rapidly rising savings rate seemed closely associated with high income growth, because high income growth boosted the savings rate as income grew faster than the consumption increase, suggesting that the high savings rate was an outcome of high income growth rather than a cause. In addition to high income growth, a variety of other policy measures including financial and fiscal policy also facilitated high levels of savings.

Fourth, efforts were made to facilitate manpower and technology development in tandem with industrial development to enhance the absorptive capacity of investment. Industrial policy was consistently supported by human resource development and technology policy, placing a different emphasis at different stages of industrial development. In the 1960s, an emphasis was placed on skill formation, which shifted to engineering education in the 1970s and to the industrial innovation of the private sector in the 1980s. This policy played a decisive role in improving industrial competitiveness, which in turn led to sustained growth and accumulation.

Fifth, capital accumulation began to decelerate from the early 1990s, reflecting the falling profitability of investment. The investment rate rose rapidly until the end of the 1980s but began to decline from the early 1990s. As a result, the growth of fixed capital formation, which had been major source of growth, fell significantly since the early 1990s, imposing a negative impact on growth. Economic growth thus began to slow down since the early 1990s. The deceleration of capital accumulation seemed largely attributable to falling profitability, which was pronounced entering the 1990s. As shown in Table 3.8, the rate of return on assets and equity in the

Table 3.8   Returns on Assets and Returns on Equity in the Manufacturing Sector, 1986–1999 (Unit: percent)

	Returns on Assets			Returns on Equity		
	All firms	Big 30	Non-chaebol	All firms	Big 30	Non-chaebol
1986	4.45	3.03	6.66	20.02	15.11	26.38
1988	4.93	4.99	7.91	20.48	21.88	28.60
1990	2.52	1.67	3.65	9.39	7.15	10.98
1992	1.37	1.01	1.97	5.78	4.64	6.83
1994	2.69	2.88	2.79	10.75	11.93	10.17
1996	0.93	0.68	1.45	3.73	2.90	5.45
1997	−0.31	−0.88	0.12	−1.41	−4.59	0.46
1998	−1.51	−1.94	−1.19	−6.71	−9.71	−4.37
1999	1.41	0.95	2.82	5.03	3.43	8.77

Source: Krueger and Yoo (2006, p. 184).

manufacturing sector fell continuously in the 1990s except for a few years, and in this regard, chaebols which were highly leveraged were hit harder than non-chaebols.

Chapter 4

Growth and Structural Change

4.1 Investment-Led Growth

The Korean economy achieved rapid growth over the past half century. GDP grew at an average annual rate of 8 percent during the period 1954–1997. It is remarkable that, as shown in Table 4.1, almost all sectors except agriculture showed performances of high growth. The manufacturing sector recorded the highest growth of 13.2 percent, followed by 8.3 percent in services and 7.8 percent in social overhead capital (SOC). The agricultural sector showed a relatively slow growth rate of 3.2 percent.

Although the growth rate slowed down considerably after the financial crisis in 1997, the Korean economy continued to maintain moderate growth with per capita GNI (Gross National Income) jumping to USD 26,205 in 2013 from USD 67 in 1953, an almost 400-fold increase in 60 years.[1] The exports had a dramatic growth, rising from less than USD 30 million to over USD 560 billion in the same period. In 2013, Korea's total trade amounted to more than USD 1 trillion, leading Korea to be ranked as the seventh largest trade economy in the world.

The remarkable performance of the Korean economy was largely driven by exports and investment, which grew in real terms annually at 17.8 percent and 14.1 percent, respectively, (Table 4.2). Which one played the more important role in Korea's growth process? In

---

[1]See National Accounts 2014, The Bank of Korea.

Table 4.1   Economic Growth by Industrial Sector, 1954–2010 (Unit: percent)

	1954–1960	1961–1970	1971–1980	1981–1990	1991–1997	1954–1997	1998–2010
GDP	3.9	8.5	9.1	8.7	7.5	8.0	4.5
Agriculture and fishery	2.4	4.6	1.6	3.7	1.1	3.2	1.1
Mining and manufacturing	12.1	15.9	14.2	11.8	7.5	12.5	7.3
	(12.8)	(17.0)	(16.2)	(12.3)	(7.7)	(13.2)	(7.4)
Service	3.8	8.7	8.6	9.2	8.0	7.8	4.2
Electricity, gas, water, and construction	9.8	19.7	10.8	10.6	6.2	8.3	0.9

Note: Figures in parentheses indicate growth rate of manufacturing.
Source: National Accounts 2009, 2014. The Bank of Korea.

Table 4.2   Growth Rate of GDP, Consumption, Investment, Exports, and Employment, 1954–2010 (Unit: percent)

	1954–1960	1961–1970	1971–1980	1981–1990	1991–1997	1954–1997	1998–2010
GDP	3.9	8.5	9.1	8.7	7.5	8.0	4.5
Consumption	4.3	6.6	6.7	7.9	6.9	6.6	3.6
Investment	9.2	22.3	14.9	12.8	8.0	14.1	2.5
Exports	9.8	29.0	22.8	12.1	15.0	17.8	10.9
Employment	—	3.5[a]	3.7	2.7	2.3	2.9[b]	−0.1

Notes: [a] 1964–1970; [b] 1964–1997.
Source: National Accounts 2009, 2014. The Bank of Korea.

this regard, the neoclassical view is that Korea's rapid growth was export-led, because the export-oriented policy made exports highly profitable, which led the economy to specialize in accordance with its comparative advantage, resulting in rising incomes, savings and investment, and growth. In other words, there was a virtuous circle between export-oriented policy and growth.

Although exports played a crucial role in Korea's rapid growth process, the export-led growth hypothesis seemed to overstate the role of exports in growth, because exports accounted for a rather small part of the economy in the early stage, which meant that the contribution of exports to growth could not have been very high until the 1970s. The high growth rate of exports in the 1960s and 1970s is also somewhat misleading, given the extremely low initial base of exports. More importantly, there is no clear empirical evidence supporting the higher profitability of exports compared to non-export activities. The relative price of exports remained fairly stable in the 1960s and even fell in the 1970s, implying that the profitability of exports was unlikely to be higher than non-export activities during this period.[2]

In the 1960s and 1970s, it was generally understood among the Korean business firms that they engaged in export activities not because of higher profitability but because of the easy access to subsidized credits, the availability of which was critical for running their business. They attempted to export whatever was exportable to acquire export credits, implying that the consideration of profitability did not play a decisive role in exports. Therefore, the argument that export-oriented policies made exports highly profitable, leading to high savings, investment, and growth, is not convincing.

This is further supported by the fact that the export sector revealed less productivity growth than the non-export sector. During 1966–1970, for example, the total factor productivity (TFP) growth of the export sector averaged 5.4 percent, while that of import substituting and domestic industries averaged 8.5 percent and 14 percent, respectively.[3] In this period, despite lower productivity growth, exports grew at 36.7 percent per annum, suggesting that productivity growth did not play an important role in export growth.

There were certainly export industries which displayed higher productivity growth, for instance, labor-intensive industries such as textiles, leather products, rubber products, and electrical machinery and appliances, but they did not affect the overall productivity performance of the export sector much. The reason behind the low productivity growth of the export sector was largely due to inefficiency, arising from a variety of direct and indirect subsidies extended to export industries. In fact, many Korean exporters were making negative profits during the 1960s and 1970s, and the losses were compensated by subsidies and high profits from their domestic sales.

---

[2]For a detailed discussion, see Rodrik (1995, pp. 61–64).

[3]For more details, see Kim (1972, p. 29).

It is further noted that the rapid growth of investment was largely driven by HCI-oriented policies rather than export-oriented policies because the government began to provide massive support to HCIs which brought about huge investment boom in the 1960s and 1970s, which in turn enabled the Korean economy to have sustained high income and export growth in the subsequent periods. The extensive export incentives certainly made an important contribution to stimulating investment, but they were not likely to have a significant impact on overall investment rate. Therefore, it seems better to say that Korea's rapid growth was investment-led rather than export-led.[4] It is also worth mentioning that investment is the important source of export growth as it contributes to augment capacity to export. Even from this dynamic perspective, it is logical to say that high growth should have been led by investment rather than by exports.

The investment-led growth process is also discernable when we look at the movement of the investment rate and GDP growth rate. As shown in Fig. 4.1, GDP growth rate and investment rate revealed more or less a similar movement except around early 1980s and late 1980s in which the Korean economy suffered greatly from the non-economic factors. The similar movement of investment rate and growth rate seems to reflect investment-led growth process, implying that capital accumulation was the major source of economic growth.

Although investment played a major role in pushing growth, the contribution of exports to growth should not be understated because exports have grown very fast, increasing at a double-digit rate since the 1960s (Table 4.2). According to demand side analysis of output growth, the contribution of exports expansion to growth has shown

---

[4]According to Rodrik, the rapid rise in the export to GDP ratio in the 1960s and 1970s cannot be explained by the export-oriented policy, but better by the investment boom that generated import demand for capital goods, which in turn generated exports. Thus, causality runs from investment to import and from import to export. His argument is quite plausible, since exports during this period were constrained more by capacity to produce than by relative profitability of exports. For a detailed discussion, see Rodrik (1995, pp. 72–74).

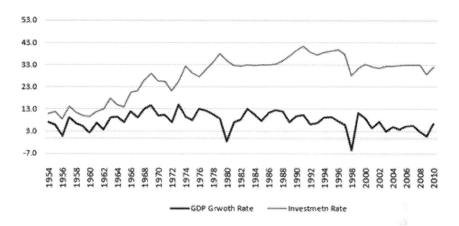

Figure 4.1 GDP Growth and Investment Rate, 1954–2010 (Unit: percent)

Source: National Accounts 2014. The Bank of Korea.

a rising trend until 1980s, although it was much lower than that of domestic demand expansion.[5]

The question is how could exports grow so fast? In this regard, it is important to realize that the Korean government deliberately promoted HCIs from the second five-year plan, the objective of which was to transform them into competitive export industries. To enhance competitiveness of HCIs which were mostly import substituting industries, a variety of manpower and technology policy measures were taken along with massive financial and fiscal supports, which enabled them to grow into export industries, as reflected in the rapidly rising share of HCI exports. The share of HCI products in total exports increased from 12.8 percent in 1970 to 41.8 percent in 1980 and 56.6 percent in 1990. Since export incentives were almost terminated in the 1980s, the rapid export growth in the 1980s and

---

[5]According to the demand-side decomposition of output growth, export expansion accounted for 9.2 percent of output growth, much lower than that of domestic demand expansion which accounted for 78 percent during 1955–1963. The contribution of export expansion increased to 32.4 percent from 1963 to 1975 and 41.7 percent from 1975 to 1985, while contribution of domestic demand expansion fell to 64.4 percent and 52.5 percent during the same period. See Kim (2001, pp. 60–61).

thereafter had little to do with export-oriented policy and more to do with the rapid development of the HCI sector which became increasingly export-oriented.

4.2   The Slowing Growth Rate

After three decades of rapid economic growth, the Korean economy began to slow down entering the 1990s. The growth rate fell from 9.8 percent in the 1980s to 7.5 percent in the 1990s. This trend was evident in almost all sectors, including mining and manufacturing, service and SOC sectors, as well as consumption, investment, and employment. Exports alone maintained the growth pace of the previous decade (Table 4.2).

The slow growth performance in the 1990s was largely due to sluggish investment. The investment rate began to decrease after it reached a record high 40 percent in 1991, resulting in falling capital accumulation. Fixed capital formation, which recorded double-digit growth in the 1980s, dropped to single-digit growth in the 1990s. The falling investment rate was, to some extent, unavoidable because the investment rate was unusually high, so it was not likely to be sustainable.

It is important to note that other factors also contributed to the falling investment rate. The political democratization movement and concomitant labor disputes that occurred from the late 1980s led to wage hikes, which negatively affected the competitiveness of Korean industries. The most labor-intensive industries lost their competitiveness to other developing countries which were quickly catching up with the Korean export market. Thus, Korean firms started to relocate their production facilities to countries with lower wages. On the other hand, Korean firms were increasingly exposed to foreign competition, as markets were opened at a faster pace while no longer being covered by government subsidies and protection. Thus, the profitability of investment continued to fall further in the 1990s, leading to slower accumulation and growth.

The situation became much worse after the financial crisis in 1997, as the Korean economy underwent major structural reforms that led to a sharp decline in investment activities followed by a slowdown in growth, and there were no signs of sustained growth after the short recovery in 1999 and 2000. The growth rate almost halved, falling from 7.5 percent in the 1991–1997 to 4.5 percent in the 1998–2010. The investment rate also dropped to 28.9 percent from 37.2 percent during the same period. The more striking fact is that in real terms, investment increased only 2.5 percent per year during the period 1998–2010 against the 8 percent increase of the 1991–1997 (Table 4.2).

A number of complex factors contributed to the slowdown of investment and growth in the post-crisis period. First of all, the massive restructuring of big conglomerates left little room for active private investment. Most firms were pressed to restore financial soundness to reduce excessively high indebtedness, which was blamed as a major cause of the financial crisis. The macroeconomic environment was also unfavorable for investment, as the government implemented tight monetary and fiscal policies to stabilize the economy. The massive unemployment and increased income inequality caused by the crisis led to a drastic policy change, emphasizing equity rather than growth. Social expenditures were thus greatly expanded while reducing economic expenditures, which did not leave much room for public-sector investment.

Private-sector investment also contracted considerably due to financial sector reform aimed at strengthening the supervisory and regulatory system, which forced financial institutions to pursue a conservative credit lending policy based on profitability and stability. Large enterprises also knew that the "too big to fail" system no longer worked, which made them very cautious in undertaking investment. The pro-labor government which came into being in the early 2000s continued to press chaebols to reduce their economic power. The lack of labor market flexibility also prevented private firms from investing at home, making them favor overseas investment.

This resulted in the prolonged slowdown of growth. The SOC sector including electricity, gas, water supply, and construction suffered the most from the government's austerity program and grew less than 1 percent against the 6.2 percent growth of the

1990s. The service sector also suffered from low growth due to the massive unemployment brought about by the restructuring of big corporations and financial institutions; thus, the growth rate dropped to 4.2 percent from the 8 percent of the 1991–1997. Only the manufacturing sector maintained a relatively high growth of 7.4 percent, thanks mainly to the sustained growth of exports which averaged 10.9 percent in the 1998–2010.

4.3   Structural Changes

The rapid economic growth over the past half century accompanied drastic changes in the structure of the Korean economy. The value-added share of agriculture and fisheries in GDP fell from around 50 percent to 2.9 percent between 1953 and 2007. The share of the mining and manufacturing sector rapidly increased, rising from 10.1 percent in 1953 to 28.6 percent in 2000 and then slightly dropped in 2007. The share of the SOC and service sector steadily grew from 42.6 percent to 69.6 percent during the same period.

This rapid structural change indicates that the Korean economy is gradually approaching the economic structure of advanced industrial countries, in which the service sector is dominant. A comparison of the Korean production structure with that of Japan, as shown in Table 4.3, shows that the Japanese production structure of 2006 is not particularly different from Korea's in 2007. The share of agriculture and that of mining and manufacturing are slightly higher in Korea, whereas the share of the service sector is higher in Japan; however, the difference is insignificant.

Similar changes can be found in the employment structure. The employment share of the agriculture, forestry, and fisheries sector continued to decrease and dropped to 7.4 percent in 2007. The employment share of the mining and manufacturing sector grew until 1990, and then started to decrease thereafter. The share of SOC and services has continued to rise since 1970 and is likely to grow further.

It is interesting that the employment share of each sector differed from its production share, reflecting its relative labor productivity change. For example, in 2007, the employment share of the mining

Table 4.3   Structural Changes of Production and Employment, 1953–2007 (Unit: percent)

Year	Agriculture and Fisheries		Mining and Manufacturing		SOC and Services	
	Value added	Emp.	Value added	Emp.	Value added	Emp.
1953	47.3	—	10.1	—	42.6(40.8)	—
1960	36.8	63.0	15.9	8.7[a]	47.3(43.2)	28.3[a]
1970	29.1	50.4	20.1	14.3	50.8(44.3)	25.3
1980	16.1	34.0	26.0	22.5	58.0(48.0)	43.5
1990	8.7	17.9	27.4	27.6	63.9(51.5)	54.5
2000	4.6	10.6	28.6	20.4	66.8(57.3)	69.0
2007	2.9	7.4	27.5	17.7	69.6(60.0)	75.0
2006(Japan)	1.5	—	21.7	—	76.8(68.1)	—

Notes: [a]1963. Figures in parentheses indicate value added in the service sector.
Sources: National Accounts 2009, The Bank of Korea; The 60-Year History of the Korean Economy-I (2010, p. 205).

and manufacturing sector was much lower than that of its production share, implying that its labor productivity is higher than other sectors of the economy, followed by the SOC and service sector. The agriculture sector is likely to display the lowest productivity, since its production share is far lower than its employment share.

It is also interesting to see that the employment share of the mining and manufacturing sector was falling much faster than its production share since 2000, suggesting that its productivity should have increased faster than other sectors of the economy. In contrast, the employment share of the SOC and service sector continued to increase faster than its production share, indicating the relative decline of its productivity. The relative decline of labor productivity can also be found in the agriculture sector, since its production share was falling much faster than its employment share.

4.4   Sources of Growth

The previous chapter mentioned that capital accumulation played a major role in Korea's economic growth. Since economic growth is determined not only by capital, but also by labor and technology, it is necessary to examine in detail the sources of growth using the growth accounting method. Although the growth accounting method does not explain the causality of growth, it is useful for identifying the contribution of production factors to economic growth.

Numerous attempts have been made to analyze the sources of Korea's economic growth using the growth accounting method. The findings differed considerably depending on the methodology and data used, but the general conclusion was that Korea's rapid growth in the past was largely driven by factor inputs, particularly capital input, which played a far greater role than labor input and TFP growth. As labor was abundant while skills and capital were deficient in the early stage of development, it seems natural that capital accumulation played a major role, while productivity growth played an insignificant role in the growth process. This is confirmed by a study by Hahn and Shin, as shown in Table 4.4, in which capital accumulation was shown in terms of per worker capital.

The pre-crisis and post-crisis period should be distinguished when examining sources of growth, because government policy differed significantly before and after the crisis. In the pre-crisis period, the government pursued a growth-first policy by placing top priority on

Table 4.4   Sources of Growth in Major Regions, 1961–2004 (Unit: percent)

	GDP Growth	Per Worker GDP Growth	Contribution from	
			Per Worker Capital	TFP Growth
World (83)	4.0	2.4	1.2	1.3
Advanced (22)	3.3	2.1	1.1	1.1
China	7.2	5.4	2.1	3.4
Korea				
(1961–2004)	7.1	4.7	2.9	1.8
(2001–2004)	4.5	2.9	1.3	1.5
East Asia (5)	5.7	2.8	1.8	1.0
Latin America (22)	3.7	1.0	0.6	0.4
South Asia (4)	4.9	3.0	1.1	1.8

Note: Figures in parentheses indicate the number of countries covered.

Source: Hahn and Shin (2010), quoted from Sakong and Koh (2010, p. 93).

growth while leaving distribution largely to market forces. On the contrary, in the post-crisis period, government policy shifted toward emphasizing welfare and distribution, so that growth became of second concern.

As mentioned earlier, there was a significant slowdown in the investment rate after the crisis, which in turn led to slowing growth. As shown in Table 4.4, per worker capital increased only 1.3 percent per year in the 2001–2004 during which per worker GDP grew 2.9 percent, accounting for 44.8 percent of per worker GDP growth. The rest was contributed by TFP which grew 1.5 percent in the same period. The striking fact is that TFP growth contributed more than capital accumulation to economic growth, implying that capital accumulation was no longer a major driver of growth in the post-crisis period.

This is in great contrast to the pre-crisis period during which capital accumulation was the major contributor to growth. Between 1961 and 2000, per worker capital increased roughly 3 percent per year while TFP growth increased, on average, 1.8 percent per year, indicating that capital accumulation played a major role in the growth process. Due to the dominant role of capital accumulation in the pre-crisis period, the contribution of capital accumulation to economic growth was much higher than that of productivity growth during entire period under review. The per worker capital growth rate was 2.9 percent, while the per worker GDP growth rate averaged 4.7 percent during this period. This indicates that capital accumulation accounted for 61.7 percent of per worker GDP growth, with the rest being contributed by productivity growth.

As mentioned above, in the post-crisis period productivity growth played a more important role than capital accumulation in sustaining growth, and this is likely to continue in the future unless investment rate is substantially raised. Since a substantial increase in capital accumulation is not likely to occur in the future, Korea's growth will to a greater extent depend on productivity growth, which in the past seemed rather high compared to countries in other regions (Table 4.4).

Korea's relatively high productivity growth in the past owed much to economic liberalization, increasing human capital formation and

R&D expenditures, and the improvement of industrial structure. The problem is that these efficiency-enhancing factors have more or less reached their limits, at least in quantitative terms, implying that it may not be easy to further facilitate productivity growth. The Korean economy is fully liberalized as far as market opening is concerned, leaving little room for further liberalization. Korea's R&D/GDP ratio reached 3.47 percent in 2010, almost as high as that of advanced countries, so that any substantial increase in the R&D/GDP ratio seems unlikely, thereby constraining the capacity for innovation and technology development.

The same holds true for human capital formation and industrial structure, as far as quantitative expansion is concerned. This, of course, is not meant to exclude any possibility of further productivity improvement, but to suggest that special efforts are needed to enhance the overall efficiency of the economy based on qualitative improvement rather than the quantitative expansion of these factors.

4.5   Institutional and Policy Factors

The growth accounting method is a simple *ex post* analysis of sources of growth aimed at identifying the quantitative contribution of production factors to growth. This kind of quantitative analysis alone is too simple to explain the complex process of growth which involves many institutional and policy problems. Therefore, the growth accounting method should be complemented by qualitative analysis for a better understanding of the growth process. There were numerous institutional and policy factors that affected Korea's rapid growth. Since we cannot deal with all the problems, our discussion is confined to key areas considered critical for the successful implementation of development plans.

4.5.1 *Strong Leadership Commitment*

Korea implemented six consecutive five-year economic plans until 1991 since the introduction of the first plan in 1962. Development plans were introduced in most newly independent countries after the Second World War, but the majority of them were not particularly successful excluding a few East Asian countries. Korea was one of those that achieved success. The design of the development plan itself was not so important; more crucial was its successful implementation, which depends very much on the leadership's commitment to development.

In this respect, the late President Park Chung Hee made an important contribution because he laid the institutional basis for the successful design and implementation of the development plans. His strong commitment to economic development was reflected in many aspects. The first was organizational reform for planning, which led to the establishment of a central planning agency called the Economic Planning Board (EPB) in 1961. At the beginning, the EPB was responsible for economic planning, budgeting, and government statistics. In 1963, the status of the minister of the EPB was promoted to Deputy Prime Minister (DPM), to assume the responsibility of inter-ministerial policy coordination. The function of the EPB was considerably expanded in the 1970s and 1980s, becoming responsible for monopoly regulation, investment project appraisal and performance monitoring, and international policy coordination. Thus, the EPB became very powerful with resource allocation completely under its control irrespective of financing sources.

The integration of the planning, budgeting, and coordination function into one agency played a pivotal role in the effective coordination and implementation of development plans and policies. Since the minister of the EPB held the position of DPM, the EPB could easily exercise coordination through various means and methods. Budgetary control was no doubt the most effective means to control other ministries. Besides budgetary control, there were other mechanisms through which the EPB exercised coordination. Important policy issues that required inter-ministry coordination and consultation were discussed at ministerial meetings, all chaired by the DPM.

Consultative ministerial meetings were often held to discuss policy issues and exchange views to build a consensus before policy proposals were submitted to formal ministerial meetings such as the

Economic Ministers Meeting. The meeting was held whenever the DPM considered it necessary, usually once a week. The meeting provided the DPM with an important vehicle for coordinating economic policies at the policy planning stage. When the EPB faced a deadlock in the coordination process, the president's office stepped in so that the EPB could implement policy coordination effectively.

The growing importance of the EPB in the process of Korea's development made it easy to draw elites of the Korean society into the institution. Since the EPB was staffed with elites and generally free from pressure groups, it could design development strategies and policies based on rational economic reasoning, thereby providing the institutional basis on which Korea was able to grow fast. In this process, the EPB was greatly supported by think tanks such as the Korea Development Institute.

However, the status of the EPB weakened from the late 1980s as Korea underwent drastic political and socio-economic transformation, which had a significant impact on development policy planning. The state-led development strategy was increasingly challenged in tandem with the rapidly growing size of the economy coupled with the political democratization movement. This led to the dismantling of the central planning system, as the EPB merged with the Ministry of Finance to become the Ministry of Finance and Economy in 1994. While the dismantling of the central planning system was unavoidable, we should recognize the contribution the EPB made to the growth and development of the Korean economy from the 1960s through the 1980s.

Another important institutional factor reflecting the strong leadership commitment was the Monthly Economic Review Meeting and Monthly Export Promotion Meeting, both initiated by President Park. The former was first launched under the military government and then was held regularly from 1965. The meeting was held every month at the EPB, and leaders of the ruling party, top economic advisers to the president, and cabinet members participated to discuss the overall economic situation and policy agenda. In the meeting, President Park was briefed on current economic trends and policy issues and gave directions and checked on follow-up measures in the next meetings.

The meeting was very effective in implementing various economic policy agendas. Cabinet members and policymakers had to be prepared not only to report on progress, but also to answer questions from President Park. A former high official from Park's government describes Park's passion and commitment to economic success, saying, "I really respect his (Park) passionate attitude. If a goal was not achieved, he demanded full explanations until he was satisfied. We constantly had to do our best to meet his expectations." A media report on President Park's regime once evaluated that "Park's resolution and commitment were so strong that once a goal was set, he pushed forward to achieve it no matter how big and difficult the challenge was. His extraordinary resolution and determination were the true locomotion of Korea's economic development."[6] The Monthly Economic Review Meeting was not held under the Chun Doo Hwan government, as the government policy shifted toward a market-oriented development strategy in the 1980s.

The Monthly Economic Review Meeting in earlier days provided a good opportunity for President Park to learn about the economy. Later, he himself became an economic expert and led the economic development policy in the 1960s and 1970s. The biggest SOC project of the Seoul–Busan Highway and the construction of the Pohang Integrated Steel Mill (POSCO) in the 1960s were his ideas and had initially faced strong opposition by most economists and politicians.

The "Monthly Export Promotion Meeting" was another crucial pillar of the institutions that represented President Park's strong will to develop the Korean economy. In the early years of the Park administration, Korea faced a severe foreign exchange crisis due to the sharp reduction of US aid. Export promotion emerged as the most important strategy to secure sufficient foreign exchange reserves, which was essential not only for successful implementation

---

[6]For more details, see Kang *et al.* (2008, pp. 134–135).

of development plan, but also for the stability of the regime. Thus, the government introduced various measures for export promotion including the Export Promotion Act of 1962 and the Committee for Export Promotion. In 1964, the Committee was expanded to the "Extended Export Promotion Meeting" with the inclusion of experts from private sectors. The meeting convened monthly between 1966 and 1979. President Park himself made sure to attend the meeting.

The role of the Extended Export Promotion Meeting included the following: an analysis and assessment of export performance, awards to business firms of high export performance, and discussions on difficulties in export activities faced by private sectors. The meeting first started as an inter-governmental body, but private business firms started participating shortly after. The manifestation of President Park's strong will for export promotion strengthened the credibility of government policy in the market, which helped promote exports and private investment. Furthermore, the export drive created a strong belief in the business community that exporting was a profitable economic activity. The Korean government set an export target every year during the period of 1962–1981, and the target was always surpassed except for in the first year, 1962.

4.5.2   *Transforming Import Substitution Industries into Export Industries*

Korea's success story stems from its outstanding industrialization which enabled Korea to maintain high growth over the past half century. Many institutional and policy factors have contributed to Korea's success in industrial development. Korea is now a major producer of automobiles, computer chips, steel, and shipbuilding, among others, and emerged as a new industrial power within a relatively short span of time. The essence of this success story lies in the fact that Korea succeeded in transforming the import-substituting heavy and chemical industries into competitive export industries. In other words, Korea succeeded in completing the so-called second stage of import substitution, which many developing countries attempted to do but failed.

In this regard, most experts have ascribed Korea's successful industrial development to the outward-looking development strategy, highlighting export policy as a key factor of the success, while understating the role import substitution policy played in Korea's industrialization. Import substitution policy was often criticized in terms of efficiency because it advocates protection. Such a static view is unrealistic because an industry can rarely start off as an export industry from the beginning, as far as the manufacturing sector is concerned. Therefore, protection is a prerequisite for industrial development, as it enables industries under certain conditions to grow into export industries. In this sense, import substitution is a precondition for manufactured exports.

It is evident that Korea, with no significant natural resources, needed to develop industries to export, and in order to do so had to protect the domestic market so that they could grow first. The question is not, *per se*, whether or not to protect domestic industries, but how to transform protected industries into export industries. Korea succeeded in this regard because Korean export industries mostly started as import-substituting industries and then grew into exporting industries.

Korea's import substitution policy began with nondurable consumer goods, mostly processed foods and textiles using various tariff and non-tariff measures in the 1950s, and many of them turned into export industries in the 1960s. Entering the 1960s, the government promoted import substitution for basic materials and intermediate products such as oil refinery, synthetic fiber, cement, and fertilizers, which were required not only to meet the rapidly rising domestic demand but also to provide materials for export industries.

In the 1970s, heavy and chemical industries were promoted to facilitate industrialization and improve the structure of exports toward capital and technology-intensive industries. A number of supportive policies were provided while protecting them, so they could grow and then develop into export industries. In the 1980s, emphasis was placed on promoting capital goods industries, particularly the machinery industry, to satisfy growing domestic demand. A localization program for the machinery industry was launched aimed at the domestic production of machine tools and supported the industry with incentives. The program continued into the 1990s with intensive R&D support, which led to considerable improvement of the quality of domestically produced machinery, enabling it to grow as an export industry from the 1990s.

As briefly mentioned above, Korea took a phased approach to import substitution, starting with nondurable consumer goods, followed by intermediate products and durable consumer goods, and then moving on to producer and capital goods. Different incentive schemes were applied at different phases of import substitution to enhance industrial competitiveness. A detailed analysis of industrial policy development will follow in the next chapter. The factors that contributed to transforming import substitution industries into competitive export industries can be summarized as follows.

First, import substitution policy has evolved with the progress of industrialization. Tariff and non-tariff measures were primarily used to protect domestic markets in the 1950s and 1960s. Entering the 1970s, the government policy focused on stimulating investment in HCIs through fiscal and financial measures while protecting the domestic market. In the 1980s, the policy shifted toward enhancing industrial competitiveness by supporting manpower and technology development and opening the market.

Second, the inefficiency and rent-seeking activity usually associated with protectionism was relatively small, since the government pursued protectionism only for a limited period. The protectionist policy, widely used until the 1970s, was gradually replaced by import liberalization and the reduction of government support to promote the market mechanism and competition.

Third, the massive support for HCIs in the 1970s incurred the structural problems such as overinvestment in many heavy industries and the deterioration of industrial competitiveness, which led to an industrial policy shift. The selective industrial policy was replaced by functional industrial policy supporting manpower and technology development. The industrial rationalization program was introduced to cure ailing industries suffering from excess capacity or lack of competitiveness through various tax incentives, investment realignment, and so forth. The industrial policy shift combined with the rationalization program greatly contributed to improving the international competitiveness of HCIs.

Fourth, science and technology policy played a crucial role in transforming import substitution industries into export industries, because industrial competitiveness ultimately depends on skill and technology. Therefore, science and technology policy adapted to satisfy the changing needs of industrial development. In the 1960s, for example, emphasis was placed on skill formation to support labor-intensive export industries. In the 1970s, science and technology policy was directed to support the HCI drive. Specifically, the government set up various specialized state-funded research institutes, invited Korean scientists from abroad, and continued to strengthen the supply of technicians and engineers to meet the increasing demand for them. In the 1980s, the science and technology policy shifted toward promoting R&D activities and technology development of the private sector to enhance industrial competitiveness.

Fifth, government assistance to private firms was provided based on "reciprocity" to make it effective. Export credit was provided in exchange for export performance, tax incentives, and financial assistance for investment in HCIs. Government support under the rationalization program was implemented, provided that recipient firms agreed to capacity reduction and the demolition of outdated facilities, among others. In the case of government support for technology development, the matching fund system was used to oblige participating firms to contribute a certain proportion of the required R&D investment. This kind of performance- or reciprocity-based assistance helped make government support more effective and productive.

Finally, it should be mentioned that sustained high economic growth over several decades provided an ever-growing domestic market for HCIs, which enabled them to enjoy economies of scale and accumulate their technological competence, which in turn led them to grow as export industries. The rapid growth of the Korean economy with a population of over 40 million provided an explosive surge in domestic demand for cars, electronics, petrochemicals, steel, etc., which enabled them to grow fast and improve their competitiveness. In other words, without the sustained high growth of the economy, it would have hardly been possible to build competitive HCIs, suggesting that the expansion of the domestic market was the basis on which HCIs could transform themselves into export industries.

Chapter 5

Industrial Development and Structural Transformation

5.1 Evolution of Industrial Development Policy

Industrial development policy is a very broad concept covering monetary and fiscal policy, trade policy as well as technology and manpower development policy affecting the growth and structural change of manufacturing industries. It is a more general and broader concept than "industrial policy," which is usually defined as a policy aimed at the promotion of particular industries.[1] When we examine the industrialization process from a long-term development perspective, industrial policy should cover broader policy issue such as manpower and technology development because it plays a key role in industrial development. Based on this broader concept, we analyze Korea's industrial development policy, examining specific policy measures undertaken and their impacts on industrial development. Korea's industrial development policy over the past half century can be, broadly speaking, divided into five phases of evolution, as follows:

(1) Easy Import Substitution (1950s);
(2) Export Drive and Selective Import Substitution (1960s);
(3) Heavy and Chemical Industry (HCI) Promotion and Second-stage Import Substitution (1970s);

---

[1] For various definitions of the industrial policy concept, see Chang (1994, pp. 58–61).

(4) Structural Adjustment and Technology-oriented Industrial Policy (1980s);
(5) Globalization and Promotion of High-tech Industries (1990s).

5.1.1 *Easy Import Substitution (1950s)*

The first phase of industrial development in Korea covers the period from 1953 to 1960, in which the easy import substitution policy was implemented. The major concern of the government policy during this period was to provide basic daily necessities for the population, and hence focused on the import substitution of nondurable consumer goods. Since the major source of financing imports was foreign aid, industrial policy was geared to utilizing aid goods, which comprised mostly raw materials and intermediate goods. As a result, raw material-processing industries such as processed foods, apparel, and fabricated textiles flourished during this period.

Protectionist policy measures were carried out to promote domestic industries. Tariff reforms were undertaken to increase tariff revenue while providing stronger protection for domestic industries. The simple average tariff rate was raised from a uniform 10 percent to around 40 percent in 1949. No duty was levied on food grains, non-competitive equipment, and raw material imports. Lower tariff rates were applied to essential and unfinished goods not domestically produced, higher rates were applied to finished goods produced in Korea, and the highest rates were reserved for luxury goods.

To promote domestic industries, tariffs were exempted for imports of machinery and equipment in the case of certain major industries including electric power, machinery and metal-working, chemicals, and textiles. In 1957, tariffs were further raised to protect domestic industries, but the basic structure remained unchanged since lower rates were applied to raw materials and non-competitive finished goods, while higher rates were applied to semi-finished goods and competitive finished goods.

Imports were controlled through a quota system and foreign exchange allocation. Quantitative controls on imports were implemented, based on the comprehensive demand and supply program which was announced semi-annually. Importable commodities were classified under three levels: automatic approval, restricted, and prohibited items. Foreign exchange was allocated to private traders and end-users through auction and bidding procedures, the lottery, and foreign exchange tax.[2] Since private exports were very small compared to total foreign exchange receipts, imports in the 1950s had to be financed by foreign aid or by the government-held foreign exchange (KFX). Foreign aid financed approximately 72 percent of total imports from 1953 to 1960.

A multiple exchange rate system was adopted with an overvalued official rate, which enabled the import of necessary raw materials and machinery at low prices, while offering a preferential rate for exports. The export–import link system was also used to favor exporters and various incentives were provided to promote exports, but these measures were mostly ineffective because exports comprised primary products which were not very responsive to price incentives.

The import substitution policy led to the rapid growth of imports of raw materials and intermediate goods while dampening imports of consumer goods, reflecting the rapid import substitution of nondurable consumer goods (Table 5.1). As a result, the import coefficient, defined as a ratio of imports divided by domestic demand, fell for consumer industries such as apparel and fabricated textiles, leather and leather products, and paper and paper products, except

Table 5.1   Composition of Imports by Category of Final Demand, 1953–1960 (Unit: percent)

	1953	1954	1955	1956	1957	1958	1959	1960
Consumer goods	70.4	59.2	34.3	34.8	40.5	36.5	23.6	24.6
Intermediate goods and raw materials	22.4	21.0	39.5	43.4	41.0	47.0	48.5	49.6
Investment goods	3.4	13.6	16.8	11.1	9.6	9.7	13.7	11.7

Source: Krueger (1979, p. 72).

---

[2]For more details, see Frank, Jr., *et al.* (1975, pp. 29–35).

Table 5.2   Import Coefficient[a] by Manufacturing Industry, 1953–1960

	1953	1954	1955	1956	1957	1958	1959	1960
Food and beverages	0.019	0.013	0.012	0.003	0.022	0.078	0.058	0.044
Textiles	0.108	0.135	0.146	0.051	0.037	0.053	0.055	0.071
Wearing apparel	0.015	0.003	0.004	0.018	0.013	0.044	0.008	0.004
Leather and its products	—	0.007	—	—	0.002	0.001	0.001	0.001
Paper and its products	0.428	0.372	0.414	0.181	0.208	0.475	0.341	0.304
Basic chemical products	0.145	0.127	0.162	0.092	0.077	0.414	0.310	0.303
Petroleum and coal products	0.152	0.066	0.089	0.010	0.045	0.600	0.561	0.336
Glass and Clay	—	0.066	0.047	0.065	0.003	0.140	0.116	0.024
Chemical fertilizer	1.000	1.000	1.000	1.000	1.000	1.000	1.000	0.967
Basic metal products	—	0.401	0.311	0.169	0.085	0.448	0.273	0.211
Fabricated metal products	0.001	0.061	0.047	0.042	0.021	0.099	0.043	0.095
Machinery	0.388	0.359	0.236	0.222	0.007	0.405	0.441	0.450
Electrical machinery	0.155	0.413	0.291	0.122	0.194	0.549	0.388	0.435

Note: [a]Import/Domestic demand.
Source: Suh (1975, pp. 77–81).

food and beverages in which import coefficient did not decline because despite increasing domestic production the imports continued to rise due to growing domestic demand (Table 5.2).

Falling import coefficients were also found in some intermediate products such as glass and clay, chemical fertilizer, and basic metal products. On the other hand, import dependency in heavy industries steadily increased due to a lack of domestic production. The upward trend of import coefficients was observed in most heavy industries, including basic chemical products, coal and petroleum products, fabricated metal products, machinery, and electrical machinery.

Import substitution for nondurable consumer goods such as processed food, beverages and tobacco, finished textiles, and leather products characterized industrial growth in the 1950s. They

Table 5.3   Growth of HCI and Light Industry, 1954–2000[a] (Unit: percent)

	1954–1960	1961–1970	1971–1980	1981–1990	1991–2000	1954–2000
Manufacturing	12.8	17.0	16.2 (18.2)	12.3	8.7	13.1
Light Industry	11.1	13.4	12.9 (14.2)	7.1	1.6	8.8
HCI	18.5	25.2	17.7 (20.0)	14.6	10.1	15.5

Note: [a]Figures in parentheses indicate growth rates during the period 1971–1979. For the classification of HCI and the light industry, see Table 5.4.

Source: National Accounts 2009, The Bank of Korea.

accounted for more than 70 percent of total manufacturing production in the 1950s, and most of them became export industries in the 1960s. Since these industries are all labor-intensive and do not require complicated technology, the 1950s are usually described as the period of easy import substitution in the light manufacturing consumer goods sector. Besides these nondurable consumer goods, some intermediate goods including plate glass, cement, and steel products also grew rapidly, but they did not affect the structure of production due to their insignificant production.

Thanks to rapid import substitution in consumer goods as well as some intermediate goods, the manufacturing sector recorded a relatively high growth rate of 12.8 percent per year and made an important contribution to improving the structure of production toward the manufacturing sector. Heavy industries grew faster than light industries, but the industrial structure did not change much due to the dominant role of light industries.

5.1.2   *Export Drive and Selective Import Substitution (1960s)*

As mentioned earlier in Chapter 1, the military government initially attempted to pursue an ambitious import substitution policy in the early 1960s, but failed due to the foreign exchange crisis in 1963. Thus, from 1964, the government was forced to shift the industrial policy from import substitution to export promotion. A total of

13 labor-intensive products were selected for export promotion.[3] They included cotton fabrics, wearing apparel, leather products, rubber products, radio, electric apparatus, plywood, ceramic ware, canned mushrooms, silk products, and woolen fabrics. Various incentives were provided including the introduction of a unitary floating exchange rate system after a drastic devaluation in 1964. These policy measures led to phenomenal export growth in the 1960s.

While promoting exports, the Korean government began to encourage import substitution in selected key industries such as cement, fertilizer, oil refinery, and synthetic fiber during the first five-year plan period. They were protected through quantitative restrictions and high tariffs and promoted with incentives including tariff exemptions on imported raw materials and capital goods, access to preferential credit, and a lower direct tax rate.

As the balance of payments improved in the mid-1960s, the government resumed efforts to promote HCIs including machinery, shipbuilding, electronics, petrochemicals, and steel. They were designated as strategic industries to be promoted, and special laws were introduced to support them through various incentives.

Thanks to government support for both exports and import substitution, the manufacturing sector grew rapidly at 17 percent per annum during 1961–1970, with HCIs growing faster than light industries. Thus, there was a marked structural shift toward HCIs, whose share in manufacturing value added increased from 28 percent in 1960 to 39.7 percent in 1970 (Table 5.4). It should be noted, however, that this structural shift was largely due to the rapid growth of chemical industries, such as rubber and plastic products. Since these products are labor-intensive rather than capital-intensive, labor-intensive light industries continued to play a dominant role in the manufacturing sector until the end of the 1960s.

---

[3]For details, see Kim (1990, p. 115).

Table 5.4   Structural Change of Production and Employment in Manufacturing, 1953–2000 (Unit: percent)

	1953	1960	1970	1980	1990	2000
Light industry	73.8	72.0	60.3	41.7	29.4	21.2
		(66.8)	(61.3)	(51.2)	(34.7)	(33.1)
Food, beverages, and	33.3	36.4	28.8	10.8	7.4	6.3
tobacco		(15.7)	(13.6)	(9.0)	(7.1)	(6.8)
Textile, garments, and	28.6	25.1	21.3	23.3	13.5	8.3
leather		(35.4)	(31.1)	(30.9)	(22.1)	(16.5)
Wood, paper, and	9.5	9.0	7.9	4.8	5.1	4.3
paper products		(13.4)	(11.0)	(7.8)	(7.4)	(6.4)
Others	2.4	1.5	2.3	2.9	3.3	2.3
		(2.3)	(5.6)	(3.5)	(3.1)	(3.4)
HCI	26.2	28.0	39.7	58.3	70.6	78.8
		(33.2)	(38.7)	(48.9)	(60.3)	(66.9)
Chemicals, coal, and	9.4	9.9	19.7	19.8	14.5	15.3
petroleum products		(12.1)	(11.8)	(13.2)	(14.4)	(11.6)
Non-metallic mineral	7.6	5.1	4.9	6.5	6.7	4.2
products		(6.0)	(5.8)	(4.7)	(4.2)	(3.2)
Basic metals	—	2.7	2.5	10.2	13.9	12.8
		(2.6)	(3.7)	(4.5)	(4.0)	(3.9)
Fabricated metals and	9.3	10.4	12.6	21.8	35.6	46.5
machinery		(12.5)	(17.4)	(26.5)	(37.7)	(48.2)
Total manufacturing	100.0	100.0	100.0	100.0	100.0	100.0

Note: Production is value added in current prices and figures in parenthesis indicate shares of employment. The HCI share of manufacturing production differs slightly from the one in Table 5.9 due to the difference in industrial classification. For details, see Kim (2016, p. 153).

Sources: National Accounts 2009. The Bank of Korea; Korea Statistical Office.

Similar patterns can be found in the export and employment structure. As shown in Table 5.5, the share of light manufacturing exports increased from 45.4 percent in 1964 to almost 70 percent of total exports, while the export share of heavy and chemical products witnessed a moderate increase, rising from 9.2 percent to 12.8 percent during the same period. The textile industry led manufacturing exports, accounting for 40.8 percent of total exports in 1970. In other words, labor-intensive light industries turned themselves from

Table 5.5   Structural Change of Exports, 1964–2008 (Unit: percent)

	Primary Products	Manufactured	HCI	Light Industry
1964	45.4	54.6	9.2	45.4 (27.7)
1970	19.5	82.4	12.8	69.6 (40.8)
1980	11.7	88.2	41.8	46.4 (29.1)
1990	4.9	95.1	56.6	38.5 (22.7)
2000	2.8	97.2	81.0	16.2 (10.9)
2005	1.5	98.5	89.6	8.9 (4.9)
2008	1.8	98.1	91.7	6.4 (3.2)

Note: Figures in parentheses indicate the share of textile products.
Source: Institute for International Trade, Korea Traders Association.

Table 5.6   Export and Import Ratios of HCI and Light Industry, 1960–1970 (Unit: %)

	Light Industry		HCI	
	E/DO	M/DD	E/DO	M/DD
1960	0.009	0.050	0.006	0.333
1961	0.013	0.053	0.009	0.289
1962	0.018	0.052	0.010	0.359
1963	0.033	0.052	0.021	0.366
1964	0.055	0.038	0.021	0.245
1965	0.063	0.037	0.035	0.236
1966	0.082	0.050	0.029	0.361
1967	0.104	0.056	0.030	0.345
1968	0.122	0.078	0.031	0.344
1969	0.116	0.084	0.047	0.320
1970	0.161	0.079	0.055	0.313

Notes: E: Export; M: Import; DD: Domestic Demand; DO: Domestic Output.
Source: Suh (1975, pp. 84–85).

import substitution into export industries; this is reflected in their increasing export ratios (Table 5.6). Apparel and fabricated textile products, leather and leather products, and wood and furniture displayed rapidly rising export ratios in the 1960s.[4]

---

[4]For more details, see Suh (1975, pp. 77–81).

It is remarkable that, unlike in the 1950s, the import coefficients of light manufacturing industries rose in the 1960s, implying that the growing import demand offset more than the import substitution effect. This is because in a rapidly growing economy like the Korean economy in the 1960s, import demand increased so quickly that the import coefficient could rise despite growing domestic production. The rising import coefficient of light manufacturing industries seemed largely due to rapidly growing import demand for raw materials and intermediate goods associated with export growth.

Unlike light manufacturing industries, which became export industries in the 1960s, no similar phenomenon was found in HCIs. While there was a slight upward trend in the export ratios of HCIs, it was far from significant, indicating that the HCIs were still in the stage of import substitution in the 1960s. This was reflected in the movement of the import coefficient of HCI which showed a slight downward trend since the early 1960s (Table 5.6).

The employment structure also advanced toward HCIs, but the shift was insignificant so that the light industries were the major source of employment creation in the 1960s, accounting for 61.3 percent of total manufacturing employment in 1970 (Table 5.4).

In conclusion, the 1960s can be explained as a period marked by the simultaneous promotion of exports and selective import substitution. This is confirmed by the industrial incentive system. As shown in Table 5.7, heavy industries for domestic sales, such as consumer durables, machinery, and transport equipment, had a high effective protection rate. In contrast, most exporting industries including processed foods, construction materials, intermediate products, and consumer nondurables had either a negative or very low effective protection rate. Most heavy industries had high effective subsidies favoring the domestic market, whereas in the rest of industries they favored exports. This indicates that although overall incentives in the manufacturing sector were in favor of exports, some selected heavy industries were highly protected by offering them an exclusive domestic market. In other words, the incentive system was not neutral, as contended by the neoclassical.

Table 5.7   Korea's Effective Protection and Effective Subsidy Rates, 1968 (Unit: percent)

Industry Group (ISIC)	Effective Protection Rate		Effective Subsidy Rate	
	E	D	E	D
Primary activities	−16	18	−3	22
Processed foods	−3	−18	2	−25
Beverages and tobacco	−2	−19	15	−26
Construction material	−5	−11	6	−17
Intermediate products |	31	−25	43	−30
Intermediate products ||	0	26	17	20
Consumer non-durables	−2	−11	5	−21
Consumer durables	−5	64	2	38
Machinery	−13	44	5	31
Transport equipment	−53	163	−23	159
Manufacturing	3	−1	12	−9
All industries	0	11	9	10

Notes: D and E stand for domestic and export sales, respectively.
Intermediate products \| and \|\| correspond to intermediate products at lower and higher levels of fabrication, respectively.
Source: Westphal and Kim (1982), quoted from Moreira (1995, p. 40).

5.1.3   HCI Promotion and Second-Stage Import Substitution (1970s)

Moving into the 1970s, the government began to intensify its support for HCIs. Rising protectionism against labor-intensive products in developed countries prompted Korean policymakers to advance the structure of exports toward products with high income and growth elasticity, suggesting the urgent need for developing capital and technology-intensive industries.

The catch-up development strategy also played an important role in promoting HCIs. In the early 1970s, there was a general understanding among the policymakers that Korea was around 20–30 years behind Japan in industrial development. Therefore, they believed it was possible for Korea to catch up with Japan, provided that Korea successfully promoted HCIs. Thus, tremendous efforts were made to study the Japanese industrial development policy and its performance. Security concerns also played an important role in the HCI drive due to the heightening tension with North Korea and the US government's withdrawal of its troops from Asia in the early 1970s.

The year 1972, in which the third five-year plan began, marked a turning point for Korea's political and economic development, as reflected in the introduction of the new Constitution in 1972 and the official declaration to promote the HCI in 1973. In his 1973 New Year's address, President Park announced his intention to launch the HCI plan which required a total investment of USD 9.6 billion between 1973 and 1981. By promoting HCIs, the government aimed to achieve the goal of USD 1,000 per capita income and USD 10 billion of exports by 1981, which was very ambitious since Korea's per capita income in 1972 was a little over USD 300, with exports amounting to only USD 1.6 billion. The six HCIs mentioned earlier were designated as key industries to be promoted. The government intended to develop most of these industries as leading export industries and expected their share in commodity exports to reach more than 50 percent of total exports by 1981.

As the emphasis of the industrial and trade policy shifted toward promoting HCIs, a number of important policy changes occurred in financial and fiscal policy, as well as manpower and technology policy. The incentive system, which favored exports over domestic sales, was reformed to support HCIs. While gradually reducing incentives for exports, the preferential tax and credit system was increasingly intensified for the benefit of HCIs. The preferential tax treatment of export earnings was abolished in 1973. Tariff exemption on the import of capital equipment for export production was switched to an installment payment system in 1974. In 1975, tariff exemptions on raw material imports for export production was replaced by a tariff rebate system, under which duties on imported raw material for export production were rebated at the time of export. Thus, the only remaining features of the export incentive system were commodity tax exemption and preferential export credits.

A series of preferential financial and tax incentives were devised to induce investment in HCIs. The government established the National Investment Fund (NIF) in 1974 to facilitate investment in the HCI sector. The idea of the NIF was to channel savings and idle public funds into more productive activities, such as

HCIs and long-term export financing. The NIF, which consisted of funds from government contributions, various public funds, and savings from banking institutions, was made available mostly for HCIs at a preferential rate, and the interest rate differences were subsidized by the government. The interest rate on equipment loans for HCI projects was in general 2–3 percentage points lower than the commercial lending rate, and the repayment period was also long, ranging from 8 to 10 years.

Credit allocation for the HCI sector by banking institutions increased rapidly since the early 1970s, with the sector's share in total incremental lending rising from 35.6 percent in 1973 to 59.8 percent in 1980. Thus, 75 percent of facility investment in the manufacturing sector went to HCIs during the period 1973–1979, leaving only 25 percent of investment to the light industry.[5] This led to overinvestment in many heavy industries generating bottlenecks in light industries.

Besides the indirect financing through the NIF, the government made direct investments in the HCI sector in the form of constructing industrial complexes and equity investment. As a result, public expenditures in the HCI sector expanded rapidly, accounting for 3.8 percent of the total central government expenditure and 15.6 percent of the economic services expenditure during 1970–1980.[6] The government also provided various tax incentives for the promotion of HCIs. Those who invested in the so-called "important industries" were exempted completely from corporate income tax for the first 3 years, and 50 percent for the following 2 years. Alternatively, they could either receive an 8 percent investment credit (10 percent in the case of domestically produced machinery and equipment) or an extra 100 percent of the special depreciation allowance.

The "important industries" included the six strategic HCIs (petrochemicals, shipbuilding, machinery, electronics, steel, and non-ferrous metal) plus fertilizers, the defense industry, electric power generation, aircraft, and mining. Tax reforms were also undertaken to increase

---

[5]Lee (1991, p. 452).
[6]See Lee (1991, p. 451).

fiscal revenue by introducing the resident tax and telephone tax in 1973, the defense tax in 1975, and value added tax in 1976. Thus, the tax/GDP ratio rose from 12.3 percent in 1972 to 16.7 percent in 1979. Despite tax reform efforts, the fiscal deficit continued to aggravate, threatening economic stability.

There was also a change in the tariff exemption system for imported machinery and equipment. While exporters had received duty exemption on their imports in the past, exemptions since 1974 were granted only for the import of capital goods that were used for new facility installations of important industries, regardless of whether they produced for exports or the domestic market. Since the important industries were mostly import-substituting industries, providing duty-free entry of capital goods for these industries removed the advantage the exporters had previously possessed. Since major export industries such as textiles, clothing, and shoes were not included in the important industries, the policy was in favor of import substitution while discriminating against exports.

The tariff system gradually changed in the direction of raising tariffs for the intermediate and capital goods, while reducing tariffs for consumer goods. In the 1973 tariff reform, tariff rates on heavy and chemical products and intermediate goods were raised, whereas the previously high rates on finished consumer goods such as textiles were generally cut by approximately 10–50 percentage points. Duties on capital goods such as machinery and machine elements and recently established industries were further raised in the 1976 tariff reform, although the tariff structure had been simplified and the average tariff rate was overall lowered.

Besides financing problems, manpower and technology was another critical policy issue faced by the Korean government, because a large number of skilled manpower including engineers and scientists were required to carry out HCI projects. At that time, Korea did not have enough skilled manpower to run modern machinery, not to mention engineers and scientists to assimilate and adapt imported technology. President Park set up the Korea Institute of Science and Technology (KIST) in 1966 and invited dozens of scientists and engineers working abroad back to Korea for KIST.

Korea's research level was very modest at the beginning of the 1970s, with the R&D/GNP ratio standing at no more than 0.3 percent in 1971. Only 2,477 persons were classified as researchers working in the science and technology field. There was no other research institute aside from KIST that could carry out any substantial research. Various policy measures were undertaken to solve the manpower and technology problem, which are further discussed in Chapter 11.

The massive support for HCIs spurred an investment boom, leading to the rapid growth of manufacturing and structural shift toward the HCI sector. As shown in Table 5.3, the manufacturing sector grew at an annual rate of 16.2 percent during 1970–1980 with heavy industries growing faster than light industries. Extremely rapid growth was observed in heavy industries such as basic metal, fabricated metal products, machinery, equipment, and chemicals, followed by light industries such as textiles, wearing apparel, leather products, and other manufacturing industries, which were mostly export-oriented. Traditional domestic market-oriented industries such as beverages, tobacco, food, wood products, printing and publishing, and paper and paper products recorded the least output growth.[7]

As the HCI sector grew much faster than light industries, a rapid structural shift took place in production, exports, and employment. As shown in Table 5.4, the share of HCIs in total value added in manufacturing climbed from 39.7 percent in 1970 to 58.3 percent in 1980. The sector's employment share also increased, from 38.7 percent to 48.9 percent during the same period. Exports experienced a distinct structural improvement as the share of HCI exports increased from 12.8 percent in 1970 to 41.8 percent in 1980, indicating that HCIs became increasingly export-oriented by the end of the 1970s.

The HCI policy was often criticized by the neoclassical with the argument that the credit allocation in favor of HCIs led to overcapacity and damaged light industry performance, adversely affecting economic and export growth.[8] It is true that excessive

---

[7]For more details, see Kim (1983, p. 112).
[8]Balassa (1990, p. 16).

Table 5.8   Output and Productivity Growth of Manufacturing
Sector, 1967–1979 (Unit: percent)

	1967–1979	1967–1973	1973–1979
Output (A)	23.6	28.0	19.4
Labor productivity	12.0	16.2	7.9
Capital productivity	1.9	4.5	−0.5
TFP (B)	5.5	8.5	2.5
B/A	23.3	30.4	12.9

Source: Kim *et al.* (1984, pp. 50, 94–95).

incentives for the HCIs led to overinvestment in the HCI sector, resulting in low productivity growth. As shown in Table 5.8, the total factor productivity growth of the manufacturing sector in the 1970s was much lower than in the 1960s. Particularly striking is the negative growth of capital productivity due to excess capacity and the resulting capacity underutilization in many heavy industries.

For this reason, it is often argued that the costs of the HCI policy could have been higher than its benefits. When viewed from the dynamic perspective, however, the benefits would be higher than the costs because the HCI policy was consistent with Korea's dynamic comparative advantage. This long-term dynamic viewpoint was proved true as the HCIs became Korea's leading export industries in the 1980s and 1990s. In sum, despite some negative effects, the HCI policy in the 1970s should be considered a success because it paved the way for sustained growth by upgrading the industrial structure toward capital and technology-intensive industries.

5.1.4   *Structural Adjustment and Technology-Oriented Industrial Policy (1980s)*

Although the HCI drive in the 1970s was very successful in terms of growth, it entailed, as noted earlier, a number of undesirable side effects such as high inflation, weakening industrial competitiveness, and a sectoral imbalance within manufacturing sector. The death of President Park in 1979 and the ensuing political turmoil made the situation worse; thus, the economy plunged into negative growth in 1980 accompanied by soaring inflation and serious balance of payments difficulties. Consequently, the Korean economy underwent a sharp recession from 1980 to 1982, which led many HCI enterprises into deep financial difficulties.

The major concern of industrial policy in the 1980s was how to enhance industrial competitiveness while solving the excess capacity problem of the HCI sector, which was particularly serious in the areas of heavy electrical equipment, automobiles, heavy machinery, and fertilizer. Thus, the structural adjustment program was carried out for these industries by reducing production capacity, building entry barriers, and encouraging mergers. The heavy electrical equipment producers were merged in 1980 and were granted monopoly. Automobile producers were forced to specialize in the production of certain designated categories of vehicles. The Hyundai Heavy Machinery Company was nationalized, broken into smaller firms, and then later handed over to the management of Samsung and the Korea Electric Power Company (KEPCO). Firms in the fertilizer industry were also merged, and overall production capacity was reduced. Various fiscal and financial supports were provided to these industries to expedite the implementation of the adjustment program.

The government began to overhaul the industrial incentive system and replaced industry-specific support with functional support, providing incentives for R&D activities and manpower development. A number of tax and financial incentives were newly introduced while existing ones were strengthened. This policy stance led to the enactment of the Industrial Development Act in 1986, which replaced all seven industry-specific laws, signaling the shift of industrial policy from industrial targeting to productivity and technology-oriented policy. The core objective of the new law was to provide incentives for productivity improvement and technology development, while supporting the rationalization of industries that were losing competitiveness or industries that required support to improve their competitiveness. The Industrial Development Fund was created to support industrial rationalization.

In 1986, the Korean government designated six industries for the rationalization program: textile fabrics, ferroalloy, automobiles, naval diesel engines, heavy electrical machinery, and heavy construction machinery. Except for textile fabrics, all other industries were heavy industries covered by the structural adjustment program in the early 1980s, indicating that these troubled industries required further support for rationalization. In 1987, the fertilizer and dyeing industries were also designated for the rationalization program.

The rationalization program was offered only for limited years, normally two to three, and focused on enhancing industrial competitiveness. The government offered entry barriers to capital-intensive heavy industries such as automobiles, ferroalloy, diesel engines, etc., which were suffering from excess capacity, while encouraging them to specialize in the production of specific products. For labor-intensive industries such as dyeing and textile fabrics, the rationalization program focused on facility modernization, assisting technology development through automation, and the replacement of obsolete facilities. The designated industries were given preferential credits from the Industrial Development Fund.

Apart from the HCI support under the rationalization program, efforts were also made to enhance overall industrial competitiveness by promoting competition and industrial innovation. In 1983, a comprehensive import liberalization program was introduced to induce foreign competition, and various tax and financial support programs were devised to facilitate R&D activities and manpower development. In other words, the government used the "carrot and stick" approach by placing private firms under strong pressure through import liberalization, while offering them various incentives for industrial innovation.[9]

Thanks to these combined policy efforts, the HCI sector began to regain its competitiveness from the mid-1980s. As shown in Table 5.3, the HCI sector grew at an annual growth rate of 14.6 percent during the 1980s, twice as high as that of the light industry sector. The rapid expansion of investment and exports in the HCI sector served as key contributing factors in this remarkable growth performance. External economic conditions, such as the low dollar against the Japanese yen

---

[9]For more details, see Chapter 11.

in the wake of the Plaza Accord in 1985, also helped Korean heavy industries acquire international competitiveness.

In this regard, it seems worthwhile to note that the success of the HCI promotion policy did not solely rely on direct government support such as subsidies and protection. Indirect support such as price stabilization, import liberalization, manpower, and technology development also played an important role in enhancing the competitiveness of heavy industries. These indirect supports may have in fact contributed more strongly to enhancing the competitiveness of heavy industries, because the HCI promotion policy could hardly have been successful without the government's systematic policy efforts for skill formation and local technological capability building in the 1960s and 1970s and the facilitation of the industrial innovation of the private sector in the 1980s. This is because the competitiveness of heavy industries depends ultimately on skill and technology.[10] This seems to be the most important lesson to be learned from the Korean experience in promoting heavy industries.

5.1.5   *Globalization and Promotion of High-Tech Industries (1990s)*

Entering the 1990s, the Korean economy faced new challenges. Korea's traditional export industries were gradually losing their competitiveness due to rapidly rising wages, whereas the import of foreign technology became increasingly constrained due to rising technology protectionism in advanced countries. In other words, industrialization based on imported technology no longer appeared sustainable. Such changing circumstances led the Korean government to reinforce the technology-oriented industrial policy initiated in the late 1980s and to look to high-tech industries as a new driving force of industrial growth.

Thus, the thrust of industrial development policy was directed toward supporting industrial technology development including the

---

[10]For a detailed discussion on incentives for industrial innovation and technology development in the 1970s and 1980s, see Chapter 11.

promotion of high-tech industries and enhancing industrial competitiveness. Since industry-specific support was no longer permitted under the WTO system, government policy focused on stimulating private R&D activities, facilitating the growth of high-tech industries as well as small venture firms.

A variety of incentives introduced in the 1980s were further strengthened to stimulate private-sector R&D efforts. The technological capability building of the private sector was continuously supported by facilitating the establishment of private sector research laboratories. Thus, the number of corporate research institutes soared dramatically from 53 in 1980 to 966 in 1990 and 7,100 in 2000. Many efforts were also made to facilitate the technological infrastructure building of the private sector by providing information and standardization, R&D facilities, testing and evaluation equipment, technical manpower training, etc. Up to 70 percent of the costs required for these purposes were subsidized by the government (60 percent in the case of manpower training). These policy measures gave rise to the swift expansion of private R&D expenditures, accounting for almost 70–80 percent of total national R&D expenditures in the 1990s.

To enhance industrial competitiveness, the five-year production technology development plan (1991–1995) was launched in 1990 to develop product design technology, processing technology, design technology, and automation technology. To facilitate high-tech industries, the five-year industrial technology development plan (1996–2001) was launched in 1995, to promote industrial technology of strategic importance with a view to producing new world-class industrial products. The private sector was encouraged to participate in the project through the matching fund system under which private firms provided a certain portion of the research funds, so they could claim ownership of the research outcomes.

As technology development became the national agenda, many ministries began to develop their own R&D programs. The most notable among them was the telecommunication technology program launched by the Ministry of Information and Communication in 1992, which had significant impacts on the development of ICT industry.

Immense efforts were made to promote the IT industry in view of its growing importance in the economy. The government deregulated the telecommunication service industry to stimulate competition, and this led to an explosive increase in demand for mobile telephone services and internet start-ups.

Various tax and financial incentives were provided to induce FDI in the Korean IT industry. Numerous foreign investment zones and exclusive complexes for foreign investors were established to attract foreign IT investment. As a result, FDI in the IT industry increased rapidly from USD 64 million in 1996 to USD 2.7 billion in 2000.

The government also intensified its support for venture business by enacting the Act on Special Measures for the Promotion of Venture Business in 1997. The 1997 financial crisis demonstrated that rapid growth driven by large-scale enterprises was no longer sustainable. Therefore, the government was pressed to find a new driving force for growth and realized that small high-tech firms, particularly in the information and communication sector, could play such a role. Consequently, various incentives were provided for investment in venture business and venture capital. The KOSDAQ securities market was opened in 1996 to enable high-tech start-ups to access equity funding, and a large number of venture business incubators were also established across the country to accommodate and nurture new venture start-ups. The government also constructed a number of techno parks to attract venture business.

The result was a dramatic rise in the number of venture companies, which increased from 2,042 in 1998 to 11,392 in 2001. Venture capital investment as a percentage of GDP increased to almost 0.6 percent in 2001, a four-fold increase from 1998, and the information and communication sector including computer software, internet, and information systems accounted for 64 percent of total venture capital investment in 2001.[11] Thanks to the government support policy, the ICT industry as a whole grew rapidly since the mid-1990s and became major sources of economic growth and exports, accounting for almost 30–40 percent of GDP growth and

---

[11]See Baygan (2003, p. 11).

30 percent of exports in the early 2000s.[12] Korea's trade surplus after the financial crisis in 1997 was largely attributable to trade surplus in the ICT sector.

The 1990s were a turning point for Korea's industrial development because Korea began to develop its own industrial technology, reflecting the shift of technology policy from imitation to innovation. Technology development became the focal point of industrial development policy, implying the pursuit of technology-led industrial development. The industrial development policy was thus focused on promoting innovative firms and high-tech industries and brought about many successful results. In consequence, Korea emerged as a global leader of the ICT industry including semiconductors, liquid crystal digital displays, and mobile phones, to name a few. Therefore, the 1990s can be characterized as a period of technology-led industrial development with significant progress in the development of high-tech industries.

5.2 Industrial Growth and Structural Transformation

5.2.1 *Growth of Manufacturing Sector*

Korea's rapid growth over the past half century was largely driven by the phenomenal growth of the manufacturing sector, which averaged 13.1 percent per year, almost twice as high as the GDP growth of 7.1 percent during the period 1954–2000 (Table 5.3). This led to a rapid structural shift in the economy toward the manufacturing sector whose share in GDP jumped from 9.0 percent in 1953 to 24.5 percent in 2007, higher than that of advanced industrial countries including Germany and Japan (Fig. 5.1). However, the manufacturing share of GDP has stabilized around 28 percent in recent years, reflecting its slowing growth.

This structural change was accompanied by the steep rise of the HCI sector whose share in manufacturing output rose from

---

[12]The 60-Year History of the Korean Economy-II (2010, p. 425).

Table 5.9   Trends of the Industrialization Ratio, 1953–2013 (Unit: percent)

	Industrialization Ratio[a]	Heavy Industrialization Ratio[b]
1953	9.0	21.1
1960	13.8	23.4
1970	16.9	37.8
1980	21.9	57.5
1990	24.0	69.3
2000	25.2	77.1
2007	24.5	82.3
2013	28.4	86.8

Notes: [a]Manufacturing share of GDP at current prices.
[b]HCI share of manufacturing value added at current prices. The ratios from 1953 to 2007 are from the National Accounts 2009, and the 2013 ratio is computed based on the National Accounts 2014.
Source: National Accounts, 2009, 2014, The Bank of Korea.

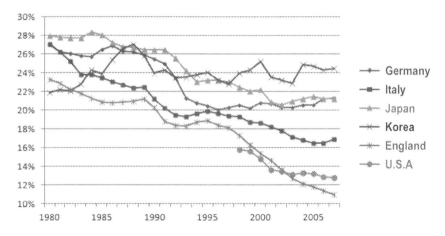

Figure 5.1   International Comparison of Industrialization Ratio,[a] 1980–2007
Note: [a]Manufacturing share of GDP at current prices.
Source: OECD Statistical Analysis (STAN) data.

21.1 percent in 1953 to 82.3 percent in 2007. The high level of manufacturing growth was largely driven by HCI growth, which averaged 15.5 percent per year during the period 1954–2000. It is remarkable that Korea's HCI share in manufacturing output was higher than

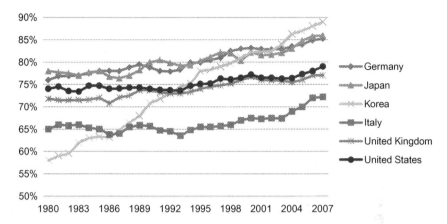

Figure 5.2   International Comparison of Heavy Industrialization Ratio,[a] 1980–2007

Note: [a]HCI share of manufacturing production computed based on ISIC Rev.3 covering C21T22 (paper, pulp, etc.), C23T25 (chemical, rubber, plastic products), C26 (non-metallic mineral products), C27T28 (basic metal, fabricated metal products), C29T33 (machinery, equipment) and C34T35 (transportation equipment). The Korean ratio in 2007 differs slightly from the one in Table 5.9 which is based on value added.

Source: OECD Statistical Analysis (STAN) data.

Germany and Japan in 2007 (Fig. 5.2). The successful transformation of HCIs into competitive export industries made higher HCI growth possible, which in turn led to higher manufacturing growth and higher economic growth. As shown in Table 5.10, the contribution of manufacturing growth to GDP has tended to increase continuously over the last five decades and accounted for almost one-third of output growth in the 1990s.

An international comparison of the manufacturing share of GDP is provided in Fig. 5.1. It is interesting that the manufacturing share of output in advanced industrial countries has shown a tendency to decrease since the early 1980s. The declining trend was not very steep in manufacturing powerhouses like Germany and Japan, whereas sharp declines were observed in England and Italy, reflecting their weakening industrial competitiveness. Another important phenomenon is that like in Korea, the HCI share in manufacturing production has tended to increase in all major industrial countries,

Table 5.10 Growth of the Manufacturing Sector and Its Contribution to
GDP Growth (Unit: percent)

	GDP Growth (A)	Manufacturing Growth	Contribution Degree[a] (B)	Contribution Rate (B/A)
1954–1960	3.85	12.8	0.75	19.5
1961–1970	8.45	17.0	2.24	26.5
1971–1980	9.05	16.2	2.44	27.0
1981–1990	8.66	12.3	2.40	27.7
1991–2000	6.63	8.7	2.10	31.7

Note: [a]Manufacturing growth rate multiplied by the composition ratio of the
manufacturing industry.
Source: National Accounts 2009, The Bank of Korea.

reflecting the structural shift within manufacturing toward high value
added and high-tech industries.

While the diminishing role of the manufacturing sector is unavoidable in the course of development, its sharp deterioration seems
undesirable because it could play a crucial role in a country's
economic decline, as experienced by Italy. Italy used to have a strong
manufacturing sector with output share of GDP around 26 percent,
almost as high as Germany in the early 1980s. However, this fell
to almost 16 percent in the early 2000s, which greatly hampered
the growth of the Italian economy. This has important implications
for countries like Korea with a strong manufacturing basis, because
unless the manufacturing sector remains competitive, it could seriously damage the country's sustained growth and development.

The fact that Korea's rapid growth was largely driven by manufacturing growth can be confirmed by looking at the historical
trend of its growth rate. As shown in Table 5.10, GDP growth
seems to be closely associated with manufacturing growth since the
growth rate was higher when manufacturing growth was higher and
vice versa.[13] It is also notable that manufacturing growth tended

---

[13]The year 1980 was an exceptional year affected by political turmoil after the
death of President Park. If we drop the year 1980, manufacturing growth in the
1970s was 18.2 percent, higher than in the 1960s.

to increase until the 1970s and began to slow down from the 1980s. This was largely due to the relative decline of light industries which were losing their competitiveness in the international market.

In contrast, the HCI sector continued to grow fast as it gradually gained competitiveness through productivity improvement, as evidenced by the high export ratio. As shown in Table 5.11, most heavy industries revealed a high output and productivity growth during 1985–2001. Particularly high TFP growth was observed in the IT industry (semiconductors, electronics and parts, IT equipment, and home appliances), accounting for almost half of the output growth. It is also remarkable that TFP growth in the manufacturing sector as a whole was 4.3 percent during 1985–2001, higher than the 2.5 percent of the 1973–1979. This suggests that the manufacturing

Table 5.11   Output and Productivity Growth and Export Ratios of Manufacturing Industries, 1985–2001 (Unit: percent)

Subsector	Output	Export Ratio[a]	TFP
Food and beverages	5.7	5.2	1.0
Textile and textile articles	0.0	49.2	1.1
Paper and paper products	6.2	10.0	1.5
Chemicals	10.6	22.5	1.9
Coal and petroleum products	9.0	22.7	4.3
Non-metallic mineral products	6.6	6.1	3.6
Basic metal	9.7	17.6	3.0
Metal products	6.9	14.7	1.1
Machinery	13.0	22.7	4.8
Semiconductors	28.9	82.3	9.3
Electrical machinery	21.1	28.1	9.8
IT machinery	20.0	46.1	14.0
Appliances	12.0	33.8	6.9
Transport equipment — motor vehicle	14.6	28.6	3.0
Transport equipment — without motor vehicle	10.6	89.5	5.6
Precision machinery	7.2	53.8	1.5
Other manufacturing industries	4.3	23.0	3.3
Manufacturing total	10.6	29.8	4.3

Note: [a]Data for the year 2000.

Source: Korea Development Institute (2003, p. 68, 102, 103).

sector became more productive and competitive in the 1980s and
1990s compared to the 1970s.

The dramatic growth of the manufacturing sector also had significant impacts on exports, employment, and balance of payments.
Korea's exports today are almost completely driven by manufactured
exports, which accounted for 98.1 percent of total exports in 2008,
with HCI exports comprising 91.7 percent. The rapid growth of
manufactured exports enabled Korea to solve balance of payments
difficulties, which Korea had been suffering from until the outbreak
of the financial crisis in 1997. Since the early 2000s, Korea has
continuously recorded a current account surplus.

The rapid growth of the manufacturing sector has also been a
major source of employment creation. During 1966–2000, as shown
in Table 5.12, employment in the manufacturing sector increased
4.2 percent per year, which is much higher than the overall employment growth of 2.9 percent. The manufacturing sector employment
was largely contributed by HCI sector in which employment grew
6.2 percent per year, twice as high as that of light industries.

However, it should be noted that employment growth in the
manufacturing sector has been continuously falling since the 1970s,
in both heavy and light industries. The decline was steeper in
light industries than in heavy industries. Although growth rate
mattered most, the movement of the wage rental ratio in favor of
wages and the resulting labor-saving technical progress seems to
have played no less an important role in the employment growth
of manufacturing industries. In the 1990s, the manufacturing sector

Table 5.12   Growth of Manufacturing Employment, 1966–2000 (Unit: percent)

	Manufacturing	Light Industry	HCI
1966–1970	11.1	10.9	11.6
1971–1980	9.4	7.2	10.1
1981–1990	4.2	1.6	6.5
1991–2000	−1.1	−2.6	−0.1
1966–2000	4.2	3.1	6.2

Source: Mining and Manufacturing Survey Report, Korea Statistical Office.

experienced negative growth in employment due in part to the financial crisis, indicating growth without employment.

5.2.2 *Structural Changes*

The rapid growth of the manufacturing sector brought about dramatic changes in the structure of production, employment, and exports. As noted earlier, there was a rapid structural shift in production toward the HCI sector. Its share in the manufacturing sector rose from 28 percent in 1960 to almost 79 percent in 2000, bringing the share of light industries from 72 percent down to 21 percent during the same period.

Until the 1970s, Korean manufacturing was dominated by light industries. Their production and employment shares were as high as 60.3 percent and 61.3 percent in 1970, respectively, and then fell continuously thereafter to 21.2 percent and 33.1 percent in 2000. This was mainly due to the drastic decline of textile industries including leather products, once key export industries in Korea. The output share of these industries fell drastically from 21.3 percent in 1970 to 8.3 percent in 2000, and their employment share also fell from 31.1 percent to 16.5 percent during the same period.

It is important to note that this swift structural change was brought about by the dramatic growth of heavy industries such as metal products, machinery, precision equipment, and transport equipment, whose production and employment shares increased from 10.4 and 12.5 percent in 1960 to 46.5 and 48.2 percent in 2000, respectively. Since these industries are mostly technology-intensive industries, their speedy growth indicates the structural shift of the manufacturing sector toward technology-intensive industries. In other words, a notable structural advancement took place within the manufacturing sector, geared toward high-tech and technology-intensive industries, which enabled the Korean economy to sustain high growth until the 1990s. As shown in Table 5.13, high-tech industries including medium-high technology have taken up an increasing share of manufacturing production since 1980, accounting for more than one-third in 1995, whereas the share of low-tech industries dropped by more than 50 percent to 26.2 percent in 1995.

Table 5.13   Growth and Structural Changes of Manufacturing by Technology Level, 1985–1995 (Unit: percent)

	1980	1986	1990	1995	Annual Growth Rate 1980–1986	1986–1990	1990–1995
High-tech industries (IT industries)	5.2 (2.6)	7.8 (4.9)	9.8 (6.3)	12.7 (9.4)	20.6 (25.2)	17.0 (18.2)	14.1 (17.2)
Mid-high-tech industries	9.0	12.7	18.1	24.0	19.3	20.9	14.6
Mid-low-tech industries	27.3	32.6	34.6	37.1	16.1	12.4	9.7
Low-tech industries	58.4	46.8	37.6	26.2	8.6	4.8	0.7
Manufacturing industries	100.0	100.0	100.0	100.0	12.7	10.8	8.2

Source: The 60-Year History of the Korean Economy-II (2010, p. 240).

This implies that Korean manufacturing was completely transformed from labor-intensive light industries to capital and technology-intensive heavy industries in the span of 30 years. This kind of rapid structural change can seldom be observed in the history of economic development. As Fig. 5.2 shows, no advanced industrial country experienced such a rapid structural transformation in such a short period. The rapid structural change was also witnessed in the employment structure, although it did not change as fast as the production structure. In 2000, for example, two-thirds of manufacturing employment was generated by the HCI sector.

Dramatic change was also observed in the structure of exports, reflecting the changing production structure. As mentioned earlier, the HCI sector became increasingly competitive since the mid-1980s and turned itself into an export industry, accounting for 91.7 percent of total exports in 2000. Most of the capital-intensive heavy industries have become very competitive, as reflected in their high export ratios. Extremely high export/output ratios were observed in semiconductors, IT equipment, home appliances, automobiles and other transport equipment, and precision equipment. In 2000, semiconductor and transport equipment exported 82.3 percent and 89.5 percent of their production, respectively. IT equipment, home appliances, automobiles, and precision equipment exported 30 to 55 percent of their production (Table 5.11). This indicates that technology-intensive industries have emerged as the leading export industries in Korea.

5.3   Industrialization Process

As mentioned earlier, the Korean government took a dual approach to industrialization by pursuing an import substitution policy while promoting exports. This policy enabled Korea to sustain high industrial and export growth. The rapid export growth, however, was usually explained by the export promotion policy without referring to its industrial policy aspect of export growth.

Exports not only need export incentives but also require the growth of new export industries for sustained growth. For this reason, the Korean government deliberately pursued an import substitution policy while promoting exports. Most Korean export industries started off as import substitution industries and then grew into export industries. The import substitution policy started with labor-intensive nondurable consumer goods in the 1950s, followed by import substitution for durable consumer goods and intermediate goods in the 1960s and 1970s. The import substitution of capital goods started in the 1970s took longer largely due to technological difficulties. The capital goods industry transformed, however, itself into an export industry starting from the 2000s by overcoming technological difficulties through localization programs and intensive R&D support. This section analyzes the import substitution process in nondurable consumer goods, intermediate and durable consumer goods, and capital goods, and then explains how they were able to grow into export industries.

5.3.1   *Nondurable Consumer Goods*

In the 1950s, Korea pursued an inward-looking industrial policy focused on the import substitution of nondurable consumer goods including textiles, rubber products, and plywood, which became major export industries in the 1960s. Export incentives certainly played an important role in boosting exports, but unless these industries were promoted in the 1950s, it would have hardly been possible for them to achieve rapid export growth in the 1960s. This is because there were virtually no other manufactured products to be exported in the 1960s, suggesting that import substitution policy in the 1950s provided an industrial base for export growth in the 1960s.

In 1953, the government set up a five-year cotton textile industry rehabilitation plan (1953–1957), and supported facility investment while protecting the domestic industry. This enabled the cotton textile industry to grow swiftly, meeting domestic demand by the end of the 1950s and then began to export in the 1960s. In the beginning, exports consisted mainly of simple labor-intensive cotton fabrics, followed by exports of highly processed knitted products which took up an increasing share of total textile exports. Textile exports, which amounted to USD 24 million in 1964, grew to USD 100 million in 1967, becoming the leading export industry in the 1960s. In this process, vocational training institutes played an important role in supplying the skilled labor force which, coupled with low wages, was the major source of comparative advantage.

The rubber industry was another example which turned itself into an export industry in the 1960s. Until the end of 1950s, the rubber industry was represented only by the manufacturing of rubber footwear to meet domestic demand. Thanks to various export incentives in the 1960s, the labor-intensive rubber footwear sector grew rapidly into an export industry benefiting from low labor costs and exported more than USD 100 million in 1973. The other rubber goods such as tires and rubber belts witnessed also a remarkable growth owing to rapid expansion of automobiles in the 1960s and began to export, amounting to USD 19 million in 1973. Korean tires were very popular in Southeast Asia and the Middle East due to their low price and high quality.

The plywood industry also first began as domestic market-oriented industry and then grew into an export industry. The Dongmyung Timber Company established in Busan in 1954 produced plywood to meet domestic demand until the end of the 1950s. In 1964, plywood was designated as an export industry and supported by preferential financing, which led to the industry's rapid development. Plywood exports amounted to USD 100 million in 1970 and 286 million in 1973, making Korea one of the world's leading plywood exporters.

5.3.2   *Durable Consumer Goods and Intermediate Goods*

Korea began to promote intermediate goods and durable consumer goods from the second five-year plan to meet increasing domestic demand for them. For example, chemical fibers such as nylon, acryl, polyester, polypropylene, etc., were supplied entirely by imports until the mid-1960s. As demand for these goods rose quickly in the early 1960s, domestic production started from the late 1960s with the production of nylon, followed by viscose rayon, acrylic fiber, polypropylene fiber, polyester fiber, etc. The rapid growth of domestic demand for them led the government to develop the petrochemical industry and launch the construction of the Ulsan Petrochemical Complex in 1968. The Complex began with the construction of thirteen petrochemical plants including a naphtha cracking center.

Following the completion of the complex in 1973, the petrochemical industry, such as the chemical fiber industry which used intermediate petrochemical products as raw materials, developed fast owing to rapidly rising domestic demand. The continued growth of domestic demand on the back of high economic growth led to capacity expansion, thereby reducing production costs, which in turn enabled the chemical fiber industry to grow as an export industry. For example, the export ratio of chemical fibers soared significantly, while their import ratio dropped considerably in the 1970s (Table 5.14).[14]

---

[14]Balassa argues that plywood and chemical fiber began as export-oriented industries from the very beginning, but this is not true, as explained. See Balassa (1981, p. 17).

Table 5.14 Export and Import Ratios of Major Chemical Fibers, 1963–1974 (Unit: percent)

	Viscose Filament		Polypropylene		Nylon		Polyester		Acryl	
	M/DD	E/DO	M/DD	E/DO	M/DD	E/DO	M/DD	E/DO	M/DD	E/DO
1963	100.0	—	—	—	98.6	—	100.0	—	100.0	—
1965	100.0	—	—	—	69.0	—	100.0	—	100.0	—
1967	55.8	—	100.0	—	87.4	—	100.0	—	66.6	—
1969	21.5	—	21.8	3.0	56.9	1.4	55.5	1.1	24.8	18.4
1971	34.8	31.6	0.3	1.6	48.8	41.3	33.8	65.9	43.6	43.3
1973	47.6	53.1	0.1	36.2	47.5	52.8	45.4	65.8	75.1	77.2
1974	23.2	40.6	1.3	40.0	27.4	56.3	12.9	58.8	40.6	58.5

Notes: M = Import; DD = Domestic Demand; E = Export; DO = Domestic Output.
Source: Suh (1975, pp. 143–149).

Iron and steel products were another major intermediate industry that started as import substitution and then grew into an export industry. Prior to liberation from Japanese colonial rule, Korea had an annual production capacity of 600,000 tons of iron and 160,000 tons of steel, but most of the plants were located in North Korea. Therefore, Korea had to rely on imports to meet domestic demand during the 1950s. In the first five-year plan, the government aimed to build a steel plant with a capacity of 300,000 tons, but failed due to financial difficulties, and hence there was no integrated iron and steel mill until the end of the 1960s.

With the progress of industrialization, demand for steel increased rapidly, growing at 25 percent per year during 1962–1971. However, the existing domestic steel plants were ill-suited to satisfy growing demand because they were mostly specialized in the final rolling facilities. They were also small in scale, relying on simple outdated technologies which meant they could hardly compete with foreign steel products. Consequently, domestic demand was largely met by imports until the end of the 1960s and large quantities of semi-finished iron and steel products were imported and processed by small and medium-sized producers for domestic use.

With the completion of the Pohang integrated steel mill (POSCO) in 1973, which had a capacity of 1.03 million tons of crude steel, the imbalance among iron-making, steelmaking, and rolling facilities was greatly reduced and the steel industry continued to grow fast, reflecting the growth of shipbuilding, automobiles, and other heavy industries. Even after the completion of POSCO, the domestic demand for steel continued to outstrip its production capacity. Therefore, POSCO had to expand its production capacity continuously based on the long-term expansion plan. When POSCO's fourth expansion phase was completed in May 1983, the company's total capacity reached 9 million tons. With the completion of POSCO's fourth expansion in 1983, Korea produced nearly 2 percent of the world's crude steel and POSCO became the tenth-largest steel producer among non-communist countries. Modern facilities combined with its favorable location in the coastal region allowed POSCO to attain the world's lowest unit production costs for steel.

In 1987, for example, the production cost per ton of hot-rolled steel was USD 259.50, or 80 percent of the US and 60 percent of Japanese costs (Stern *et al.*, 1995, p. 176).

The rapid growth of the steel industry thus enabled Korea not only to meet domestic demand but also to export substantial quantities of steel. Steel exports have increased rapidly since the early 1970s, rising from 0.8 million tons in 1972 to 7.1 million tons in 1987, accounting for 38 percent of total production. Export items were also considerably diversified, ranging from plates to sheets, pipes, bars, etc., which in turn enabled the steel industry to grow into export industry in the 1980s. As production continued to expand rapidly, the self-sufficiency ratio reached about 77 percent in 1987 while producing steel at internationally competitive prices (Stern *et al.*, p. 172).

The Korean electronics industry started its development earlier than other industries in the HCI sector, because it began with labor-intensive assembly production. As early as the 1960s, Korea began to produce labor-intensive products such as radios, refrigerators, black and white TV sets, etc., as well as various labor-intensive parts and components. Thus, prior to the 1973 HCI declaration, the electronics industry had made considerable progress, with exports accounting for as much as 23 percent of total production in 1970 (Table 5.15).

Table 5.15   Export, Import, and Intermediate Input Ratios of the Electronics Industry, 1960–1995 (Unit: percent)

	Import/ Supply	Imported Intermediate Inputs/Output	Imported Intermediate Inputs/Total Intermediate Inputs	Export/ Output
1960	67.6	16.3	21.2	17.2
1965	27.5	17.4	26.5	10.3
1970	41.2	26.7	39.6	22.7
1975	31.1	29.3	42.1	38.1
1980	27.0	23.0	31.8	34.7
1985	27.8	27.4	38.0	44.2
1990	21.3	23.2	32.3	39.3
1995	21.1	23.3	35.1	47.5

Source: ECOS System, The Bank of Korea.

The electronics industry was designated as a strategic industry to be promoted in the late 1960s, and government support was intensified in the 1970s while protection was reinforced with high tariffs and quantitative restrictions. Korea began to produce color TVs in 1974, microwaves in 1978, and VTRs in 1979, thereby gradually shifting the production structure from simple labor-intensive consumer products to more skill-intensive consumer products. In the 1970s, however, production was dominated by simple home electronics including radios and black and white TVs and depended upon foreign technology and imported parts and components. As shown in Table 5.15, import dependency was as high as 41.2 percent in 1970 due to the high import dependency of intermediate inputs, which increased from 21 percent in 1960 to nearly 40 percent in 1970.

Thus, entering the 1980s, great efforts were made to promote the local production of parts and components to enhance international competitiveness. For example, the government began to launch color TV broadcasting, which was not permitted in the 1970s. This led to an explosive increase in domestic demand for color TVs, which strongly facilitated the localization of parts and components. On the other hand, import liberalization and the weakening competitiveness of labor-intensive products due to rapidly rising wages pushed local producers to invest in technology-intensive products such as industrial electronics. The government provided various support to this end, which enabled Korean firms to produce personal computers in 1982, 64K DRAM semiconductors in 1984, and electronic switching systems in 1986. Thus, the electronics industry continued to grow fast in the 1980s, with many products growing more than 20 percent per year.

The rapid growth of the electronics industry was accompanied by a structural shift from consumer electronics toward industrial electronics such as telephones, electronic switching systems, and computer monitors in the 1980s. The share of consumer electronics in total production fell from 40.3 percent in 1980 to 21.8 percent in 1995, while that of industrial electronics increased from 12.8 percent in 1980 to 20.4 percent in 1995. The share of parts and components

Table 5.16   Structural Change of Electronics Industry, 1980–2000 (Unit: percent)

	1980	1985	1990	1995	2000
Production					
Consumer Electronics	40.3	33.1	35.1	21.8	13.0
Industrial Electronics	12.8	20.8	21.9	20.4	39.9
Parts and Components	46.9	46.1	43.0	57.8	47.1
Total	100.0	100.0	100.0	100.0	100.0
Export					
Consumer Electronics	51.9	40.5	33.3	18.0	11.6
Industrial Electronics	8.6	19.7	20.0	17.6	36.7
Parts and Components	39.5	39.8	46.5	64.4	51.7
Total	100.0	100.0	100.0	100.0	100.0

Source: Park (2003, p. 15).

also increased during the same period, rising from 46.9 percent to 57.8 percent. A similar structural shift was observed in exports. The export share of consumer electronics fell from 51.9 percent to 18 percent, while the shares of industrial electronics and parts and components gained significantly, rising from 8.6 percent and 39.5 percent to 17.6 percent and 64.4 percent during the same period, respectively (Table 5.16).

Exports were a major contributor to the growth process, as reflected by the steadily rising export ratio which reached almost 50 percent in 1995 (Table 5.15). In the early period, the cheap labor cost associated with mass production was the major source of international competitiveness. In the later years, the cost advantage of cheap labor was almost exhausted, and as the production structure became more technology-intensive there was a pressing need for in-house R&D activities which led to process as well as product innovation, enabling the electronics industry to become Korea's largest export sector. Significant progress was also made in the local-ization of parts and components, reducing the import dependency of intermediate inputs and consequently leading to a substantial decrease in the overall import dependency of the electronics industry (Table 5.15). As briefly explained above, the Korean electronics industry, which started as a simple assembly production industry, went through import substitution process of intermediate inputs and raw materials and then developed into a leading export industry.

The automobile industry is another major durable consumer goods industry that started as an import substitution industry and then developed into an export industry.[15] Before Korea's independence in 1945, the limited domestic demand for automobiles and parts was met completely by imports from Japan. However, as Japan's need for parts for military vehicles increased after the outbreak of the Second World War, Japan began to produce certain automobile parts in Korea and supplied them to Manchuria, North China, and Korea. This parts industry was largely owned by the Japanese. In addition, there were a large number of maintenance and repair shops, some of which were directly operated by major Japanese automobile producers such as Toyota, Nissan, and Isuzu. Thus, the automobile industry before 1945 was characterized by the production of a very limited number of auto parts, so Korea merely remained as a market for finished cars produced in Japan.

After 1945, technicians and salesmen who had worked either at parts manufacturing factories or in repair shops resumed the production of parts such as piston rings and pins, gaskets, springs, bolts and nuts, and brake linings, which had already been produced before 1945. After 1950, automobile parts production proliferated rapidly, largely due to the growing repair and replacement demand for military vehicles as well as for civilian motor vehicles, which were mostly rebuilt from the military vehicles. Due to increasing repair and replacement demand, the number of different types of auto parts domestically produced rose to 500 in 1962. Thus, the replacement demand for easily made parts could be mostly met by domestic production. It should be noted that a considerable number of items were supplied not only to the Korean army but also to the US Army, in competition with Japanese products. Thus, the growing military demand for repair and replacement after the Korean War

---

[15]This part is largely drawn from the author's earlier paper, "Ancillary Firm Development in the Korean Automotive Industry" in K. Odaka (ed.), *The Motor Vehicle Industry in Asia*, Singapore University Press, 1983.

led not only to the proliferation of auto parts production but also to that of repair and rebuilding shops, which had a far-reaching impact on the domestic production of motor vehicles in Korea.

The Korean automobile industry reached a turning point in 1962 when the government undertook a series of measures to promote the automobile industry as a part of the first five-year development plan. One of the first measures was the enactment of the Automobile Industry Protection Law, which prohibited the import of complete cars as well as parts and components not intended for assembly production, while providing tariff exemption and various tax benefits to assemblers.

The government also set up a five-year automobile development plan aimed at the domestic production of motor vehicles in Korea. The first modern assembly production started with semi-knocked down (SKD) assembly in 1962, but soon shifted to completely knocked down (CKD) assembly production with a view to replacing parts and components through gradual local production. The policy shift was taken in due consideration of the fact that Korea had already made considerable progress in the manufacture of parts and components as well as automobile manufacturing technology. There were many small-scale automobile assemblers in the early 1960s that engaged in rebuilding military vehicles for civilian use, such as passenger cars used for taxis, buses and trucks.

In order to implement the new automobile promotion policy, the government selected a local automobile manufacturer and urged it to subcontract work out as much as possible to local parts producers. The Shinjin Industrial Company was selected as an assembler in 1964 and authorized to manufacture passenger cars. Shinjin started with 21 percent localization of parts and components in 1966. To accelerate the domestic content program, the government set up the Automobile Industry Basic Promotion Plan at the end of 1969.

The main objective of the plan was to achieve the complete domestic manufacture of small passenger cars by the end of 1972, and motor vehicles in general by the end of 1974. Thus, a strong emphasis was placed on the localization of parts and components. The government set a domestic content schedule along with the designation of items to be localized. This was implemented through a variety of incentives including preferential loans which led to the rapid rise of the domestic content ratio to over 70 percent in 1974, although the ratio was far behind the original target set in the basic promotion plan.

The oil crisis and the changing pattern of demand in the world automobile market compelled the Korean government to make a major shift in its development strategy. In 1974, the government announced the Long-Term Automobile Promotion Plan, the main objective of which was to develop Korean models with 100 percent domestic content, aimed at promoting the automobile industry as an export industry. The new strategy called for the production of "citizen cars" by three designated manufacturing firms named Hyundai, Kia, and Saehan.

These firms were requested to produce newly designed models with more than 95 percent domestic content and with engine capacity limited to less than 1.5 liters. The production of citizen cars was scheduled to begin in 1975 with an annual capacity of over 50,000 units for each model. More than 80 percent of the total domestic demand for passenger cars was planned to be met by these three citizen cars, while the remaining 20 percent was expected to be met by foreign models. The production of foreign models was permitted only for medium-sized passenger cars with an engine capacity of more than 1.5 liters.

Another important feature of the new strategy was to actively promote ancillary firm development independent of the primary firms on which government policy had so far concentrated, because the parts and components industry was considered a potential export industry. Korea began to export some auto parts such as piston rings and pins, springs, and axle shafts to meet replacement demand from the early 1960s, but most ancillary firms were small in scale and produced low-quality products. Therefore, the government believed that the development of ancillary firms based on specialization and large-scale production was indispensable for the successful implementation of the citizen car program and stimulated vigorous investment in supplier industries.

Three different cars were developed and assembled out of mostly domestic parts and components: Pony (Hyundai), Brisa (Kia), and Camina (GM-Korea). Pony was an original model developed by an Italian designer, while other cars were based on old models previously produced elsewhere. The production of motor vehicles increased sharply after 1975, largely due to the explosive increase in domestic demand, and reached 202,532 units in 1979. It is also noteworthy that Korea began to export motor vehicles in 1975 and more than 30,000 units were exported in 1979.

The rapid growth in the production of citizen cars coupled with the domestic production of major functional items stepped up the domestic content ratio to over 90 percent in the case of small passenger cars. Although almost all parts and components were produced domestically, their quality was, in most cases, still below international standards, while prices tended to be higher than international standards, which in turn made Korean automobiles less competitive in the international market. This was well reflected in the TFP of the automobile industry which displayed negative growth during the period 1966–1977, implying that the industry was suffering from significant inefficiencies mainly caused by the underutilization of capacity and failure to achieve optimal economies of scale.

The problem became far more serious when Korea was hit by the second oil crisis in 1979, which led automobile industry into deep recession. Thus, in 1981 the government introduced the rationalization program which reduced the number of passenger car producers from three to two in order to reorganize car manufacturing into a mass production system. As the domestic as well as world economy gradually recovered from 1983, Korean car producers began to expand production capacity to meet increasing domestic and export demand. The production capacity expanded significantly, doubling from 337,000 units in 1983 to 683,000 units in 1986. Exports of automobiles increased rapidly, rising from 25,000 units in 1980 to 347,000 units in 1990, benefiting from the appreciation of the yen against the dollar following the Plaza Accord in 1985. Encouraged by substantial improvement in production efficiency, the government began to liberalize the automobile market from 1987, and the Korean automobile industry responded with further capacity expansion and increased R&D efforts. Thus, the Korean car industry was able to improve its competitiveness so that exports continued to grow fast and reached more than 3 million units in 2000, accounting for more than 50 percent of total production.

As mentioned above, the Korean government pursued the policy of Korean-owned domestic manufacture of motor vehicles patterned after the Japanese development model, which enabled the Korean automobile industry to grow into an export industry. The success or failure of this type of development strategy depends very much on the growth of efficient supplier industries and the size of the domestic market. Korea succeeded in solving these problems. As far as supplier industries were concerned, the rapidly growing repair and replacement demand following the Korean War played a vital role in facilitating the growth of ancillary firms which led to the rapid localization of parts and components, enabling the indigenous development of motor vehicles. In this respect, the Korean development strategy differed from those of other developing countries, in which completed cars were assembled by subsidiaries of foreign firms, usually multinationals, or by joint ventures with foreign firms that supplied parts and components, thereby undermining the development of local supplier industries.

It is also noted that the development of the Korean automobile industry was not smooth but was marked by fluctuations inherent in a small market crowded by numerous vehicle producers. Therefore, it was not until the early 1980s when the per capita income reached over USD 1,000 that the automobile industry gained real growth momentum, as it benefited from the swiftly expanding domestic market, implying that sustained high economic growth was critical for the advancement of the automobile industry.

5.3.3 *Capital Goods*

Despite the rapid growth of domestic demand, the import substitution of the capital goods industry started much later due to technological difficulties and the underdeveloped components and materials industry. The capital goods industry is defined here as the general machinery sector that supplies production facilities for other industries.

The government began to promote machinery industry in the second five-year plan to increase the degree of self-sufficiency of the capital goods industry. The Machinery Industry Promotion Law was enacted in March 1967, and preferential loans were provided to facilitate the procurement of locally produced machinery while restricting the import of machinery. Despite these promotional measures, the import of machinery rose rapidly due to the low quality of domestically produced machinery, thereby causing a growing import dependency, as high as 77.8 percent in 1970. Until the early 1970s, the local production of machinery was limited mostly to agricultural machines such as power tillers, power sprayers, water pumps, and some simple textile machinery such as sewing machines.

The turning point for the machinery industry came when the government announced the Long-Term Machinery Industry Promotion Plan in 1973 which included the construction of the ambitious Changwon integrated machinery complex.[16] The major objective of the plan was to raise the self-sufficiency of the machinery sector while promoting exports through the development of production technology. Emphasis was placed on import substitution, aimed at replacing imported machinery with locally produced machinery. The standard localization ratio was set for imported machinery to facilitate the use of locally produced machinery and a report system was adopted to restrict the import of foreign machinery. Thanks to government support policy, the general machinery sector experienced a rapid expansion, growing at 29.1 percent per annum during the period 1967–1979. As a result, the self-sufficiency ratio defined as

---

[16]The Changwon machinery industry complex comprised 26 material plants, 39 general machinery plants, seven electrical equipment plants, and eight precision equipment plants. The complex was originally initiated by Hyundai International Incorporated but was transferred to Hyundai Heavy Machinery Company, which was nationalized in 1980. The restructuring of the company continued throughout 1980s and split into smaller firms that were handed over to Samsung, LG, and KEPCO. See Lee (1991, pp. 433–454).

output divided by total supply increased from 20.4 percent in 1970 to 48.6 percent in 1980, thereby reducing import dependency from 77.8 percent to 59.0 percent during the same period (Table 5.17).

Entering the 1980s, the government policy shifted toward raising the localization ratio and promoting the parts and materials industry. In 1986, the government announced the five-year localization plan (1986–1991) for machinery, parts, and materials to achieve the local production of 13,435 items by 1991. Although the plan was very comprehensive, covering not only the machinery sector but also other sectors including automobile and electrical parts, the machinery sector represented a large proportion of the designated items. The items to be locally produced were supported by various public funds for investment and technology development. Technical assistance was also extended in terms of providing testing facilities and technical consultancy, etc.[17]

The localization policy continued in the 1990s. Considerable progress was made in the self-sufficiency of the machinery sector, which increased from 48.6 percent in 1980 to 65.9 percent in 2000, as shown in Table 5.17. It is also notable that machinery exports began to take off in the 1990s, reflecting the improvement of quality as well as price competitiveness due to appreciation of the yen against the dollar following the Plaza Accord. Exports in the general machinery sector which amounted to no more than USD 30 million in the early 1980s increased sharply from the second half of the 1980s, reaching USD 3.3 billion in 1991 and USD 11.2 billion in 2000. Accordingly, the export ratio rose from 10.7 percent in 1980 to 29.9 percent in 2000, and the machines exported were considerably upgraded and diversified, including automatic weaving machines, elevators, bulldozers, loaders, NC machine tools, etc.

Despite the remarkable achievement of localization and export growth, much remained to be done to develop the machinery sector as an export industry which relies very much on the quality of parts and materials. Thus, entering the 2000s the thrust of government policy shifted from import substitution and localization

---

[17]For more details, see Korea Development Bank (1989, pp. 46–47).

Table 5.17   Export, Import, and Intermediate Input Ratios of the General
Machinery Sector, 1960–2008 (Unit: percent)

	Import/ Supply	Imported Intermediate Inputs/Output	Export/ Output	Output/ Supply
1960	12.1	10.3	1.5	—
1970	77.8	12.1	3.3	20.4
1980	59.0	15.8	10.7	48.6
1990	36.9	16.6	19.2	62.3
2000	34.1	11.9	29.9	65.9
2008	29.7	16.3	46.0	56.1

Source: ECOS system, The Bank of Korea.

to export promotion. The government believed the promotion of
specialized firms was essential for quality improvement as well as
the technological development of parts and components. For this
purpose, the government enacted the Act for Special Measures for
Assisting Specialized Enterprises in Parts and Materials in 2001
which stipulated various financial and technical supports. A series
of policy measures were further taken to build the institutional basis
to support the policy, including the launching of the basic promotion
plan for parts and materials development and the establishment of
parts and materials development institute.

These policy efforts led to the rapid growth of the parts and
materials industry, accompanied by substantial technology improvement. According to a survey conducted by the parts and materials
development institute, the overall technology level of Korea's parts
and materials in 2007 was evaluated at 88.5 percent of US technology.
This is slightly lower than that of Japan, which was estimated to
be 98.3 percent of US technology.[18] This remarkable technological
progress led to the rapid growth of machinery exports. The exports
ratio climbed to 46 percent in 2008 from 29.9 percent in 2000,
implying that the parts and materials industry grew into an export
industry in the 2000s (Table 5.17).

---

[18]For more details, see The 60-Year History of the Korean Economy-II (2010,
p. 331).

Chapter 6

Industrialization and SME Development

6.1 An Overview of the SME Development Policy

The small and medium-sized enterprises (SMEs) development policy in Korea has to be understood in the context of Korea's overall industrial development policy, which underwent several major changes from the 1960s to 1990s. SMEs are defined here as manufacturing firms that employ no more than 300 persons, while firms with more than 300 employees are defined as large-scale enterprises (LSEs).

The export promotion policy in the 1960s, which allowed the duty-free import of raw materials and intermediate goods, stimulated processing and assembly production, thereby favoring large-scale production. This policy had a negative impact on the development of SMEs because they were mostly oriented toward the domestic market. Thus, LSEs grew much faster than SMEs in the 1960s. The HCI drive in the 1970s also favored big firms. So, SMEs suffered a considerable setback relative to LSEs until the 1970s.

There were, however, some efforts to promote SMEs in the 1960s and 1970s. The Small and Medium Industry Bank was established in 1961 to help the financial problems of SMEs. Under the Small Business Coordination Act of 1961, certain industrial subsectors considered suitable for SMEs could be reserved for SMEs, excluding the participation of large-scale firms. The Export Industrial Estate Development Act was created in 1964 to support SME exports.

From 1965, commercial banks including foreign banks were obliged to provide 35 percent of their loans to SMEs.

From the mid-1970s, the government began to pay increasing attention to the promotion of SMEs because Korea's major export industries such as electronics, cars, and shipbuilding needed efficient supplier industries to enhance their competitiveness. The government enacted the SME Subcontracting Promotion Act in 1975, aimed at supporting SMEs producing specialized products or entering a subcontracting relationship. In 1976, the Korea Credit Guarantee Fund (KCGF) was set up to help the financial needs of SMEs that lacked collateral. The Small and Medium Industry Promotion Corporation (SMIPC), a semi-governmental organization, was established in 1979 to provide various support for the promotion of SMEs. Nonetheless, these policy efforts did not have enough fueling power to bring about the rapid growth of SMEs because the overall industrial incentive system was overwhelmingly in favor of LSEs. As a result, SMEs growth lagged far behind LSEs growth in the 1960s and 1970s, with the result that SMEs share in terms of number of establishments, employment, and value added dropped significantly during this period (Table 6.1).

Entering the 1980s, the government began to reform the industrial policy with great emphasis on the promotion of SMEs, because SMEs

Table 6.1   Share of SMEs in Manufacturing, 1963–2007 (Unit: percent)

	1963	1970	1980	1990	2000	2007
No. of establishments						
SMEs	98.7	97.1	96.6	98.3	99.3	99.5
LSEs	1.3	2.9	3.4	1.7	0.7	0.5
No. of workers						
SMEs	66.4	49.0	49.6	61.7	74.0	76.9
LSEs	33.6	51.0	50.4	38.3	26.0	23.1
Value added						
SMEs	52.8	28.8	35.2	44.3	50.2	50.8
LSEs	47.2	71.2	64.8	55.7	49.8	49.2

Source: Mining and Manufacturing Survey Report, Korea Statistical Office.

emerged as a major structural problem hampering the industrial competitiveness of Korea's major export industries. The promotion of SMEs was imperative not only for enhancing the international competitiveness of HCIs, but also for balanced industrial development and reducing industrial concentration which was worsening in the late 1970s. The concentration of economic power in chaebols rose rapidly in the 1970s. The top 30 chaebols came to occupy almost one-third of manufacturing value added (30.8 percent) and one-fifth of manufacturing employment (19.8 percent) in 1981.

Thus, the government began to make comprehensive policy efforts to promote SMEs by launching 10-year SME development plan in 1982, and took a number of new policy measures to promote SMEs including picking up high growth potential firms, promoting the purchase of SME products, encouraging start-ups, facilitating structural adjustment, promoting rural industries, promoting venture capital, and supporting technology development.[1] It should be noted that liberal industrial and trade policy in the 1980s also contributed to facilitating structural adjustment and enhancing the competitiveness of SMEs.

These policy efforts brought about the rapid development of SMEs with significant structural improvement. As shown in Table 6.2, the growth of SMEs was far ahead of LSEs so that SMEs gained significantly in terms of number of firms, employment, and value added. The share of SMEs in total number of establishments, employment, and value added in manufacturing increased markedly, rising from 96.6 percent, 49.6 percent, and 35.2 percent in 1980 to 98.3 percent, 61.7 percent, and 44.3 percent in 1990, respectively.

Entering the 1990s, the Korean economy was rapidly liberalized and integrated into the world economy, which compelled policy-makers to shift the industrial policy toward enhancing industrial competitiveness and promoting the high-tech industry. Reflecting the industrial policy direction, the SMEs development policy began to

---

[1]For more details, see Kim (2008c, pp. 263–264).

Table 6.2 Output and Employment Growth of SMEs and LSEs in Manufacturing, 1981–2007 (Unit: percent)

	1981–1990		1991–2000		2001–2007	
	Value Added	Employment	Value Added	Employment	Value Added	Employment
SMEs	23.8	6.3	9.2	0.6	7.1	1.8
LSEs	11.7	1.2	7.0	−5.1	6.9	−0.4
Manufacturing	13.4	4.0	8.0	−1.3	7.0	1.2

Source: Mining and Manufacturing Survey Report, Korea Statistical Office.

focus more on supporting technology development, factory automation, information networking, and venture business. On the other hand, protective measures for SMEs were substantially reduced. The number of products reserved for SMEs, which increased to 237 subsectors by 1989, was reduced continuously in the 1990s. The number of SMEs products procured by public agencies also declined rapidly after the government signed public procurement agreement with GATT in 1993.

The 1997 financial crisis prompted the government to intensify its support for SMEs, because rapid growth driven by chaebols was no longer sustainable. Thus, the government began to promote technology-oriented venture firms as a new driving force for growth by enacting the Special Law for Venture Business Promotion in 1997. Also, a number of new programs were launched by the Small and Medium Business Administration (SMBA) to assist innovative SMEs including the SME Technology Innovation and Development Program (1997), the Industry/University/Research Institute Consortium for Technology Development (1997), the Korea Small Business Innovation Research (KOSBIR) Program in 1998, and the Innovation Business Korea (INNO BIZ KOREA) Program in 2000.[2]

Aside from the support programs provided by the SMBA, other government agencies such as the Ministry of Trade, Industry, and

---

[2]For a detailed discussion, see Kim (2008c, pp. 265–268).

Energy (MOTIE), the Ministry of Information and Communication (MIC), and the Ministry of Science and Technology (MOST) also offered various funds for SMEs technology development.

Thanks to these support policies, SMEs continued to grow faster than LSEs in the 1990s and 2000s. As shown in Table 6.1, SMEs generated more than two-thirds of total employment and about half of the total value added in the manufacturing sector in 2007. In terms of the number of establishments, SMEs accounted for 99.5 percent of total manufacturing establishments in the same year.

6.2   Growth and Structural Change of SMEs

As mentioned above, SMEs policy underwent several major changes during the last four decades, which had a significant impact on the growth and structural shift of SMEs. As shown in Table 6.2, SMEs grew faster than LSEs from the 1980s and thus became the major contributor to output and employment growth of the manufacturing sector, resulting in relative decline of LSEs. It is remarkable that LSEs have no longer been contributing to employment growth since the 1990s, indicating that employment growth in the manufacturing sector was entirely contributed by SMEs in the 1990s. In other words, SMEs have been the major contributor to the output and employment growth of the manufacturing sector since the 1980s and were also accompanied by significant structural changes which are summarized as follows.

Table 6.3   Growth of Output, Employment, and Productivity by Firm Size, 1985–2001 (Unit: percent)

Size of Firm	Value Added	Employment	Labor Productivity
5–9	16.5	8.2	7.6
10–19	14.3	5.9	8.3
20–99	11.7	2.9	9.3
100–299	9.8	−0.5	10.8
300 and more	10.0	−2.9	13.6

Source: Korea Development Institute (2003, pp. 83–85, 96–103).

First, the growth of SMEs in manufacturing was largely led by small firms with less than 100 employees, implying that Korean SMEs are overwhelmingly dominated by small firms. As shown in Table 6.3, the smaller the size of the firms, the higher was the growth of output and employment. Firms with less than 20 employees displayed the highest growth in output and employment, followed by firms with 20–99 employees. Accordingly, their share of output and employment as well as the number of firms in manufacturing continued to rise from the 1980s. In contrast, medium-sized firms with 100–299 employees experienced the least output growth, accompanied by negative employment growth (Table 6.3). Thus, their shares of output, employment, and number of firms have steadily declined since the 1980s (Table 6.4).

Second, SMEs grew much faster than LSEs in both the light and heavy industries, leading to an increase of their shares in both sectors (Table 6.5). Large-scale production based on cheap labor was no longer competitive due to a rapid rise in wages. As a result, the number of labor-intensive large firms, particularly those in the textile and footwear industries relying heavily on exports went either bankrupt or had to scale down their production lines or to relocate their facilities to low-wage countries. This led to the relative decline of LSEs and the rise of SMEs in light industries. Even in the heavy industries, SMEs grew faster than LSEs because the increasing localization of parts and components led to the faster growth of supplier industries which are mostly small and medium-sized.

Third, a rapid structural change took place in favor of heavy and chemical industries within the SME sector. Since the early 1980s, the government has taken a series of policy measures to promote start-ups, venture businesses, and small high-tech firms, which led to the rapid growth of small firms in heavy industries. While heavy SMEs grew fast, labor-intensive SMEs lost their comparative advantage due to wage hikes. This led to the rise of heavy SMEs in the SME sector, accounting for more than 50 percent in terms of number of establishments, employment, and value added in 1990 (Table 6.5).

Table 6.4 Structural Change of SMEs by Firm Size, 1980–2007 (Unit: percent)

Size of Firm	Establishment				Employment				Value Added			
	1980	1990	2000	2007	1980	1990	2000	2007	1980	1990	2000	2007
5–19	58.9	61.0	73.4	76.3	8.4	14.7	34.3	28.1	4.1	7.1	11.2	12.7
20–99	29.8	32.6	23.1	20.8	20.2	29.2	33.4	32.8	13.0	20.3	21.5	22.2
100–299	7.9	4.7	2.8	2.4	20.8	17.7	16.3	16.0	18.0	17.1	17.5	15.9
300+	3.4	1.7	0.7	0.5	50.6	38.4	26.0	23.1	64.9	55.5	49.8	49.2
Total	100.0	100.0	100.0	100.0	100.0	100.0	100.0	100.0	100.0	100.0	100.0	100.0

Source: Mining and Manufacturing Survey Report, Korea Statistical Office.

Table 6.5   Structural Changes of SMEs and LSEs, 1970–1990 (Unit: percent)

	Number of Firms				Employment				Value Added			
	1970	1975	1980	1990	1970	1975	1980	1990	1970	1975	1980	1990
Light industry												
SMEs	97.2	96.2	97.0	98.4	47.9	44.7	51.0	66.9	29.4	31.7	36.4	54.2
LSEs	2.8	3.8	3.0	1.6	52.1	55.3	49.0	33.1	70.6	68.3	63.6	45.8
Heavy and chemical industry												
SMEs	96.8	96.1	96.1	98.1	50.9	47.4	49.6	57.4	27.9	31.6	34.0	39.3
LSEs	3.2	3.9	3.9	1.9	49.1	52.6	50.4	42.6	72.1	68.4	66.0	60.7
Total SMEs												
LI	66.6	64.3	59.3	49.7	63.0	61.9	57.9	49.5	57.9	54.2	49.2	41.5
HCI	33.4	35.7	40.7	50.3	37.0	38.1	42.1	50.5	42.1	45.8	50.8	58.5

Source: Mining and Manufacturing Survey Report, Various years, Korea Statistical Office.

6.3   Problems Facing SMEs and Policy Implications

Numerous policy measures to promote SMEs since the 1980s brought about a remarkable progress in the growth and structural change of SMEs. The problem is that despite its significant progress, the SMEs sector faces a number of structural problems to be resolved for further growth and development. SMEs are suffering from a shortage of production workers, the dominance of small firms, low productivity, and low R&D, which calls for a new policy approach to SMEs development.

The strong interventionist approach has been the backbone of Korea's SMEs policy, because SMEs are considered an object of protection. For this reason, public support for SMEs in Korea has been very extensive and generous with a long duration. Influenced in part by political pressure groups, the Korean government has provided extensive supports through public funds, credit guarantees, and various support programs. The government, including local governments, and SME-related organizations ran around 1,300 programs in 2013, indicating that SMEs are overly supported (OECD, 2014a, p. 85).

While the generous public support has made a significant contribution to the growth and development of SMEs, it also entailed the negative side effects by allowing weak firms to survive. Furthermore, it encouraged small firms to remain small so as to stay eligible for public support because once they become large they lose all the benefits given to them. This seems one of reasons why medium-sized firms with 100–299 employees revealed the least growth of output and employment during the last several decades, which in turn led to retardation of the growth of mid-sized firms with 300–999 employees. As shown in Fig. 6.1, firms with 300–999 employees represent only 16.1 percent of total manufacturing sales, which is far lower compared to those of Japanese (26.8 percent) and German mid-sized firms (28.9 percent), indicating the structural weaknesses of the Korean manufacturing sector.

The generous public support also had a negative impact on productivity growth because it is likely to discourage the investment and innovative activities of SMEs. As shown in Fig. 6.2, the labor

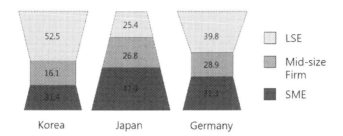

Figure 6.1   Comparison of Manufacturing Sales by Firm Size: Korea, Japan and Germany (Unit: percent)

Notes: The mid-size firm refers to firms with 300–399 workers in Korea and Japan and 250–999 workers in Germany. The sales ratio for Korea, Japan, and Germany refers to 2009, 2006, and 2005, respectively.

Source: Economic Research Institute, Industrial Bank of Korea, quoted from Maeil Business News, Korea, June 7, 2011.

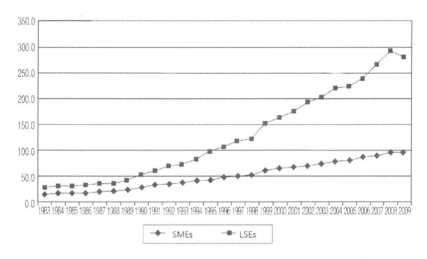

Figure 6.2   Labor Productivity[a] of SMEs and LSEs, 1983–2009 (Unit: KRW million in 2005 prices)

Note: [a]Value added per worker.

Source: Kim (2012, p. 25).

productivity growth of SMEs lagged far behind that of LSEs since the early 1990s, resulting in a widening productivity gap between SMEs and LSEs. Thus, SMEs labor productivity fell to one-third of LSEs in 2009. Since wages are, as shown in Fig. 6.3, around

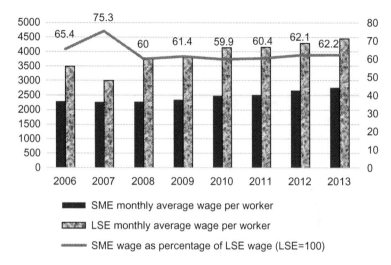

Figure 6.3   Wages of SMEs as Percentage of LSEs (Unit: KRW 1,000 in current prices, percent)

Source: SMEs Status Indicators 2014, Korea Federation of SMEs.

60 percent of LSEs wages while productivity is one-third of LSEs productivity, labor costs in SMEs are much higher than in LSEs, implying a weakening competitiveness of SMEs. The share of SMEs in Korea's total exports, which used to be as high as around 40 percent in the 1990s, dropped to around 20 percent in the 2000s and continued to fall further. The share of SMEs exports, for example, dropped from 21.1 percent in 2009 to 18.3 percent in 2012.[3]

Weak R&D activities are also important sources of lower productivity growth. Although the R&D/sales ratio of SMEs has risen slightly since the early 2000s, it is still very low due to the shortage of qualified manpower and financial resources and has tended to decline in recent years. As shown in Table 6.6, the R&D/sales ratio of SMEs was 1.09 percent in 2011, which is much lower than that of large-scale firms (1.74 percent), and more importantly only 28.1 percent of SMEs undertook R&D activities in the same year. After the financial crisis, the number of innovative SMEs has grown rapidly but they are still

---

[3]Kim *et al.* (2014, p. 55).

Table 6.6 R&D/Sales Ratio of SMEs in Manufacturing, 2000–2011 (Unit: percent)

	2000	2003	2004	2005	2006	2007	2009	2011
R&D/sales ratio	0.47	0.89	0.89	1.12	1.26	1.37	1.00	1.09
Ratio of R&D performing firms	12.0	19.6	19.5	20.8	23.2	22.6	27.6	28.1

Source: Korea Federation of SMEs.

relatively small in number, so that they did not affect much overall R&D activity and productivity growth of SMEs.

Another serious problem facing SMEs is the manpower shortage. As the Korean economy continued to grow fast, the labor shortage became very acute in almost all sectors, resulting in a sharp wage increase. The labor shortage is particularly serious in the SMEs sector, where wages are much lower and working conditions and fringe benefits are not as attractive as in large-scale firms. As a result, manpower shortages in the SME sector are far more serious than in large-scale firms.

In addition to the labor shortage, the high turnover rate of blue-collar workers poses major obstacles to the growth of SMEs. The turnover rate of blue-collar workers in SMEs is much higher than in large-scale firms. According to the Ministry of Employment and Labor, the turnover rate of SMEs production workers increased from 4.6 percent in 2010 to 5 percent in 2017, while that of LSEs dropped from 3.9 percent to 2.8 percent in the same period. This implies that the labor supply to small firms became extremely volatile, and volatility is likely to rise with the widening wage gap.

Furthermore, the business environment for SMEs has markedly deteriorated, as they face severe competition from abroad in the wake of trade liberalization. Cheap foreign products are penetrating the domestic market, successfully competing against Korean SMEs products. The competitive edge based on cheap labor has faded, compelling many SMEs to move overseas. In consequence, SMEs have been suffering from falling profit margins. Wages increased higher than productivity growth causing rising labor costs for SMEs, which

Table 6.7   Operating Profit Ratio of SMEs and LSEs (Unit: percent)

	2000	2001	2002	2003	2004	2005	2006	2007	2008	2009	2011
LSEs	8.2	6.0	7.5	8.2	9.4	7.2	6.0	6.8	6.6	6.4	6.1
SMEs	5.8	4.5	5.3	4.6	4.1	4.4	4.3	4.4	4.8	4.5	4.2

Source: The Bank of Korea.

in turn led to falling profit rates. As shown in Table 6.7, operating profits as a ratio of sales have tended to decline continuously since the early 2000s, and the gap between SMEs and LSEs does not appear to narrow. Thus, around one-third of SMEs have an interest-coverage ratio of less than 100 percent, meaning that their earnings are insufficient to cover their interest payments. Many such firms, however, survive on generous government support.

Therefore, the generous public support provided to SMEs should be streamlined by reducing the number of support programs, because it contributes to neither SMEs growth and innovation nor the performance of the firms. A study conducted by KDI comparing SMEs receiving support to those that do not over 2003–2009 found that public support failed to boost profit and sales (OECD, 2014b, p. 26). This seems to suggest that the government need to change its SMEs policy from protection-oriented to innovation-oriented support in order to enhance SMEs capacity for productivity improvement.

Chapter 7

Industrialization and Concentration of Economic Power

7.1 Rapid Industrial Growth and Concentration of Economic Power

Korea's growth-first policy which worked in favor of large-scale firms had a significant impact on the industrial organization. As shown in Fig. 7.1, the shipment share of the 100 largest mining and manufacturing firms grew rapidly until the early 1980s thanks to the HCI drive policy that facilitated the growth of large-scale firms. Entering the 1980s, this rising trend of concentration weakened considerably due to the structural adjustment policy for the HCI sector and the SME promotion policy. The falling concentration ratio started to reverse from the mid-1980s, as the economy picked up after Plaza Accord in 1985. This upward trend continued until the 1997 financial crisis because the government resumed a high growth policy in the 1990s.

The financial crisis of 1997 strongly affected the growth of large firms which underwent extensive structural reform, causing a sharp decline in the concentration ratio. After a short fall following the financial crisis, however, it rose again as the economy recovered. However, it has displayed a stabilizing tendency due to slowing economic growth and the continued control over chaebols. In other words, no long-term, upward trend of concentration could be found. In contrast to shipment-based concentration, the employment-based concentration ratio has shown a tendency to decline since the early

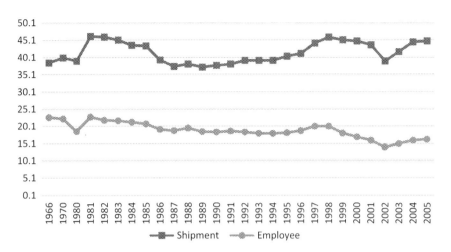

Figure 7.1   Long-Term Concentration Ratio of 100 largest Mining and Manufacturing Firms, 1966–2005 (Unit: percent)

Source: Lee (2007, p. 109).

1970s, reflecting the diminishing role of large firms in creating employment (Fig. 7.1).

The concentration of economic power is to a certain extent an inevitable phenomenon arising from the growth of capitalistic market economy. This phenomenon is, however, critically perceived in the Korean society. The reason is that economic power is concentrated in a small number of family-owned business groups known as chaebols. Since chaebols grew rapidly with the help of various forms of government support, their accumulation of capital and wealth was not fully justifiable in the eyes of the general public. Therefore, the concentration of economic power and its related problems need to be analyzed in terms of chaebol concentration, which can be divided into three aspects, namely share of chaebols in the economy, their diversification of business, and corporate ownership.

The economic power of chaebols is measured in terms of shipment and employment shares in the mining and manufacturing sector, and business groups are divided into the top 30 chaebols and top 10 chaebols. As shown in Fig. 7.2, the concentration ratio of the top 30 chaebols displays a trend similar to that of the 100 largest firms

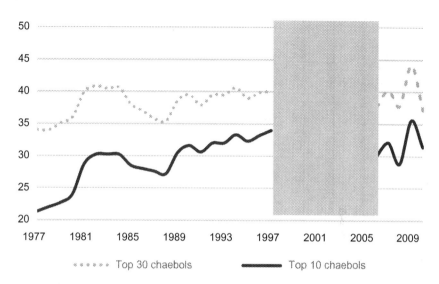

Figure 7.2   Long-Term Concentration Ratio of 30 and 10 Largest Chaebols in the Mining and Manufacturing Sector, 1977–2009 (Unit: percent)

Note: No consistent data was available for chaebol concentration during 1997–2006 due to corporate restructuring following the financial crisis.

Source: Lee (2013, p. 291).

because most of the 100 largest firms are subsidiaries of the chaebols. In 1994, for example, 83 out of the 100 largest firms in the mining and manufacturing sector were affiliates of the top 30 chaebols.[1] The concentration ratio rose rapidly until the early 1980s and after a short fall rose again from the mid-1980s, reflecting the booming economy following the Plaza Accord in 1985. Entering the 1990s, the ratio stabilized albeit with some fluctuations, indicating that a long-term upward trend no longer existed.

In contrast to the top 30 chaebols, the concentration ratio of the top 10 chaebols shows a rising trend over time until the 1997 financial crisis, indicating that the concentration of economic power was more pronounced in the top 10 groups than in the top 30 groups. This seems to suggest that the concentration of economic power in Korea is not so much the problem of big business groups in general as a small number of business groups represented by the top 10 chaebols.

---

[1]See Shin (2000, p. 65).

The 1997 financial crisis made it extremely difficult to compile consistent data for chaebols due to corporate restructuring. Therefore, no reliable data was available for chaebol concentration between 1997 and 2006. Nonetheless, there is no doubt that chaebol concentration declined following the financial crisis. This can be inferred from the concentration ratio of the 100 largest firms, which dropped considerably until the early 2000s. The chaebol concentration began to climb again from 2006 but seemed relatively stable thereafter, accompanied by some ups and downs due to business cycle.

The stabilizing tendency of chaebol concentration since the early 2000s was also observed in the non-financial corporate sector. As shown in Fig. 7.3, the sales concentration ratio of the top 30 chaebols in the non-financial sector shows a stabilizing tendency after a short decline in the early 2000s. The level is slightly lower than in the mining and manufacturing sector and ranges between roughly 33 and 36 percent due to the lower chaebol share in the service sector. In 2010, for example, the top 30 chaebols accounted for

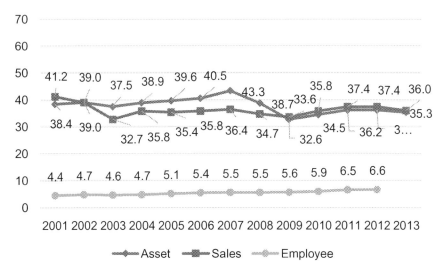

Figure 7.3   Concentration Ratio of Top 30 Chaebols in the Non-Financial Sector, 2001–2013 (Unit: percent)

Source: Korea Economic Research Institute.

16.1 percent of service sector sales while accounting for 45.5 percent of manufacturing sales. The concentration ratio in terms of assets also shows a stabilizing tendency after a short rise in the early 2000s. On the other hand, the employment concentration ratio tends to increase slightly, reflecting the increasing role of the service sector in employment creation.

In view of the importance of chaebols in the economy, it seems worthwhile to examine the chaebol concentration from the viewpoint of the national economy as a whole. In this regard, the sales or assets of chaebols are often compared to GDP in order to demonstrate the seriousness of economic concentration by chaebols. In 2010, for example, the sales of the top 30 chaebols were estimated to be as high as 76.7 percent of GDP, which gives the impression that chaebol concentration is a very serious matter. The chaebol concentration based on their sales in relation to GDP is misleading, because GDP is based on a value-added concept which differs greatly from the concept of sales. Therefore, any meaningful estimation of chaebol concentration in the national economy needs to be based on a common denominator such as value added.

There were some efforts that attempted to estimate chaebol concentration in terms of value added. As shown in Fig. 7.4, the value-added share of the top 30 chaebols in GDP, which ranged between 11 and 15 percent during 1985–2000, tended to rise slightly from the late 1980s until 1995, and began to decline thereafter. This

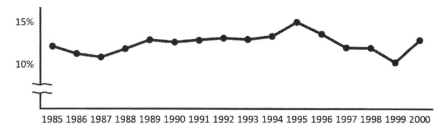

Figure 7.4   Value-Added Share of Top 30 Chaebols in GDP, 1985–2000 (Unit: percent)

Sources: Choi (2000, 2001), quoted from Lee (2013, p. 282).

is consistent with the movement of the concentration ratio of the top 30 chaebols in the mining and manufacturing sector.

Regarding the level of chaebol concentration, it is often argued that the concentration in Korea is high compared to other developing countries. Due to the lack of data reliability, it is difficult to make any meaningful international comparison. However, there was some evidence indicating that the economic concentration in Korea was relatively low by historic Asian standards.[2]

It should be further noted that the economic concentration in Korea is not so high even when compared to advanced industrial countries. During 1990–1993, for example, the average concentration ratios of the 100 largest manufacturing firms in Japan and US in terms of employment, sales, and assets were 21.1 percent, 39 percent, 34.4 percent, and 41.1 percent, 55.7 percent, 31.9 percent, respectively. In Korea, they were 18.6 percent, 41.6 percent, and 46.7 percent during the same period, indicating that Korea had either lower or similar concentration ratios except in assets concentration.[3]

The second important feature of the Korean chaebols is their highly diversified business portfolios. The growth-first policy and big business-oriented industrial policy led to the rapid development of chaebols since they were supported by the government in many ways. Thus, chaebols came to run various business lines including the manufacturing, financial, and service sectors. In 1994, the five largest chaebols had, on average, 42 subsidiaries and ran business in more than 30 industries.[4]

The diversification of business activities was to some extent desirable for the continued growth of firms, but the problem was that the chaebols expanded their business activities through the very aggressive use of leveraging which led to huge corporate debts. The debt to equity ratio of the top 30 chaebols, for example, soared from

---

[2]Korea in 1975 had substantially less business concentration than Japan at the end of World War II, Pakistan in 1959 or India in 1958 and 1968. For a detailed discussion, see Jones and Sakong (1980, pp. 261–266).
[3]See Hwang (1997, p. 84); see also Yoo and Lee (1997, p. 460).
[4]Yoo and Lee (1997, p. 460).

Table 7.1   In-Group Ownership Concentration, 1996–2014 (Unit: percent)

	1996	1998	2000	2002	2004	2006	2008	2010	2012	2014
In-group ownership	44.1	44.5	43.4	49.5	51.8	51.2	51.0	50.5	56.1	54.7
Family ownership	10.3	7.9	4.5	7.5	4.6	5.0	4.2	4.4	4.2	4.2
Subsidiary ownership	33.8	36.6	38.9	39.0	40.4	43.8	44.4	43.6	49.6	48.3
Others[a]	—	—	—	3.0	2.8	2.4	2.4	2.5	2.4	2.2

Note: [a]The sum of shares of non-profit corporations, registered executives, and treasury (own) stocks.
Source: Korea Fair Trade Commission.

347.5 percent in 1995 to 519 percent in 1997, and some of them had debt-to-equity ratios as high as 1,000 percent, which served as a major cause of the financial crisis.

The third important feature of Korean chaebols is the high ownership concentration. "In-group ownership," defined as the sum of direct shares of the controlling shareholder's family, shares of subsidiaries and other related parties, has steadily increased since the mid-1990s. In the case of the top 30 chaebols, it rose from 44.1 percent in 1996 to 54.7 percent in 2014 (Table 7.1). This is mainly due to the increase of the shares of subsidiaries, which jumped from 33.8 percent to 48.3 percent during the same period. On the other hand, the controlling family's share fell drastically during the same period because the government pushed chaebols to go public.

7.2   Economic Concentration and Chaebol Policy

The government began to regulate large firms from the mid-1970s to cope with the increasing industrial concentration which intensified the monopolistic and oligopolistic structure of the market. In 1974, for example, the monopoly and oligopoly market represented 83 percent of the industrial commodity market and 64 percent in terms of shipment (Lee and Yoon, 1993). One important consequence was the collusive pricing behavior of market dominating producers which became the major source of inflation. During 1970–1975, for example, wholesale prices increased 140 percent whereas the price of monopolistic and duopolistic producer's products rose by 200 percent (Lee, 1977).

Thus, legislative effort was required to fight inflation and regulate the unfair trade practices of big firms, which was reflected in the Price Stabilization and Fair Trade Act of 1975. Although the Act stipulated various regulations against unfair trade practices, they were not effectively implemented because the government feared that its strong enforcement would hamper the growth of HCIs. Thus, the government policy was focused on price controls rather than regulating unfair trade and anti-competitive practices. Extensive price control was adopted by regulating the prices of approximately 150 monopolistic and oligopolistic products, and this policy continued until the end of the 1970s. Some efforts were also made to regulate big firms in terms of credit control and to encourage their public listing in the stock market. However, these policies were not actively enforced and hence the chaebol share of economic power increased greatly during the 1970s.

The turning point for competition policy came in 1980 by enacting the Monopoly Regulation and Fair Trade Act (MRFTA). The Act was modeled after competition law in Japan and Germany and covered all relevant problems such as monopolistic behavior, anti-competitive mergers, cartels, and unfair trade practices. The MRFTA aimed among others to promote fair and free competition and to reduce the concentration of economic power, thereby facilitating market-oriented development. In other words, the enactment of the MRFTA was a reflection of the fundamental shift in policy orientation from state-led to market-oriented development initiated by the Chun Doo Hwan government in the early 1980s.

Since the MRFTA did not include a restrictive clause on conglomerate integration, its enforcement was directed mostly toward regulating unfair trade practices, undue international contracts, and unfair subcontracting trade. In consequence, despite their widespread practices of business integration, abuse of market dominance, and concentration of economic power, chaebols were not regulated until the mid-1980s due to the economic recession. The government was hesitant to regulate chaebols because of the potential negative impact on the economy. Instead, the government attempted to discipline big firms by means of liberalization and restructuring.

The government began to regulate chaebol concentration as the economy picked up from the mid-1980s. In 1987, business groups whose asset value exceeded KRW 400 billion were designated as large business groups subject to various government regulations. The regulation of cross shareholding within a designated business group was introduced to prevent excessive business expansion. In 1992, regulation of cross payment guarantees between chaebols' subsidiaries was also adopted. The so-called specialization policy was reinforced in 1993 to induce chaebols to concentrate on their core businesses so as to strengthen their competitiveness. In 1994, the regulation of cross shareholding within a large business group was further tightened by lowering the ceiling of equity investment from 40 percent of net assets of an investing company to 25 percent of its net assets. Besides these measures, many others were implemented to mitigate chaebol concentration in terms of credit control, restriction of real estate holdings, etc.

Nevertheless, the efforts to regulate chaebols were not very successful because actual policy implementation was considerably affected by business cycles, socio-political considerations, and pressure from the business community. As the government pursued a high growth policy from the late 1980s, the government had to rely on chaebols and thus the control on the conglomerates was eased or became less effective. The collusive relation built between businessmen and politicians also dampened the effectiveness of government policy which was typically exemplified by Samsung's entry into the already overcrowded automobile market in 1994.

A thoroughgoing and comprehensive structural reform of chaebols took place only after the financial crisis in 1997. Since the excessive leveraging of chaebols was considered a major cause of the crisis, government policy focused on the business restructuring of large chaebols, improving their corporate governance, enhancing management transparency, and eliminating cross-debt guarantees. The principal objective of the reform was to bring business practices in line with international standards, thereby enhancing the competitiveness of Korean firms. The government launched a variety of reforms to achieve its objectives, which had significant impacts on the growth and structure of chaebols.

The government pushed large business groups to reduce their excessive debt levels, improve their capital structure and eliminate the cross subsidization of their subsidiaries. To help eliminate over-capacity in key manufacturing industries, business swaps, so-called big deals, were carried out for the top five groups in the areas of semiconductors, oil refinery, aircraft, automobiles, petrochemicals, power generation, rolling stock, and vessel engines. A variety of measures were taken to improve corporate governance with a view to strengthening investor rights, enhancing the transparency of financial accounting and disclosure, and raising the accountability of managers and major shareholders.

Measures were also taken to liberalize the capital market and FDI to promote competition. The ceiling on foreign investment in equity and bonds was eliminated, and foreign ownership in most industries and financial services was liberalized. The restriction on foreigner's land procurement for investment was eliminated and a one-stop service for foreign investment was instituted.

These reform policies made a significant contribution to improving the financial structure of chaebols and bringing Korean accounting standards closer to international ones. The top 30 chaebols could reduce their debt-to-equity ratios from 519 percent on average to 380 percent at the end of 1998. The top five chaebols except for Daewoo group lowered their debt equity ratios to below 200 percent by 2000. A significant progress was made in implementing their overall restructuring plans. By the end of 1999, the number of subsidiaries and affiliates of the top four chaebols had fallen to 165 from 232 at the end of 1997. Business swaps were completed in the areas of semiconductors, oil refinery, aircraft, rolling stock, power generation, and vessel engines.

Entering the 2000s, efforts were made under the Roh Moo Hyun government to strengthen the regulation of chaebols with an emphasis on ownership concentration. Voting rights for the stocks held by financial subsidiaries were further restricted and the establishment of holding companies was encouraged. Cross shareholding and cross payment guarantees between subsidiaries were prohibited for the business groups with asset values exceeding KRW 2 trillion. However, the efforts to reduce ownership concentration were not very successful except with regard to family ownership.

The chaebol policy was considerably eased in 2008 when the Lee Myung Bak government adopted the business-friendly policy to stimulate the economy. The MRFTA was revised toward lifting restrictions on equity investment and easing regulations on holding companies. However, the business-friendly policy turned out unsustainable due to poor economic performance and mounting anti-chaebol pressure associated with rising income inequality, which led the government to return to chaebol regulation. Thus, controls on chaebols were strengthened under the Park Geun Hye government, prohibiting new equity investment, raising penalties for unfair subcontracting practices, and so forth.

As mentioned above, the government's policy toward chaebols has frequently changed, influenced by business cycles and regime changes. This is because policy measures were taken without a firm and consistent philosophy and principle in dealing with chaebol issues. The chaebol policy moved from one extreme to another, depending on its emphasis on efficiency or equity. Most regimes attempted to regulate chaebols in their early stages, but soon retreated for economic and socio-political reasons.

The chaebol problem in Korea is a very delicate issue, involving not only economic but also social problems. Since large business groups continue to play a dominant role in the economy, they need to grow further for sustained growth of the economy. On the other hand, an anti-chaebol sentiment is widespread among the people, reflecting growing concerns over social equity and distribution. Therefore, the crucial issue regarding the chaebol policy is how to reconcile efficiency with equity in the sense that equity is enhanced within the limits of not hampering growth.

In this regard, it seems worthwhile to review the criteria of regulation which is based on the asset value of business groups. Business firms are designated as large business groups based on their asset value, and once designated they are subject to various government regulations including entry, pricing, investment, and ownership. The system was first introduced in 1987 starting with an asset value of KRW 400 billion. From 1993 onwards, the 30 largest groups were regulated until 2001 as the number of business groups with asset values exceeding KRW 400 billion was rising quickly.

In 2002, the asset value of firms subject to regulation was reintroduced and adjusted upward to KRW 2 trillion taking into account inflation and growth, and cross shareholding and cross payment guarantee were prohibited. Public enterprises were also treated as business firms subject to the same regulation. Despite the upward adjustment of asset value, the number of business groups subject to regulation has steadily climbed, reaching 59 groups in 2006. Accordingly, the asset value was further increased to KRW 5 trillion in 2008, thereby reducing the number of business groups to 28. The number once again rose to 41 in 2015, reflecting the growth of the economy.

The regulation of business firms based on asset value is unique to Korea, as it is not practiced in other countries. In the era of globalization, it seems undesirable to regulate business firms simply based on the size of assets because it is detrimental to the growth of firms. Many of Korea's small and medium-sized firms are reluctant to grow further because they do not want to be targeted by government regulation while losing the many benefits they enjoy for being small or medium-sized.

Therefore, it is not desirable for the growth of the economy to regulate business firms based on arbitrary discretion. Regulation should be based on a consistent principle whereby business firms are supervised in a way that promotes fair and free competition. Moreover, the regulation of chaebol concentration should be examined from the global market perspective, which makes the concentration of economic power far less significant and important. When overseas sales are excluded, the concentration ratio becomes much lower than otherwise.[5]

---

[5]For details, see Hwang and Choi (2013, p. 59).

Chapter 8

Liberalization Policy and Process[*]

Korea's liberalization policy is often interpreted in terms of trade liberalization. Trade liberalization has certainly played an important role in Korea's rapid industrial development and growth. There were, however, other liberalization policy efforts that played no less an important role in Korea's development process. This chapter examines the liberalization policy from broader perspectives, covering not only trade and industrial policy but also financial, investment, competition, and technology policies, and then explains how these different policies affected the growth and development of the Korean economy over the past four decades from the 1960s through the 1990s.

Korea's liberalization policy since the early 1960s has been gradual but neither smooth nor uninterrupted as Korea pursued a state-led industrialization policy. Korea's liberalization policy over the past four decades can be, broadly speaking, divided into four phases of evolution: export promotion and liberalization efforts in the 1960s, heavy and chemical industry (HCI) promotion and setback in liberalization in the 1970s, policy shift to market-oriented development and renewed liberalization efforts in the 1980s, and globalization and accelerated liberalization in the 1990s.

---

[*]Revised and updated version of the author's earlier paper: "Liberalization Policy in Korea's Development Process" in Chuk Kyo Kim (ed.), *Korea's Development Policy Experience and Implications for Developing Countries*. Seoul: KIEP, 2008.

8.1   Evolution of Liberalization Policy: An Overview

8.1.1   *Export Promotion and Liberalization Efforts (1960s)*

In the 1950s, the Korean economy faced severe macroeconomic imbalances with an extremely high inflation rate and serious balance of payments difficulties after the Korean War. The government policy thus focused on containing inflationary pressures along with post-war reconstruction. In response to chronic balance of payments difficulties, the government resorted to a protectionist trade policy with high tariffs and quantitative restrictions aimed at import substitution in nondurable consumer goods. This policy of easy import substitution was mostly completed by the end of the 1950s.

The military government, which came to power in 1961 initially attempted to pursue further import substitution in capital goods and intermediate inputs. The policy, however, was not sustainable because of the foreign exchange crisis in 1963 owing to US aid cut. Thus, from 1964, the government shifted its industrial policy from import substitution to export promotion to boost economic growth and cope with the balance of payments problem. The government adopted an outward-looking development strategy, the basic goal of which was to achieve high growth through export-oriented industrialization.

In order to attain this goal, the government implemented a package of export incentives. Income taxes on export earnings were reduced by 50 percent and business taxes were exempted for exporters, while providing them with extremely favorable export credit. Tariffs were completely exempted on imports of raw materials, intermediate goods, and capital equipment. Exporters also had the benefit of accelerated depreciation allowance and the export–import link premium. The most important incentive was the export credit system, under which exporters could automatically receive loans at an extremely low interest rate compared to the normal commercial lending rate. Besides these various incentives, the government successively devalued the Korean won to maintain the exchange rate at a realistic level in order to encourage exports.

Thanks to these policy measures, exporters could carry out their business more or less at a free trade level, because they did not pay any tariffs on imports of raw materials and intermediate goods for export production. Thus, they could buy them at world market prices and then sell their products at competitive international market prices because the exchange rate was maintained at a realistic level. There were also no quantitative restrictions on exports, as well as imports for export production. Although the export incentives were greatly expanded, subsidies that directly affected the profits of exports such as direct tax deductions and an interest rate premium as a ratio of the official exchange rate drastically declined since 1965, indicating increasing export liberalization.[1]

As the balance of payments condition improved in 1965, the government made efforts to liberalize imports by increasing the number of automatic approval (AA) items, and the import policy shifted from a positive to a negative system in 1967. Thus, the import liberalization ratio rose significantly, jumping from 12 percent to 60 percent in 1967. This policy shift, however, brought about a rapid increase in imports, deteriorating balance of payments difficulties, which prevented the government from further pursuing import liberalization. Thus, from 1968, the government returned to restrictive trade policy by raising tariffs and tightening import control and no further movement toward import liberalization was made thereafter.

As briefly mentioned above, import liberalization policy in the 1960s was short-lived, covering only 1965–1967. During this liberalization period, the number of automatically approved items rose while the number of restricted or prohibited items was reduced substantially. However, the practical significance of these reforms remained very limited because the government tried to control imports through various non-tariff barriers. Most consumer goods were either classified as restricted or prohibited items, and the restricted items were controlled through annual import ceilings.

---

[1]See Kim (1991, p. 35).

The imports of manufactured goods that competed with domestic production were only allowed to fill the gap between domestic supply and demand, and even automatically approved items were subject to control by numerous special laws. Only raw materials and food were imported relatively freely.

Although exports rose rapidly thanks to the government support policy, it was impossible to reduce the trade deficit since imports were also growing at a very fast pace. The result was an ever-increasing trade deficit due to the very small initial base of exports. Thus, the balance of payments consideration was always given top priority in trade policy, and the government intervened whenever it deemed necessary to defend the balance of payments. Therefore, non-tariff barriers were widely used to reduce trade deficits.

Aside from the balance of payments consideration, industrial policy also contributed to hampering trade liberalization because the government began to promote HCIs in the second half of the 1960s. In consequence, trade liberalization virtually stopped in the late 1960s, resulting in a falling import liberalization ratio after 1967. In short, liberalization efforts in the 1960s were largely limited to exports while efforts for import liberalization were short-lived due to balance of payments constraints and industrial policy considerations.

8.1.2   *Heavy and Chemical Industry Promotion and Setback in Liberalization (1970s)*

The promotion of heavy industries was reinforced from the third five-year plan which began in 1972. The government announced the promotion of HCIs as a top policy goal in 1973. The protectionist trade regime was strengthened, as the focus of industrial policy shifted from export promotion to import substitution policy. Export incentives were gradually reduced while incentives for HCIs were strengthened.

The tariff structure was reformed and non-tariff barriers (NTBs) were tightened. The tariff rate for HCIs was raised, while it was lowered for the rest of the industry. A number of heavy and chemical products were shifted from AA to restricted status, increasing the number of restricted import items. As a result, the liberalization

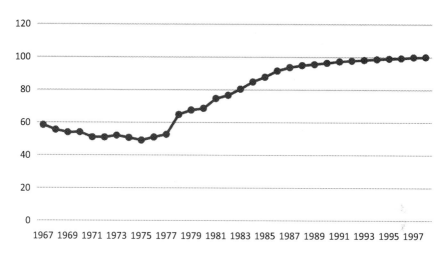

Figure 8.1   Import Liberalization Ratio, 1967–2001 (Unit: percent)
Source: Ministry of Trade, Industry and Energy (2003).

efforts initiated in the 1960s suffered a considerable setback in the
1970s leading to a decline in the import liberalization ratio (Fig. 8.1).

It should, however, be noted that an attempt was made to
liberalize imports in the late 1970s as the current account improved in
1976 and 1977. Thus, the import liberalization ratio rose slightly from
52.7 percent in 1977 to 67.6 percent in 1979. Nonetheless, this policy
could not be continued due to the death of President Park and the
ensuing political crisis and second oil shock in 1979. Consequently,
overall trade liberalization remained at a standstill during the 1970s,
and for this reason the 1970s are often portrayed as the dark ages of
Korea's trade policy regime. However, this should not be interpreted
as a policy reversal toward an inward-looking development strategy
because export promotion continued to remain an important policy
goal in the 1970s.

Although incentives for exports were cut back considerably
in the 1970s, the export finance, the key incentive for exports,
remained unchanged. The long-term export finance was strengthened
to promote the exports of HCI products such as plants, vessels and
locomotives by establishing the Export and Import Bank of Korea in
1976. Thus, long-term export finance began to play an increasingly

important role in export credit, accounting for more than 60 percent of total export finance in 1979. Therefore, the HCI drive should be regarded as a strategic policy adjustment designed to improve the structure of exports toward skill- and capital-intensive products.

8.1.3   *Policy Shift toward Market-Oriented Development and Renewed Liberalization Efforts (1980s)*

Liberalization efforts were resumed and strengthened when President Chun Doo Hwan came to power in 1980. The underlying philosophy was that market forces should play an increasingly important role in resource allocation. Thus, along with stabilization efforts, development policy was directed to liberalize trade, investment and the financial market. Key reform measures implemented to this end were as follows.

First, the government announced a multi-year trade liberalization program in 1983. The program consisted of a five-year advanced liberalization schedule for both imports and tariffs. The import liberalization ratio was to be increased from 80.4 percent in 1983 to 95.4 percent by 1988. Since the goal of import liberalization was to strengthen industrial competitiveness, a gradual and selective approach was adopted so that industries concerned could prepare for foreign competition.

Products with high competitiveness and products requiring no protection were liberalized first, whereas products with potential comparative advantages were liberalized later to enhance their competitiveness. In general, light and intermediate products were to be liberalized first, followed by heavy and chemical industrial products. Since the import of liberalized items was often restricted by special laws, efforts were made to eliminate them so as to facilitate import liberalization. For example, over 800 products were subject to control by 17 different special laws. However, they were liberalized as these laws were eliminated between 1987 and 1988.[2]

---

[2]See Sakong (1993, p. 89).

As for tariffs, the simple arithmetic average tariff rate was scheduled to be lowered from 23.7 percent in 1983 to 16.9 percent by 1988. The tariff deduction scheme was focused on reducing the dispersion of tariff rates, bringing the overall range of 0–150 percent down to the ranges of 5–10 percent for raw materials, 20 percent for intermediate products and capital goods, and 20–30 percent for consumer goods by 1988. The second five-year tariff reduction program was launched in 1988, covering up to 1993, which led to a further reduction in tariffs in the 1990s (Table 8.1).

For export liberalization, in 1982 the government abolished preferential loans for exports by raising the interest rate on export loans to the level of the commercial lending rate. Direct subsidies for exports no longer existed, except for overseas market development and long-term export credit. This policy change was carried out as part of a financial policy reform aimed at dismantling policy loans, which were widely used for industrial development until the end of the 1970s.

The floating exchange rate system, which was virtually suspended in the 1970s, was actively reintroduced from the early 1980s to stimulate exports. The nominal exchange rate continued to rise until 1985, keeping the real exchange rate at a competitive level. From 1986, however, the Korean won appreciated because of a huge trade surplus with the US, and this led to a decline in the real exchange rate, reflecting high inflation in the subsequent years.

Second, the industrial incentive system was reformed to enhance industrial competitiveness. Industry-specific support was replaced

Table 8.1   Average Tariff Rate, 1983–2007 (Unit: percent)

	1983	1988	1989	1990–1991	1992	1993	1994–1998	1999–2006	After 2007
Total	23.7	18.1	12.7	11.4	10.1	8.9	7.9	8.6	8.5
Industrial Product	22.6	16.9	11.2	9.7	8.4	7.1	6.2	6.3	6.9
Agricultural Product	31.4	25.2	20.6	19.9	18.5	17.8	16.9	18.6	16.9

Source: Ministry of Strategy and Finance.

by a functional support system in which all industries were, in principle, treated equally, and incentives were given to manpower and technology development, while restructuring troubled industries through the rationalization program. A total of eight industries (cars, heavy construction machinery, heavy electrical machinery, ferroalloys, naval diesel engines, dyeing, textiles, and coal mining) were designated for rationalization. The government worked to assist the rationalization of these industries by providing subsidized loans, restricting market entry, reducing capacity, and facilitating mergers. The support for troubled industries was, however, limited to 2–3 years, implying the end of the selective industrial policy which had been the backbone of industrial policy until the 1970s.

Third, FDI and technology imports were significantly liberalized. Until the 1970s, the government policy toward FDI was rather restrictive, limiting equity share, enforcing export requirements, restricting market entry, etc. These conditions were greatly relaxed since 1984 when the government changed its FDI policy from a positive to a negative system to facilitate the inflow of foreign investment. The number of sectors on the list has been reduced continuously thereafter. Thus, the overall liberalization ratio of FDI increased from 60.9 percent in 1983 to 79.2 percent in 1990. The liberalization ratio in the manufacturing sector grew faster, rising from 80 percent to 97.7 percent in the same period.[3]

The government policy for technology imports, like the FDI policy, was also restrictive until the 1970s, because licensing agreements were strictly controlled in terms of royalty payments and contract period and were subject to government approval. However, this restrictive policy was gradually relaxed since the late 1970s to facilitate the growth of the HCIs. A major policy change occurred in 1984 when the policy shifted from an approval to a report system. Unless rejected by the authorities within 20 days, the licensing agreements were automatically approved. Thus, the licensing agreements rose rapidly in the 1980s and were concentrated in HCIs.

---

[3]See Sakong (1993, p. 116).

Fourth, along with external liberalization, an important policy action was undertaken to promote fair trade and competition in the domestic market. In 1981, the government enacted the Monopoly Regulation and Fair Trade Act (MRFTA) to deal with the monopolistic market structure and abuse of market power by chaebols. The promotion of HCIs had led to the rapid growth of large firms, resulting in the concentration of market power in chaebols. This urgently called for regulation of the growing economic power of chaebols.

The major objective of the law was to regulate the abuse of market power, business integration, unfair trade practices, undue collaborative activities, etc. The law was amended several times, strengthening its control over chaebols. It was later followed by other anti-chaebol measures that included freezing chaebols' share of total bank credit. Nevertheless, these various anti-chaebol measures were not very effective in controlling the rising economic power of chaebols due to the many exceptions in the law, weak enforcement, and the frequent policy changes toward chaebols. However, the law marked an important turning point in economic policy in the sense that it signaled a departure from previous chaebol-friendly policies, instituting fair competition as the new rule of the game.[4]

Fifth, efforts were made to liberalize the financial market. The government had undertaken a series of measures aimed at reducing government control over financial institutions and credit allocation since the early 1980s. Liberalization began in 1981 with the privatization of government-owned nationwide commercial banks. Equity shares held by the government were sold to the private sector, but no individual shareholder was allowed to hold more than 10 percent share of a bank. Although some autonomy was provided in terms of relaxing personnel, budgeting and branching management, the banks remained under government control since the government continued to retain the appointment of chief executives and directors.

Entry barriers were also reduced for both banks and non-banking financial institutions. A number of new banks including foreign

---

[4]See Yoo (1997, p. 26).

bank branches as well as finance and investment companies were
established in the early 1980s. The interest rates on bank loans
were unified into a single rate in 1982 with a view to dismantling
policy loans, the share of which had reached over 50 percent of total
domestic credit in the late 1970s. The share of policy loans thus
began to decline in the 1980s and reached less than 40 percent in
the mid-1980s.[5] In December 1988, the government announced an
ambitious plan to deregulate most of the lending rates of banks
and non-banking institutions, including some of the deposit rates.
However, the plan was not implemented due to worsening economic
conditions in subsequent years.

As briefly mentioned above, the Korean government expended
considerable energy pursuing liberalization policies in trade, industry,
technology, and the financial sector. However, not much progress
was made aside from import liberalization, because the liberalization
policies were in most cases incomplete in that they were limited
in scope and depth and were mostly launched in the latter half of
the 1980s. Even in the case of import liberalization, a considerable
number of items remained under the so-called import diversification
program which was designed to restrict imports from Japan, not
to mention the many restricted agricultural products. In 1990, for
example, 268 items were still subject to the import diversification
program and 351 agricultural products were restricted.[6]

The service sector was largely barred from liberalization until the
1980s except for hotels, trading, and some financial services, which
in turn hindered the inflow of FDI. As a consequence, the FDI inflow
in Korea was very small, amounting to a little over USD 4 billion
during the period of 1982–1990 and being concentrated mostly in
the manufacturing sector. Despite privatization, bank operations
were still under the control of the government and interest rate
liberalization was delayed. Korea joined the IMF Article VIII nations
in November 1988, but no substantial progress was made regarding
the liberalization of the payments regime and the capital market.

---

[5]See Sakong (1993, p. 73).
[6]See Kim (1996, p. 10).

8.1.4 *Globalization and Accelerated Liberalization (1990s)*

The early 1990s witnessed a big push toward liberalization, because complete market opening was unavoidable in the face of global movement toward liberalization and Korea's strong commitment to a multilateral trade regime. Therefore, President Kim announced globalization to be the top policy goal of the new government in 1993 and began to undertake a series of reform measures aimed at liberalization and deregulation, which were accelerated after the financial crisis in 1997. The new policy reform was designed to shift the development strategy from state-led toward market-led development. Key policy actions implemented to this end were as follows.

First, the most important policy action was dismantling the five-year development planning system which was the foundation of the state-led development strategy. The government organization was reformed with the intention of creating a smaller but stronger government. The Economic Planning Board was merged with the Ministry of Finance to become the Ministry of Finance and Economy (MOFE). Many government ministries and agencies were either merged with other agencies or restructured for the purpose of deregulation, decentralization, and reducing red tape. The number of government agencies and employees was significantly reduced.

The demise of the five-year development plan had a far-reaching impact on the economic policymaking process, since a strong control tower for policy coordination no longer existed. Individual line ministries exercised greater autonomy in the decision-making process, and government intervention in the private sector was significantly reduced, as the government relaxed its control over chaebols. For example, the number of chaebols to which the credit ceiling system applied was scaled down from the top 50 to the top 30 in 1993, and further reduced to the top 10 in 1996. They were also given more freedom regarding the ownership of non-financial banking institutions. This kind of deregulation, combined with the dismantling of selective industrial policy, triggered the ambitious investment activities of chaebols, leading to overinvestment in many areas such as petrochemicals, automobiles, semiconductors, and steel.

Second, another important policy action toward this direction was the privatization of public enterprises. The size of public enterprise had grown considerably in the 1960s and 1970s as the government pursued state-led development. In the early 1980s, the government began to privatize some of the public enterprises, reflecting the shift of government policy toward reducing government intervention in the economy. However, the privatization policy in the 1980s was limited because the government maintained control over the management of privatized corporations even after liquidating their equity shares, as manifested in the privatization of commercial banks.

The Kim Young Sam government announced an ambitious privatization plan in December 1993 covering 58 public enterprises. Its objective was to enhance the managerial efficiency of corporations while preventing a concentration of economic power. The progress, however, was slow and limited because the government feared the growing concentration of economic power in the hands of chaebols. As a result, privatization was limited to 12 public enterprises in which the government had either minority shares or whose size was relatively small.[7]

Significant progress toward privatization was made only after the 1997 financial crisis. The Kim Dae Jung government announced a comprehensive plan covering 11 large public enterprises in the summer of 1998. Unlike previous efforts which dealt with the partial sale of government equity shares, the plan was aimed at the complete transfer of control of public enterprises to the private sector.[8] The plan was to a large extent successfully implemented as scheduled. Most of Korea's large public enterprises such as Pohang Iron and Steel Company, Korea Telecom Corporation, Korea Tobacco & Ginseng Corporation, and Korea Heavy Industry Corporation were privatized during this period.

Third, import liberalization was accelerated beginning in the early 1990s as Korea participated actively in the Uruguay Round (UR) negotiations. Market opening was greatly facilitated by reducing

---

[7]See Lee and Moon (2001, p. 344).
[8]See Lim (2003, p. 40).

tariff rates and dismantling non-tariff barriers. The second five-year tariff reduction program introduced in 1988 brought about substantial tariff cuts; the simple average tariff rate for all products dropped from 18.1 percent in 1988 to 7.9 percent in 1994, which was slightly higher than the average in advanced countries such as the US, Japan, and the European Union.

The tariff rates for manufactured and agricultural products were reduced from 16.9 percent and 25.2 percent to 6.2 percent and 16.6 percent during the same period, respectively. As far as manufactured goods were concerned, tariffs no longer played an important role in industrial protection. It is also remarkable that tariff dispersion was significantly reduced as the tariff structure shifted toward a uniform rate system. The central tariff rate was lowered from 20 percent in 1988 to 8 percent in 1994, so that tariff rates below 10 percent reached 93.4 percent in 1994.[9] The number of restricted items under the import diversification program was gradually reduced, and the program was completely abolished by the end of 1999.

The agriculture sector was highly liberalized in accordance with the agreement under the UR negotiations. The Korean government began to accelerate the trade liberalization of the agricultural market through tariffication and gradual tariff cuts. The restrictions were converted into the tariff equivalents of quantitative restrictions, and tariff rates were then reduced by 10 percent over 10 years. For example, in the case of beef, in 1995 the tariff rate was raised to 43.6 percent from the pre-UR level of 20 percent. This was lowered to 40 percent in 2004, and import quotas on beef were completely removed after 2000. The tariffication for rice, however, was delayed for 10 years and in the meantime, minimum market access of 1 percent was permitted in 1995, increasing to four percent by 2004. Thus, as shown in Fig. 8.1, imports of all products except rice were completely liberalized by the early 2000s.

Fourth, liberalization efforts were extended to the service sector which had been relatively closed until the 1980s. The government, partially or completely, liberalized 154 service subsectors at Korea

---

[9]See Kim (1996, p. 15).

Standard Industrial Classification (KSIC) five-digit levels between 1993 and 2000. Many of them were liberalized as a result of the UR negotiations and Korea's accession to the OECD in 1996. After the financial crisis in 1997, the liberalization of the service sector was accelerated to enhance its efficiency and to attract FDI. As shown in Table 8.2, as of February 2008, only three business categories (radio, television broadcasting, and atomic energy) were completely restricted.

Fifth, along with service sector liberalization the inflow of FDI was greatly facilitated since the 1997 financial crisis. The government has taken a series of measures designed to attract FDI. Foreign ownership of land was greatly liberalized. Foreigners were permitted to acquire or purchase land with almost no restrictions on size and site whether for business or not. Previously, foreigners were allowed only to acquire land for business purposes. The Foreign Investment Zones (FIZ) was established, offering extra incentives with regard to provision of infrastructure. Foreign investors who bring in specified state-of-the-art technology were offered a special treatment of 7 years' tax holiday and a 50 percent tax reduction for the following 5 years.

One-stop service system was set up to provide much simplified procedures and related assistance, and the Office of Investment Ombudsman was created to deal with foreign investors' difficulties and grievances concerning investment in Korea. Restrictions on M&A of Korean firms by foreign investors were substantially relaxed. The ceiling on foreign equity ownership for M&A purposes has been eliminated. As a result, foreign investors became the largest

Table 8.2   Liberalization Ratio of Foreign Direct Investment, 1993–2008

	1993	JAN 1998	DEC 1999	MAR 2001	FEB 2008
Business Categories opened for FDI (A)	1,148	1,148	1,148	1,058	1,083
Completely restricted (B)	177	21	7	4	3
Liberalization Ratio (C) %	84.6	98.2	99.4	99.6	99.7

Note: C = (A-B)/A includes both complete and partial liberalization.
Source: The 60-Year History of the Korean Economy-III (2010, p. 130).

shareholders in an increasing number of Korean firms. The opening of service sector coupled with various FDI-friendly measures led to a rapid inflow of FDI after the financial crisis.

Despite these efforts, as shown in Fig. 8.2, FDI inflow has been disappointing by global standards, fluctuating around USD10 billion a year until the early 2010s. Korea's business environment for FDI is considered less competitive than other countries due to the lack of policy transparency and labor market flexibility, as well as other restrictive regulations. According to OECD, Korea's index of barriers to trade and investment was the highest among OECD countries in 2015, making Korea the third-lowest holder of FDI stock among OECD countries, at 13 percent of GDP in 2012 (OECD 2014a, p. 79).

The government policy toward outward investment has also been greatly liberalized since the early 1990s to cope with the rising labor cost and the growing regional trade agreements. The policy switched from a positive system to a negative system in 1994 and from an approval to a report system in 1997, followed by a complete liberalization in 1998. Outward direct investment has thus grown dramatically since the early 1990s, soaring from a little over USD 1 billion in 1990 to USD 30 billion in 2015. Korean multinational firms were the main driver of overseas investment, which was mainly concentrated in the manufacturing and service sectors. Since Korea's

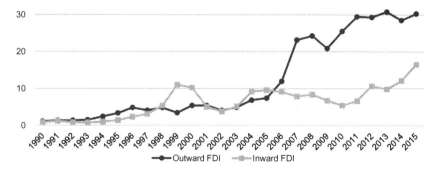

Figure 8.2 Trends of Inward and Outward FDI, 1990–2015 (Unit: USD billion)

Source: The Export-Import Bank of Korea and Ministry of Trade, Industry, and Energy.

outward investment is, as shown in Fig. 8.2, far greater than inward investment, there is growing apprehension about its potential crowding-out effect on domestic investment and employment.

Sixth, the government announced the comprehensive financial sector liberalization program in 1993 and began deregulating interest rates, liberalizing the issuance of corporate bonds and commercial papers, and reducing subsidized policy loans. The government also undertook a series of capital market liberalization measures such as the liberalization of trade-related short-term borrowing, the issuance of foreign currency-denominated bonds by corporations and financial institutions, foreign borrowing by corporations and banks, and foreign currency loans by financial institutions.

These measures largely benefited short-term transactions as they were fully liberalized, while long-term transactions were strictly controlled. Since long-term borrowing was tightly controlled, both commercial and merchant banks were heavily engaged in cheap short-term foreign borrowings to finance long-term investment projects, causing a serious maturity mismatch, which became a major cause of the financial crisis in 1997.

Following the financial crisis of 1997, the government liberalized long-term foreign borrowing in order to help firms attract foreign capital and abolished restrictions on trade-related financing. In April 1999, the foreign exchange transaction system was changed from a positive system to a negative system. The security and bond markets were completely liberalized. The security market, which first opened in January 1992 by allowing foreign investors to purchase up to 10 percent of each security item, was gradually liberalized until it was completely opened in May 1998. The opening of the bond market came later in July 1994. All regulations on the purchase of corporate and government bonds were abolished in December 1997.

8.2   Major Features and Sequencing of the Liberalization Policy

As explained above, Korea's liberalization policy underwent several major changes over the past four decades, reflecting shifting development policy. The major features of Korea's liberalization policy and its sequencing can be illustrated as follows.

First, export liberalization was pursued prior to import liberalization due to balance of payments constraints. Since Korea was suffering from a huge trade deficit in the 1960s, the government had to push forward with an export drive policy prior to import liberalization. As the balance of payments situation improved in the mid-1960s, the government attempted to liberalize imports by shifting the import policy from a positive to a negative system. However, import liberalization efforts in the 1960s were short-lived, because balance of payments difficulties resurged in the latter half of the 1960s. The setback of import liberalization policy continued into the 1970s as the government pursued the HCI promotion policy.

Second, the government began to resume import liberalization in the early 1980s, but unlike in the 1960s, engaged in a gradual and multi-stage approach. The five-year import liberalization program was announced in 1983 covering 1984–1988 and products to be liberalized were pre-announced. Monopolistic and oligopolistic products were liberalized first, and SME products were allowed a slower pace of import liberalization. Most agricultural products were not included in the schedule. Along with the import liberalization program, a five-year tariff reduction program was introduced to reduce protection for domestic industries. An advance notice system was adopted to give private firms time to prepare for foreign competition.

Third, stabilization policy preceded or at least accompanied import liberalization policy to facilitate the smooth implementation of the latter. At the beginning of the 1980s, the Korean economy suffered from serious inflationary pressure. Therefore, the government implemented tight monetary and fiscal policy measures to curb inflation before launching its import liberalization program in 1984. The overall expansion of money supply was tightly controlled and government expenditures were cut drastically by introducing a zero-based budgeting system. An incomes policy was also introduced to control wage increases.

Thanks to stabilization policy efforts, the government was able to bring inflation under control by 1983. Consumer price, which increased to double-digit level during the 1970s, was brought down to 3.4 percent increase in 1983, and wages, which had also increased at double-digit level, were brought to single-digit increase. The real exchange rate was also maintained at a competitive level since the exchange rate was constantly adjusted. These combined policy efforts enabled the Korean economy to regain its industrial competitiveness, improving balance of payments. The current account deficit/GDP ratio dropped markedly from 6.4 percent in 1981 to 1.8 percent in 1983, enabling the government to successfully implement its import liberalization program as scheduled.

Fourth, trade liberalization was carried out first, followed by capital market liberalization and then by foreign exchange market liberalization. As an outward-oriented industrialization strategy was pursued, Korea had to rely on foreign trade as an engine of growth and began to develop industries in which Korea had a comparative advantage. Thus, trade policy focused first on the promotion of labor-intensive industries and then moved to stimulating heavy and capital-intensive industries to upgrade the structure of exports. In this process, the government attempted to pursue import liberalization but did not succeed until the end of the 1970s due to balance of payments difficulties. As the balance of payments began to improve in the early 1980s, the government carried out active import liberalization. Policymakers believed import liberalization was inevitable in order to enhance industrial competitiveness.

Capital market liberalization came later because Korea suffered from a current account deficit until the mid-1980s. From 1986, however, Korea enjoyed a considerable surplus in the current account, which encouraged policymakers to open the capital market. In December 1988, the government announced a capital market liberalization plan with a detailed timetable beginning with the opening of the stock market. The stock market, opened first to foreigners in January 1992, was gradually liberalized until it was completely liberalized in May 1998. The opening of the bond market took place in July 1994 when foreigners were permitted to purchase corporate bonds of SMEs, and all regulations regarding corporate and government bonds were abolished in December 1997.

The opening of the money market for CPs and CDs was completed in May 1998.

Foreign exchange transactions were heavily regulated until 1997 as the government adopted the positive system under the Foreign Exchange Management Act, which only allowed transactions that were explicitly permitted. Foreign currency borrowings were liberalized slowly in the 1990s. Overseas bond issuance by financial institutions and corporations was deregulated in 1991, and trade-related short-term financing was gradually liberalized in the early 1990s. Foreign borrowings by banks and corporations were also permitted in 1995. The liberalization of foreign exchange transactions was accelerated only after the 1997 financial crisis. Long-term foreign borrowing was liberalized in 1998, and the negative system was adopted by replacing the restrictive Foreign Exchange Management Act with the Foreign Exchange Transaction Act in 1999.

Fifth, as far as the liberalization of the real sector was concerned, the liberalization of manufacturing preceded the liberalization of the service and agriculture sectors. This is because Korea's development policy focused on the manufacturing sector in which Korea held a comparative advantage relative to services and agriculture. An active liberalization policy was pursued since the early 1980s to enhance the international competitiveness of manufacturing, and as a result, liberalization in this sector was almost complete by the end of the 1980s with 99.7 percent import liberalization ratio in 1990. Tariff protection was not particularly high either as the simple average tariff rate of manufactured products was 9.7 percent in the same year.

The liberalization of the service sector began much later at a slower pace due mainly to the restrictive FDI policy implemented until the end of 1980s. Moving into the 1990s, the government began to speed up the liberalization of service sector as Korea participated in the UR negotiations and accelerated it to attract FDI in the wake of the 1997 financial crisis. FDI inflow was strongly encouraged by allowing hostile cross-border M&A, relaxing the foreigner equity share, streamlining foreign investment procedures, providing FIZs and strengthening investment incentives.

The liberalization of the agriculture sector also arrived later because the government attempted to achieve self-sufficiency in food supply by protecting domestic producers. However, the rising cost of agricultural support and mounting international pressure since the mid-1980s led to changes in the import policy for agricultural products, namely a gradual reduction in tariffs and non-tariff barriers. As in the service sector, the UR negotiations were instrumental in accelerating the opening of the agricultural market with the result that the import liberalization ratio went up from 80.4 percent in 1990 to 99.6 percent in 1997. Only eight items were under import restrictions in 1997. The simple average tariff rate was also lowered from 19.9 percent in 1990 to 16.6 percent in 1994.

As mentioned above, Korea's liberalization policy began with export liberalization followed by import liberalization and then extended to other sectors of the economy, as the development policy shifted toward market-led development. Despite some interruptions and costs, as evidenced in the 1997 financial crisis, there is no doubt that the liberalization policy made a major contribution to the rapid growth and development of the Korean economy. Table 8.3 shows

Table 8.3   Export and Economic Growth of Outward- and Inward-Oriented Developing Countries, 1965–2006 (Unit: percent)

	GDP Growth	Export Growth
Outward-Oriented Country		
Singapore	8.0	10.0
Hong Kong	6.4	9.3
Korea	7.3	11.7
Thailand	6.5	10.5
Malaysia	6.5	9.2
Inward-Oriented Country		
Argentina	2.4	5.9
Mexico	4.0	7.7
Peru	2.9	4.3
Pakistan	5.3	6.6
India	5.0	10.1

Source: The 60-Year History of the Korean Economy-III (2010, p. 28).

that Korea's economic performance was impressive compared to other developing countries during the last five decades. Economic growth was the second highest (7.3 percent) next to Singapore (8 percent) and far higher than that of countries that adopted an inward-looking development strategy. Exports were the engine of growth increasing at an average annual rate of 11.7 percent, the highest among developing countries.

Chapter 9

Financial Crisis and Policy Response

9.1 Causes of the Crisis[1]

There are, broadly speaking, two different views when interpreting the causes of the Korean financial crisis, which erupted in late November of 1997. One view is that Korea's macroeconomic fundamentals were relatively sound, and the crisis itself was essentially a consequence of the short-term liquidity shortages brought about by external shock. The crisis, in other words, was mainly caused by the instability within the international financial market, which had originated from the impact of the Southeast Asian financial crises. This so-called contagion theory was strongly supported by Jeffrey Sachs.[2] This theory seems to be correct insofar as the crisis was triggered by foreign banks' denial of the rollover of Korea's short-term debt. This view is supported by the fact that Korea had high economic growth, high savings rate, and low inflation prior to the crisis.

Another view is that the crisis was caused by the inherent structural weaknesses of the Korean economy combined with some policy mistakes. This view argues that the Korean economy had structural weaknesses and hence the possibility of a crisis already existed, even if there were no currency crises in Southeast Asia. According to this

---

[1]Draws on the author's earlier paper "On the Origins of Korean Financial Crisis: An Institutional Approach", Duisburg Working Papers on East Asian Studies, No. 55/2000, Duisburg University, 2000.

[2]See Radelet and Sachs (1998).

view, as shared by Paul Krugman, the fundamental cause was not liquidity shortages as such, but the structural weaknesses from which the Korean economy had been suffering for a long time.[3]

The financial crisis in 1997 was certainly not caused by a single factor such as external shock or internal weakness, instead it should be attributed to a confluence of both internal and external factors. Although both factors contributed to the crisis, structural weaknesses should be regarded as the more dominant cause of the crisis, because the Korean economy could hardly have been attacked by speculative international capital unless it had structural weaknesses such as a fragile financial system, excessive debt in the corporate sector, and high external debt.

Since these structural problems were not new and had existed in Korea for a long time, the question arises as to why the government was unable to remedy the problems earlier. We must come up with a plausible answer if we really want to understand the origins of the crisis. Unfortunately, most papers dealing with the Korean financial crisis concentrated on the analysis of structural weaknesses without paying enough attention to the underlying institutional problems that were indeed the root causes of the crisis. Based on this reasoning, an attempt was made to explain the causes of the Korean financial crisis from an institutional aspect. We will first briefly describe the nature of major structural problems and discuss why the government failed to carry out structural reform. We will then address the origins of the crisis, some of which may go far beyond the economic dimension.

9.1.1 *Structural Weaknesses*

9.1.1.1 *Macroeconomic imbalance and external debt*

The Korean economy enjoyed rapid growth until the onset of financial crisis in late 1997. The GDP growth rate averaged 7.4 percent between 1993 and 1996, and the annual inflation rate, measured by the consumer price index, remained at a relatively low level of

---

[3]See Krugman (1998).

Table 9.1   Macroeconomic Fundamentals, 1991–1996 (Unit: percent)

	1991	1992	1993	1994	1995	1996
Fiscal surplus/GDP[a]	−1.9	−0.7	0.3	0.5	0.4	0.3
Current account/GDP	−2.82	−1.25	0.29	−0.96	−1.74	−4.42
Real effective exchange rate[b]	93.5	98.8	100.9	98.3	98.0	96.0
CPI inflation	9.3	6.3	4.8	6.2	4.5	4.9
Real GDP growth	9.2	5.4	5.5	8.3	8.9	6.8
Gross savings ratio	37.3	36.4	36.2	35.5	35.5	33.8

Notes: [a]Consolidated public sector.
[b]Trade volume weighted, numbers below 100 mean overvaluation.
Source: Hahm and Mishkin (1999, p. 57).

5.1 percent during the same period. Meanwhile, monetary and fiscal policies largely remained conservative. The annual M2 growth rate had been around 15–16 percent, and the fiscal deficit had turned to a surplus since 1993. Signs of disequilibrium could only be detected in the external sector. The current account deficit had been growing since 1994, amounting to 4.4 percent of GDP (Table 9.1).

Despite the current account deficit, steady inflows of foreign capital boosted by financial market liberalization kept the overall balance in surplus. Except for the external sector, the Korean economy recorded sound macroeconomic performance. Based upon this performance, some argue that the Korean crisis is attributable to the instability of the international capital market, which originated from countries in Southeast Asia. A further argument is that Korea's current account deficit was relatively small compared to those of the other countries hit by the crisis, such as Mexico and Thailand, with the implication that current account deficit cannot be blamed for the crisis.

This argument is not very convincing. An examination of Korea's external liabilities shows that they increased rapidly due to continued current account deficits. Total external debt, which amounted to USD 88.74 billion in 1994, jumped to USD 164.34 billion in 1996, doubling within a 2-year period. The maturity structure had also been deteriorating since the early 1990s with short-term debts accounting for 56.6 percent of total external debt in 1996. As a result, short-term liabilities far exceeded Korea's foreign exchange

Table 9.2   External Liabilities, 1992–1996 (Unit: USD 100 million)

	1992	1993	1994	1995	1996
Gross external liabilities[a]	629.0	670.0	887.0	1197.0	1643.4
External Liabilities/GDP (%)	19.99	19.38	22.04	24.46	31.60
Short-term External Liabilities/Total External Liabilities (%)	58.82	60.15	65.84	65.75	56.58
Short-term External Liabilities/Foreign Exchange Reserves (%)	215.69	198.89	227.48	240.58	279.75

Note: [a]External liabilities include external debt as defined by the IBRD plus offshore borrowings of Korean banks and overseas borrowings of Korean banks' overseas branches.

Source: Hahm and Mishkin (1999, p. 57).

reserves (Table 9.2). These figures were certainly high enough to signal a potential foreign exchange crisis. Therefore, the assertion that Korea's macroeconomic fundamentals were sound before the crisis is exaggerated.

9.1.1.2   *Excessive debt financing of the corporate sector*

Another structural weakness was a large corporate indebtedness, particularly that of large business groups. The Korean government pursued the growth-first policy since the early 1960s and relied very much on large-scale firms in its policy implementation, leading to the rapid growth of chaebols. The problem was that chaebols relied heavily on bank loans to finance their investment activities. They knew the government would not allow them to go bankrupt because of their growing importance in the national economy. The banks, on the other hand, also believed the government would bail them out if the chaebols failed to service their debts. This created a moral hazard problem for both banks and chaebols.

As a result, chaebols and financial institutions did not bear the risks associated with large debts. The implicit guarantee by the government led to a rapid increase in the debt-to-equity ratios of firms, particularly those of chaebols. Debt-to-equity ratios of Korean manufacturing firms increased from 286.8 percent in 1995 to 396.5 percent in 1997. The debt-to-equity ratios of the top 30 chaebols soared from 347.5 percent to 519 percent during the same period. Some of the chaebols recorded debt-to-equity ratios higher than 1,000 percent.

This extremely high level of debt increased the financial burden of Korean firms which had traditionally maintained low levels of profitability. For almost a decade before the crisis, the average return on the equity (ROE) of chaebols had been lower than the prevailing interest rate.[4] This suggests that despite the preferential financial treatment by the government and banks, the chaebols performed worse than independent firms. The terms of trade shock in 1996 and 1997 following drastic falls in the prices of major Korean export products also contributed to a further deterioration in the profitability of Korean firms. Consequently, the number of defaulting firms rose sharply even before the financial crisis in late 1997.

9.1.1.3 *Weak financial sector*

Problems in the corporate sector spilled over to the financial sector. As noted earlier, the implicit government guarantee for banks' liabilities created the moral hazard problem. Korean banks believed the chaebols were "too big to fail." Naturally, they continued to extend credits to them despite their huge leverages. Since the banks were risk-free, they were not motivated to develop management skills and techniques for credit analysis and evaluation. The long and extensive intervention by the government had undermined the autonomy and accountability of the banking sector. The high entry barrier and strict business segmentation also contributed to the deepening inefficiency of financial institutions. Since the early 1990s, the government attempted to improve the efficiency of the financial sector through deregulation and market liberalization, but this government policy was not successful and rather worsened the balance sheet of the financial sector.

Prudential regulation was also very weak. For instance, basic regulations, such as the capital adequacy ratio, did not exist in the

---

[4]See Joh (1999, p. 7).

Table 9.3   Indicators of Bank Management Performance (Year-end value) (Average of 20 domestic commercial banks, including trust accounts) (Unit: percent, KRW million)

	1993	1994	1995	1996	1997
Return on assets	0.45	0.42	0.32	0.26	−0.93
(foreign banks)[a]	—	(1.32)	(1.17)	(1.53)	(3.89)
Return on equity	5.90	6.09	4.19	3.80	−14.18
(foreign banks)	—	(10.96)	(10.28)	(12.51)	(34.79)
Operating income/employee	31.7	52.1	39.1	40.2	26.8
(foreign banks)	—	(138.0)	(146.0)	(231.0)	(819)
Non-performing loan (NPL) ratio[b]	7.4	5.8	5.2	4.1	6.0

Notes: [a]Foreign bank branches operating in Korea.
[b]The ratio of sum of estimated loss, doubtful, and substandard loans to total loans.
Source: Hahm and Mishkin (1999, p. 58).

case of merchant banks. Regulatory control of commercial banks was also almost ineffective, given the loose accounting rules, inadequate loss provision, partial recognition of stock revaluation loss and others. In other words, financial liberalization was not accompanied by the commensurate prudential regulation and thus could not improve the management efficiency of financial institutions.

This resulted in high levels of NPLs. As Table 9.3 shows, NPLs as a percentage of total loans have been very high, ranging between 4 and 7 percent. The ratio rose from 4.1 percent in 1996 to 6 percent in 1997, indicating an upward trend prior to the currency crisis. Consequently, the returns on assets and equity have been declining from the early 1990s, implying that banking institutions faced a decline in their profitability.

9.1.2   *Failed Reform Attempts*

Korea experienced several financial crises in the past due to the similar structural problems as experienced in 1997. In 1972, Korea had serious foreign exchange shortages, high debt burden in the corporate sector, and a fragile banking sector. In the early 1980s,

Korea had also experienced a crisis due to the serious excess capacity caused by the overinvestment in heavy and chemical industries, which put many big firms almost on the brink of bankruptcy.

Korea could successfully overcome the crises largely due to the government's strong control over banks and big firms. Since the banks were under strong government control, liquidity problems were easily resolved by government intervention. The government could also effectively carry out such reform programs as investment realignment, limiting new entries, and others because businesses complied well with government policy. In the 1970s and 1980s, the government guided and supported the chaebols while monitoring and controlling their investment activities through both discretionary power and incentives. For the chaebols, compliance with the government directives was the only means to survive. Therefore, the government could effectively carry out reform policy.

Although the government was able to overcome the economic crises in the early 1970s and 1980s through direct government intervention, the fundamental structural problems of the Korean economy, such as a fragile financial sector, high leverage of chaebols and chronic balance of payments difficulties, remained unchanged because the Roh Tae Woo and Kim Young Sam governments continued to pursue a high economic growth policy relying heavily on the chaebols. If the Kim Young Sam government had not pursued the high growth policy and placed more emphasis on stability, Korea's external debt would not have been serious at all, so that Korea could have been able to ward off the attack of speculative international capital in 1997.

When the Kim Young Sam government took office in early 1993, Korea's balance of payments was more or less in equilibrium and external debt was at a manageable level. Unfortunately, the Kim Young Sam government continued to adopt the high growth policy and relaxed the control over the chaebols and financial institutions under the name of globalization and liberalization, which led to serious balance of payments difficulties and NPLs of financial institutions. In response to the deepening crisis, the Kim Young Sam government attempted a few important reform measures, beginning in December 1996. Efforts were made to reform the labor laws to enable the layoffs for structural adjustment, as well as to reform the financial sector to strengthen the prudential regulation of financial institutions. However, both attempts were not successful because the government failed to persuade the National Assembly to enact the reform bills. These failures led to a further loss of the international confidence in the Korean economy.

9.1.3   *Origins of the Crisis*

Why did the government fail to persuade the politicians to enact the reform bills and to carry out the other related reform policy? In this regard, it is worthwhile to note that the institutional weakness inherent in Korea's political system contributed to the failed reform attempts. According to Korea's constitution, the incumbent president is not allowed to run for a second term. The single presidential term has certainly its merits in that it eliminates the prolonged rule of one president, which could lead to dictatorship. The system has, however, a kind of political built-in instability with negative impact on the economy, particularly in a country where power is concentrated on the president with the political party playing an insignificant role in the policymaking process. Since the president has a relatively short 5-year fixed term, he or she would be tempted to accomplish "too many goals in too short period", leaving many reform programs unfinished. Furthermore, he or she would wish to leave an impression by making a grand achievement that is often economically unjustifiable. One good example was the Kim Young Sam government's decision to join the prestigious OECD which led to the premature liberalization of capital account. The two million housing construction plan of the Roh Tae Woo government was another good example which caused a serious inflationary pressure, undermining the economic stability accomplished under the Chun Doo Hwan administration.

The single term also impairs the constancy of economic and social policy because a 5-year period is often too short to implement reform programs which require a longer period. The unfinished reforms are not usually carried out by the next president because he or she wants his or her own reforms to be implemented, thereby creating uncertainties in policy implementation. More importantly, the lame duck phenomenon that occurs near the end of a president's term makes it extremely difficult for the president to carry out reforms. This is one of the reasons why President Kim Young Sam failed to persuade the politicians to enact the reform bills in 1997. The vested interest groups, such as labor unions and even bureaucrats, did not support him because they knew that he was set to lose his political power very soon. Therefore, it seems fair to say that the failed reform attempts by the Kim Young Sam government should be in part attributed to the inherent weakness of Korea's political system.

Apart from the political system mentioned above, there are many other institutional deficiencies which prevented the smooth transition toward a market-led development. Although the government-led high growth strategy of the last four decades brought about a significant economic progress, it entailed some serious adverse side effects. Korea's corporate management and financial system lacked transparency; moral hazard was endemic; and, overall, the economy was suffering from the absence of market discipline. Korea's commercial banks served as the main conduit of resource distribution in line with the government policy direction. This *de facto* public role of commercial banks acted as a serious impediment to the development of a genuine banking industry based on profit-oriented, accountable, and transparent management principles. Over several decades, Korea's major business groups undertook a debt-financed expansion strategy via a very aggressive use of leveraging. There was no adequate monitoring mechanism to impose management account-ability and transparency, and the lack of an effective governance structure allowed a continuation of the high-risk business strategy. These are all institutional problems that worked as a deterrent to the efficient working of a market economy.

Since the early 1990s, the Korean economy has undergone a transition from the state-led toward the market-led development. The institutional changes were required to make the transition process successful and less costly. The Kim Young Sam government attempted to carry out some reform measures to this end, but it failed to do so for the reasons mentioned above. Many government policymakers believed that the liberalization and deregulation would bring about an efficient market order. They did not realize that the efficient functioning of a market economy requires far more than just dismantling regulations, cutting subsidies, and reducing protection. This was certainly a big mistake they made in their efforts toward a market-friendly policy formulation.

Korea's rapid development in the past owed much to the authoritarian rule of a strong political leadership. Since the early 1990s, the state has retreated from directing the economy without preparing the institutional framework needed for the efficient functioning of a market economy. In other words, the old disciplining mechanism has gone without being replaced by a new one conducive to the efficient working of market economy.[5] Therefore, it would be appropriate to say that the root of the crisis lay in the institutional vacuum that occurred in the process of transition from a state-led toward a market-led development.

9.2   Policy Response and Achievements

9.2.1   *Macroeconomic Policies*

Since signing the IMF-supported assistance program, Korea has swiftly implemented a wide range of economic reform measures. These have all been directed toward rebuilding market confidence as well as expediting economic restructuring. Thus, the goal of economic policies of the Korean government under the IMF program (December 1997 through April 1998) was to stabilize the foreign exchange market and accumulate foreign reserves through the maintenance of high interest rates and tight monetary policies.[6]

---

[5]For papers stressing the importance of institutional changes, see Chang *et al.* (1998), Lee (1999a, 1999b) and Mathews (1998).

[6]For more details, see Wang and Zang (1998).

Since the onset of the crisis, the Korean government's most critical concerns have involved easing the immediate liquidity crisis and restoring international confidence. To this end, on December 3, 1997, Korea and the IMF reached an agreement on a financial aid package totaling USD 58.35 billion, which included IMF loans of USD 21 billion, USD 14 billion from the World Bank and the Asian Development Bank, and USD 23.35 from the G-7 and other countries. The accelerated disbursement of financial aid from the IMF, IBRD, and ADB has greatly eased the short-term liquidity shortage.

Korea also successfully converted USD 21.8 billion of its outstanding foreign short-term debt to medium-term debt. This led to a short-term economic rebound and allowed Korea to successfully issue USD 4 billion in global bonds in New York, April 8, 1998. Reflecting improved investor confidence, international creditor banks increased their rollovers of maturing debt from 32.2 percent in December 1997 to as high as 100 percent in early June 1998. Aside from the government initiatives, the Korean people also demonstrated their resolve and unity through various voluntary programs, most notably the nationwide campaign for gold collection.

In support of Korea's crisis resolution, the government's macroeconomic policy objectives have been three-fold: to achieve a speedy recovery from economic depression; to facilitate the implementation of sustained reforms to prevent future crises; and to strengthen the social safety net to preserve national unity in carrying out reform programs.

Korea's fiscal policy has played a pivotal role in not only stabilizing the exchange rate but also in creating momentum for rapid economic recovery. In the early stage of crisis resolution, fiscal policy was tightened in conjunction with an interest rate squeeze in order to support the stabilization of the foreign exchange market. Economic setbacks caused by the crisis, however, turned out to be far more severe than initially expected. The growth figures of real GDP and its components, except for exports and imports, plummeted into the negative in the first quarter of 1998, while more than 10,000 firms went bankrupt.

In the face of a vicious spiral of economic depression and corporate insolvency, counter-cyclical policy actions were strongly called for. Accordingly, the fiscal policy stance was changed toward expansion as early as in April 1998. The expansionary fiscal policy has continued in 1999 in order to stimulate the economy, support economic restructuring, and fund increased spending for the social safety net. The budget deficit target was set to 4 percent of GDP, and 70 percent of the resources for public investment projects were front loaded in the first half of 1999.

In the pre-crisis period, Korea's foreign exchange market was small and underdeveloped, and the exchange rate regime (the market average rate system) had a daily fluctuation band of 2.25 percent. It was difficult for Korea's exchange rate system to fully reflect its macroeconomic fundamentals. Therefore, following the expansion of the band to 10 percent in November 1997, the government adopted a free floating exchange rate system in December 1997. Since this time, the government has refrained from directly intervening in the market except to maintain a smooth fluctuation.

In the course of the crisis, Korea's monetary policy has shifted from an initial phase of tight interest rates for stabilizing the foreign exchange rate, to a period of upward adjustments for moderating the recession in 1998 and laying the foundation for economic recovery in 1999.

Upon the outbreak of the currency crisis, the Bank of Korea (BOK) announced a sharp tightening of monetary policy. By December 24, the BOK had dramatically raised short-term interest rates, which had fluctuated at around 12 percent prior to the crisis, to over 30 percent in order to facilitate a rapid stabilization of the exchange rate. This high interest rate policy was the only viable option for securing foreign currency liquidity and stabilizing the exchange rate in the face of the surging capital outflows due to the loss of international confidence.

But there were a number of adverse side effects accompanying the high interest rate policy, including the accelerated slowdown in real economic activity through the contraction of consumption and investment; the greatly increased incidence of corporate failures; and the further increase in NPLs of financial institutions. In response, the BOK steadily lowered the overnight call rate in the second quarter of 1998. By July, short-term rates were set at their pre-crisis levels, and by the end of the year were reduced further to 7 percent.

The relaxation of the monetary policy has continued in 1999. Short-term interest rates have been further lowered to support a recovery in economic activity, with the overnight call rate falling below 5 percent in April. The long-term interest rates, however, began to rise in July, although they remained at a single digit throughout the year. This was because of the more rapid-than-expected economic recovery and the uncertainties stemming from the investment trust company problems associated with the Daewoo Group. Overall, the sustained low interest rates have boosted stock prices, thereby facilitating economic restructuring and the reduction of debt-to-equity ratios through new equity offerings.

9.2.2 *Structural Reforms*

Upon the gradual stabilization of the exchange rate, the government began to carry out comprehensive structural reforms because the financial crisis was not just a temporary phenomenon of foreign exchange shortages, but was deeply rooted in the long-standing structural weaknesses of the Korean economy such as a fragile financial system, excessive corporate debt, a rigid labor market, etc.

9.2.2.1 *Financial sector reform*

The most urgent reform policy was to rehabilitate the solvency of financial institutions. The government adopted a strategy of closing non-viable financial institutions while providing recapitalization support to encourage mergers among viable institutions. Capital adequacy standards were adopted as the basis for identifying financial institutions to be resolved. Financial institutions that failed to meet the 8 percent BIS capital adequacy ratio were asked to submit rehabilitation plans. The Financial Supervisory Commission (FSC), the newly established independent supervisory agency, closely examined feasibility and settled on approval, conditional approval or disapproval.

Financial institutions whose rehabilitation plans were deemed inadequate were either subject to corrective actions or faced closure. Failed banks were ordered to transfer their business to financially sound banks. Banks with conditional approval status were required to submit revised implementation plans. In case the revised implementation plans were not approved, a mandatory merger or business transfer was ordered. The government provided fiscal support to the acquiring banks through the Korea Asset Management Corporation (KAMCO) and the Korea Deposit Insurance Corporation (KDIC). KAMCO was assigned the task of purchasing and disposing of NPLs, while KDIC was responsible for supporting recapitalization and depositor protection.

The supervisory and regulatory system was markedly reinforced. The FSC, established in April 1988, was an integrated financial supervisory body covering all financial institutions. The four existing supervisory agencies responsible for supervising banks, securities companies, insurance firms, and merchant banks were unified into the Financial Supervisory Service (FSS), and the executive body of FSC and the regulatory framework was strengthened to conform to international norms.

The accounting and disclosure standards applied to financial institutions and business firms were strengthened to conform to international best practice standards. The government spent KRW 156.2 trillion, equivalent to approximately 25 percent of GDP, for financial sector restructuring between November 1997 and March 2002, which was used for the recapitalization of commercial banks, equity injections, purchase of bad loans and assets, and depositor insurance.[7] Fiscal resources were mobilized by issuing public bonds.

Thanks to the reform measures, financial sector restructuring made significant achievements in terms of number of institutions, capital adequacy, management practices, ownership structure,

---

[7]For more details, see Yang (2002, p. 26).

Table 9.4 Financial Restructuring

	Number of Institutions as of End-1997 (A)	License Revoked	Closure through Merger	Closure & Others	Total (B)	B/A (%)
		As of End-April 2000				
Banks	33	5	5	—	10	30.3
NBFI[a]	2,069	73	110	247	430	20.8
Total	2,102	78	115	247	440	20.9

Note: [a]Non-banking financial institutions.

Source: Ministry of Finance and Economy.

and foreign capital participation. Around one-fifth of financial institutions existing as of the end of 1997 were liquidated, suspended, or merged with other financial institutions (Table 9.4). The merchant banks that were blamed for reckless foreign borrowings have been mostly disappeared. The capital adequacy ratio of banks rose from the pre-crisis level of 7 percent to over 10 percent as early as in 1999. A significant degree of operational restructuring took place in commercial bank operations. Around one-third of the workforce was downsized, along with salary reductions. Banks placed an increasing emphasis on profitability rather than asset growth and began to show positive ROE in 2001.

Foreign capital played an important role in recapitalizing the financial system. The government had to rely on foreign capital as an important source of funding due to the limited availability of capital from domestic sources. Two major commercial banks were sold to foreign capital groups. Since early 2000, several foreign financial institutions formed strategic partnerships or acquired equity holdings in financial institutions, including securities and insurance companies, thereby making a significant contribution to business decisions.

9.2.2.2 *Corporate sector reform*

The principal objective of corporate sector reform was to lower corporate indebtedness and to bring business practices in line with international standards, thereby enhancing the competitiveness of Korean firms. In January 1998, the government and the leaders of the top five chaebols agreed on the five principles of corporate sector reform. The five principles were enhancing corporate governance, prohibiting cross-debt guarantees between firms affiliated with chaebols, improving the corporate financial structure, concentrating on core business competence, and reinforcing the responsibilities of governing shareholders and management. To this end, a strong emphasis was placed on expediting banking sector reform so as to enable creditor banks to serve as a catalyst for corporate sector reform. Boosting capital market activities was also highlighted to allow new equity financing.

The government set up three different approaches corresponding to the restructuring requirements of each of the following groups: the top five chaebols and their affiliates; smaller conglomerates; and SMEs. The top five chaebols were allowed to pursue self-directed restructuring as they were believed to be capable of absorbing the resulting losses. They were asked to reduce their debt-to-equity ratios and to improve their financial structure through asset sales, recapitalization, and foreign capital inducement. To help eliminate overcapacity in key manufacturing industries, the government further called for mergers and swaps among the top five chaebols in 1998. So-called "big deals" aimed at enhancing the core competencies of conglomerates were carried out in the areas of semiconductors, petrochemicals, aircraft, rolling stock, power generation, and ship engines.

Medium-sized conglomerates, i.e. the 6th to 64th-largest chaebols, lacked the ability to restructure on their own and thus entered debt workouts with financial institutions based on the principle of fair burden-sharing. The government adopted a special program for SMEs that were hit particularly hard. The government initiated a number of schemes to help SMEs obtain working capital and trade credit, and also extended the scope of workout programs to include SMEs. Creditor banks evaluated the financial status of roughly 22,000 SMEs, and those classified as viable were selected for workout programs.

To facilitate corporate sector reform, the government implemented several policy measures designed to create an environment conducive to corporate restructuring. The government permitted 100-percent foreign ownership in listed stocks, and all forms of M&As including hostile takeovers were liberalized. The real estate market was opened to foreigners, and insolvency procedures were improved. Changes were also made to labor law, allowing layoffs and improving labor market flexibility.

As a result, considerable progress has been made in corporate restructuring over the past several years. The average debt-to-equity ratio for firms in the manufacturing sector fell from 398.3 percent in 1997 to 182.2 percent in 2001. Financial disclosure and corporate governance have improved. Large chaebols are required to produce combined financial statements covering their affiliates, indicating an important step in improving financial disclosure and transparency and bringing Korean accounting standards closer to international best practices. Chaebol affiliates have begun to separate themselves from their parent companies, becoming more independent in decision-making process.

Institutional provisions have been developed to protect the property rights of shareholders against arbitrary decisions by owner-managers. Large companies are required to bring 50 percent of their board of directors from outside the company. Foreign participation in the Korean economy has also risen substantially since the crisis, making a notable contribution to enhancing the transparency of management. Foreign ownership in Korea's listed companies increased from 13 percent in 1996 to over 30 percent in 2000. Foreigners now own more than 50 percent of equity shares of Korea's leading companies, including Samsung Electronics, POSCO, Hyundai Motor, SK Telecom, etc.

9.2.2.3 *Public sector reform*

The government set the goal of achieving a small but efficient service-oriented government and began to reform the central and local governments, government affiliates, and state-owned enterprises (SOEs). The monopolistic status of the government was one of the main factors that gave rise to inefficiency. To rectify this, the government streamlined its organizational structure. The number of ministries in the central government was reduced from 21 to 17. Also, the central government downsized its workforce by 5 percent, or 9,084 workers, while local governments reduced their workforce by 12 percent, or 35,149 workers.

In July 1998, the government announced a relatively ambitious privatization program for 11 large SOEs. Three companies, including Korea Technology Banking Co. and the National Text Book Co., were completely privatized as of November 1999. Eight other companies including Korea Electric Power Co (KEPCO)., Korea Gas Co., Korea Telecom Co., and Korea Tobacco and Ginseng Co. underwent phased privatization. Considerable stakes in Korea Telecom, POSCO, and KEPCO were sold to foreign investors through the issuance of depository receipts (DRs). The successful issuance of DRs in international financial markets boosted confidence in the Korean economy. As of November 1999, the government sold SOE assets worth KRW 7.3 trillion. Also, 32,005 jobs out of the total 41,267 jobs targeted for elimination by the end of 2000 (25 percent of total employees) were already cut from the SOE payrolls.

9.2.2.4 *Labor sector reform*

The government established the Tripartite Commission in January 1998 to enhance labor flexibility and cooperation between labor, management and government. The Tripartite Commission aimed to build a consensus system among key players to minimize the inherent social costs incurred by restructuring.

Since then, considerable progress has been made in labor market reform. The Labor Standard Act was revised in February 1998 to allow layoffs for management reasons in order to facilitate corporate restructuring. At the same time, clarifications and procedures for employment adjustment for management reasons were introduced, to prevent employers from firing employees on unjust grounds. Restrictions on the use of temporary dispatched workers were also reduced, while labor union activities were strengthened by legalizing civil servants' labor union and teachers' union. The political participation of labor unions was also permitted, which had tremendous repercussions on the development of political system in Korea.

9.2.3 *Achievements*

The Korean economy recovered rapidly from the crisis thanks to reform policies and a favorable external environment. The most impressive progress was made on the external front. Foreign exchange reserves increased rapidly due to large current account surpluses and active capital inflows, reflecting improved domestic economic prospects.

As shown in Table 9.5, Korea's total external liabilities decreased to USD 136.4 billion as of the end of 1999 from USD 159.2 billion as of the end of 1997. Not only did the size of these external liabilities show considerable improvement, but the maturity structure also improved substantially. The ratio of short-term liabilities to total liabilities decreased to 27.7 percent as of the end of October 1999, from 39.9 percent as of the end of 1997. The won/dollar exchange rate stabilized at around 1,100 to 1,200, significantly down from the 1,960 won/dollar peak at the end of 1997. This stabilization was due to the upgrading of Korea's sovereign ratings, inflows of foreign investment, continuation of the current account surplus, and the rise in international reserves.

The consequent overall macroeconomic achievements were impressive, as shown in Table 9.6. The economy, which experienced

Table 9.5   Korea's External Assets and Liabilities (Unit: USD billion)

	Sep 1997 (A)	End-1997	End-1998	End-1999	February 2002 (B)	B−A
Total external liabilities (E.L.)	180.5	159.2	148.7	136.4	138.9	−41.6
(Ratio of short-term E.L. to total E.L.)	(54.4)	(39.9)	(20.6)	(27.9)	(29.7)	(−24.7)
Total external assets	113.3	105.2	128.5	145.7	150.9	37.6
Net E.L.	67.2	54.0	20.2	−9.3	−12.0	−79.2

Source: Ministry of Finance and Economy.

Table 9.6   Key Macroeconomic Indicators, 1997–2000 (Unit: USD billion)

	1997	1998	1999	1Q 2000
GDP growth (%)	5.0	5.8	10.7	12.8
Current account	8.1	40.5	25.0	1.3
Inflation rate (%)	4.5	7.5	0.8	1.5
Won/USD rate	1,415.2	1,207.8	1,145.4	1,108.3
Corporate bond rate (%)	29.00	6.4	9.85	10.0
Total external liabilities	159.2	148.7	136.4	138.9[a]
Usable foreign reserves	8.8	48.5	74.1	83.7

Note: [a]End of February 2000.
Source: Ministry of Finance and Economy.

a severe contraction in 1997, rebounded strongly with an average growth rate of around 10 percent in 1998 and 2000, which was much faster than expected. The high growth was facilitated by a wide-ranging recovery of consumption, investment, and exports. The substantial depreciation of the currency and the surge in global demand for the IT industry led to rapid export expansion, which played a pivotal role in boosting economic recovery. With the strong exports, the current account turned to a surplus in 1998 and has remained so ever since. FDI and portfolio inflows increased markedly, reflecting the substantial progress in financial and corporate sector reform as well as the enhanced external position of the Korean economy. Inflation could be contained at a low level due to the conservative monetary policy and decline in real wages.

Although the economy recovered quickly from the crisis, it had far-reaching economic and social impacts. As noted earlier, the growth rate slowed down significantly due to the decelerating investment rate after a short recovery in 1999 and 2000. Income distribution sharply deteriorated due to massive unemployment and wage reduction, resulting in a growing income gap between the rich and poor.

The government attempted to minimize these adverse impacts of the crisis through a series of policy measures. In March 1998, the government launched a comprehensive unemployment benefit package program. The program included an expanded unemployment insurance system, subsidized loan programs to the unemployed and venture businesses, active labor market policies, and public work programs. It had some positive impact on income distribution as the Gini coefficient fell in 1999 and 2000, but this did not last long due to sluggish growth which caused the Gini coefficient to rise again from the early 2000s.

The crisis also largely undermined fiscal soundness. Korea maintained a conservative fiscal policy in the pre-crisis years. Korea's annual consolidated budget surplus was approximately 0.3 percent of GDP during the period of 1993–1997. Korea's national debt as a percentage of GDP stood at only 8.8 percent in 1996, which was far lower than the OECD average of approximately 70 percent. After the crisis, however, the government's fiscal deficit and national debt jumped drastically as the government increased its expenditures for financial restructuring, expanding social programs, and boosting the economy. The ratio of national debt to GDP rose from 11.7 percent in 1997 to 19.4 percent in 1999. If contingent liabilities such as government guarantees are reflected, the national debt total jumps from 13.3 percent in 1997 to 31.9 percent in 1998 and 36.5 percent in 1999.

Chapter 10

Education and Human Resource Development

10.1 Rapid Expansion of Education

It is generally accepted that the rapid growth of the Korean economy was, to a large extent, based on human resource development in which education played a key role. When Korea was liberated from Japanese colonial rule in 1945, the literacy rate was estimated as low as 22 percent. In 1945, the entire school population in South Korea was around 1.5 million, accounting for only 8.9 percent[1] of the total population of 16.9 million. Of all students enrolled in the school system, 93.7 percent were in primary schools, indicating the very low education level of the Korean people at the time of liberation (Lee, 1985, p. 4).

After liberation, however, educational opportunities expanded rapidly as the Korean government placed a strong emphasis on education. The compulsory public education system at the elementary level, initiated during the US military government (1945–1948), was formally adopted by the Korean government in 1948. The six-year plan of compulsory elementary education was launched in 1954 to accelerate primary school education.

The emphasis on education is reflected in the swift growth of government spending on education. As shown in Fig. 10.1, central government spending as a share of government expenditures

---

[1]This differs slightly from the figure in Table 2.1.

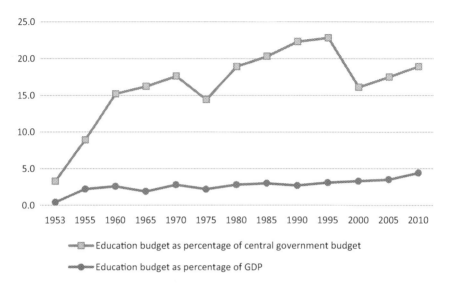

Figure 10.1   Central Government Spending on Education, 1953–2010 (Unit: percent)

Source: Korea Statistics Office and Korean Educational Statistics Service.

increased sharply in the 1950s and 1960s and continued to grow until the mid-1990s. After short fall in 2000 due to IMF crisis, it rose again in the 2000s. Thus, the size of the education sector relative to GDP also rose swiftly from 0.4 percent in 1953 to 2.6 percent in 1960 and 3.2 percent in 1980 and 4.4 percent in 2010, indicating that an increasing share of GDP was steadily spent on schooling.

As mentioned in Chapter 2, there was rapid expansion of school enrollment at all levels even in the 1950s and 1960s. The elementary enrollment ratio jumped, rising from 59.6 percent in 1953 to 86.2 percent in 1960, and rose to 91.6 percent in 1965, which was as high as that of developed countries in the same year (Table 10.1). This illustrates that Korea nearly achieved full primary school enrollment for both male and female children by the mid-1960s. As shown in Table 2.1, there was also a marked increase in the secondary and tertiary enrollment ratio during the 1950s and 1960s.

However, it should be noted that the expansion of enrollment was not entirely attributable to government action, since the private sector accounted for a large and increasing share of education. In

Table 10.1   International Comparison of School Enrollment[a] by School Level, 1960–1990 (Unit: percent)

	1960	1965	1970	1975	1980	1985	1990
Korea							
Elementary	(94)	92	96	99	100	94	100
Secondary	(27)	31	39	52	89	84	84
Higher	(4.6)	(6.2)	(8.0)	(10.3)	(15.8)	(34.2)	(39.7)
Asia							
(excluding the Arabs)							
Elementary	52.5	60.3	60.6	68.3	70.5	77.2	80.5
Secondary	41.0	31.9	37.6	43.9	41.8	42.1	44.9
Higher	8.7	5.7	11.1	14.2	15.8	13.7	12.9
Developed Countries							
Elementary	91.1	91.5	92.4	92.6	92.2	91.2	91.6
Secondary	69.3	79.1	76.1	80.7	81.0	85.6	85.8
Higher	15.1	24.5	27.2	30.0	30.8	32.8	39.5

Note: [a]Number of eligible students enrolled as a ratio of corresponding age group. Figures in parentheses indicate the total number of students enrolled as a ratio of eligible age group.
Source: Kim *et al.* (1997, p. 155).

1965, for example, around half the middle schools and high schools were private and more than one-fourth of colleges and universities belonged to private institutions.[2]

The rapid expansion of elementary education made an important contribution to the development of labor-intensive industries in the 1960s. Since around half of primary school graduates entered middle school by the mid-1960s, a large number of them were brought into the labor market, and thus female graduates in particular became the major source of labor supply in such labor-intensive fields as textiles, footwear, human hair, and plywood industries, all leading export industries in the 1960s. In 1960, 80.4 percent of production workers comprised elementary school graduates.[3]

Entering the 1960s, the government began to emphasize the expansion of secondary education to meet the growing demand for middle school enrollment, which remained at 33.3 percent in 1960.

---

[2]McGinn *et al.* (1980, p. 8).
[3]Kim *et al.* (1997, p. 171).

Compulsory elementary education led to an explosive demand for middle school enrollment, causing severe competition for middle school entrance, which in turn created many social problems. Thus, in 1968, the middle school entrance examination was abolished to facilitate school enrollment. As a result, the enrollment ratio rose rapidly, reaching 53.3 percent in 1970 (Table 2.1).

Since the government policy focused on middle school enrollment in the 1960s, high school enrollment did not improve as fast as middle school enrollment and remained at 29.3 percent in 1970. Due to a slow progress in high school enrollment, the secondary school enrollment as a whole remained at the relatively low level of 39 percent in 1970 (Table 2.1). As shown in Table 10.1, Korea's secondary school enrollment ratio in 1970 was not much higher than the average of Asian countries and far below the average of developed countries.

Another notable educational policy in the 1960s was the emphasis on vocational education which was considered critical for labor-intensive industrial development. To meet the rapidly rising demand for skilled workers, efforts were made to promote vocational education while restricting higher education the demand for which remained extremely sluggish until the 1960s. Thus, contrary to the Rhee Syngman government which was more concerned with individual knowledge and anti-communist education, educational efficiency became a major concern for the Park Chung Hee government.

Top priority was placed on the expansion of vocational schools with the objective of achieving a 70:30 split of enrollment between vocational and academic high schools by 1980.[4] Various measures were taken to promote vocational education by expanding technical high schools, providing scholarships, and promising employment to students entering vocational schools. This led to the rapid expansion of vocational high school enrollments.

As shown in Fig. 10.2, the ratio of vocational high school students relative to academic high school students jumped sharply from the mid-1960s, accounting for more than 50 percent in the early 1970s. After a short decline in the early 1970s, the ratio rose again until the end of the 1970s. The relative decline of vocational high schools and

---

[4]McGinn *et al.* (1980, p. 35).

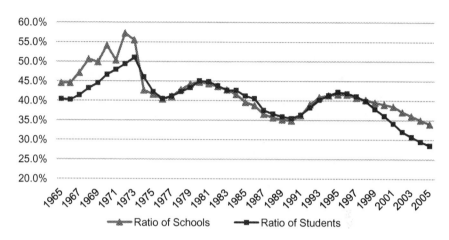

Figure 10.2   Number and Students of Vocational High Schools as Percentage of Academic High Schools, 1965–2005

Source: Kang *et al.* (2005, p. 182).

students in the early 1970s were mainly due to the rapid expansion of private high schools which were mostly academic. The private schools were encouraged to expand, which caused academic high school enrollment to grow faster than vocational high school enrollment.[5]

In the 1970s, vocational education continued to be stressed due to the HCI promotion policy, but an emphasis was placed on the expansion of overall high school enrollment, the demand for which increased sharply due to the elimination of the middle school entrance examination. The growing number of middle school students led to a corresponding increase in the number of students attending high schools, which created serious classroom shortages and severe competition for high school admission. This prompted the government to expand school facilities, as well as to adopt the high school equalization policy in 1974, which allowed middle school graduates to enter high schools through a lottery. This policy made it easier for middle school students to enter high schools, which in turn led to a rapid rise in high school enrollment.

Thus, the middle school as well as high school enrollment ratio increased sharply in the 1970s, pushing the secondary enrollment

---

[5]See McGinn *et al.* (1980, p. 6).

ratio to a level higher than that of developed countries. As shown in Table 10.1, Korea's secondary school enrollment ratio was 89 percent, higher than the 81 percent of developed countries in 1980.

The 1980s witnessed a dramatic change in the development policy which strongly affected educational policy. Until the 1970s, the government policy focused on the promotion of elementary and secondary education to satisfy increasing demand for skilled workers and technicians. Although some efforts were made to expand engineering schools in the 1970s, the government policy approach to higher education was in general conservative, imposing strict student quotas in universities.

However, entering the 1980s higher education received greater attention as the sustained high economic growth supported by rapid industrialization required a large number of students trained not only in engineering but also in a wide range of social science. The high school equalization policy and subsequent increase in the number of high school students intensified the competition for university admission, which created many problems including private tutoring and delayed higher education, incurring greater social costs. In response, efforts were made to expand enrollment in higher education; the quota system was relaxed, the enrollment system was significantly liberalized, and the entry barrier to higher education was also lowered. Thus, the tertiary school enrollment ratio increased sharply in the 1980s, rising from 15.8 percent in 1980 to 39.7 percent in 1990, which was as high as that of developed countries (Table 10.1).

On the other hand, vocational education stagnated in the 1980s since the government policy focused more on the education of engineers and scientists while eliminating the various incentives previously given to vocational schools and students. This motivated middle school graduates to prefer the academic high schools, and consequently the number of vocational schools and students relative to academic high schools and students displayed a steady downward trend in the 1980s, which later created massive shortages in skilled workers.

The liberal policy toward education was further strengthened in the 1990s as the higher education was greatly liberalized in terms of enrollment as well as the establishment of higher education institutions. The conditions required for establishing colleges and universities were eased considerably, leading to a rapid rise in the number of new colleges and universities. This policy shift together with the largely liberalized entrance quota contributed a great deal to the rapid expansion of higher education in the 1990s. Korea's ratio of high school graduates advanced to tertiary education became the highest among OECD countries. In 2010, for example, 82 percent of high school graduates advanced to higher education, far greater than the 40 percent of Europe, the 60–70 percent of the US, and the 50 percent of Japan.[6]

Although the liberal policy toward higher education adopted since the early 1980s brought about the rapid growth of higher education, its quantitative expansion was not accompanied by a corresponding qualitative improvement, as reflected in the increasing number of students per teacher. As shown in Fig. 10.3, the average number of students per teacher in higher education rose rapidly in the early

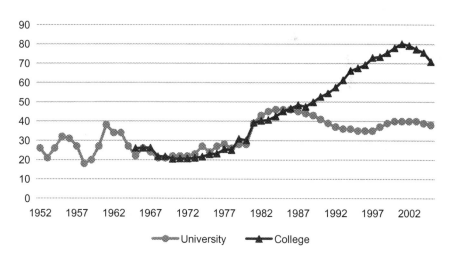

Figure 10.3   Number of Students per Teacher[a] in University and Junior College, 1952–2005

Note: [a]Full-time professor excluding lecturers and assistant professors

Source: Kang *et al.* (2005, pp. 198–199).

[6]*Chosun Ilbo*, May 24, 2011.

1980s and remained almost unchanged until the early 2000s. In the case of junior college, the number of students per teacher continued to increase until the end of the 1990s. The excessive expansion of higher education continued into the 2000s and created bubbles as the mismatch between the supply and demand of college graduates became greater due to the sluggish growth of the economy.

10.2 Human Capital Formation and Economic Growth

Despite some quality problems in higher education, there is no doubt that education played a key role in Korea's rapid growth during the last half century. In this regard, it is noteworthy that the educational plan was well coordinated with the development plan in order to provide sufficient manpower required for economic development. In the early years, efforts were focused on primary school education to increase literacy, followed by secondary education with an emphasis on vocational education to meet rapidly rising demand for skilled workers. A liberal educational policy was pursued from the 1980s, stressing higher education to cope with rising demand for professional workers in a wide range of industrial and social fields.

As a result of the swift expansion of education, remarkable progress was made in the educational attainment of the population. The average years of schooling increased steadily, rising from 5.03 years in 1966 to 10.25 years in 1995, doubling in 30 years (Table 10.2). As for the labor force aged 15–64 years old, schooling years rose from 4.6 years in 1960 to 8.3 years in 1980, and 12.6 years in 2010, which is longer than those of advanced countries except for the US (13.2) and New Zealand (13.0).[7]

Such swift development in educational attainment was reflected in the educational structure of employment. The share of employees with higher education increased rapidly, rising from 2.41 percent in 1960 to 24.01 percent in 2000, which is almost as high as the

---

[7]See Lee *et al.* (2014, p. 15).

Table 10.2   Average Years of Schooling, 1966–1995 (Unit: year)

1966	1970	1975	1980	1985	1990	1995
5.03	5.74	6.62	7.61	8.58	9.54	10.25

Source: Education Index in Korea (1997, p. 7), Korea Educational Development Institute.

Table 10.3   Composition of Employees by Educational Attainment, 1960–2000 (Unit: percent)

	Elementary School Graduation	Middle School Graduation	High School Graduation	Bachelor's Degree and Higher
1960	83.98	7.36	6.26	2.41
1970	67.43	14.93	11.51	6.13
1980	51.34	20.17	21.82	6.68
1990	29.10	19.63	37.68	13.69
2000	18.02	14.76	43.21	24.01

Source: Kim *et al.* (2002, p. 36).

OECD average of 25.6 percent.[8] On the other hand, the share of employees with elementary education dropped dramatically, falling from 83.98 percent in 1960 to 18.02 percent in 2000 (Table 10.3).

High educational attainment was accompanied by the rapid growth of public and private spending on education. Government spending on education has continued to grow fast since the late 1950s, accounting for 22.9 percent of central government expenditures and 3.6 percent of GNP in 1994. Public spending on education, which includes government spending and tuition fees, has climbed steadily, rising from 4.4 percent in 1966 to 5.5 percent of GNP in 1994 (Table 10.4). According to OECD data, public spending on education as a percentage of GDP was as high as 6.2 percent in 1994, which is not only higher than the OECD average of 5.6 percent but also higher than that of Japan and France (Table 10.5).

---

[8]Chang *et al.* (2004, p. 64).

Table 10.4   Public and Private Spending on Education as Percentage of GNP, 1966–1994

	1966	1972	1975	1982	1985	1990	1994
Total spending	8.8	9.7	7.7	10.7	11.8	10.2	11.3
Public spending	4.4	6.1	4.5	6.6	5.9	4.9	5.5
Private spending	4.4	3.7	3.2	4.1	5.9	5.3	5.8

Sources: McGinn *et al.* (1980, pp. 21–22) for 1966–1975; Kim *et al.* (1997, p. 296) for 1982–1994.

Table 10.5   International Comparison of Public Spending on Education as Percentage of GDP, 1994 (Unit: percent)

	All Levels of Education	Primary and Secondary Education	Tertiary Education
Korea	6.2	3.9	1.8
Japan	4.9	3.1	1.1
United States	6.6	3.9	2.4
France	6.2	3.8	1.1
OECD	5.6	3.7	1.3

Source: OECD, Education at a Glance (1997), quoted from Education Index in Korea (1997, p. 58), Korea Educational Development Institute.

Private spending on education also grew as fast as public spending, reaching 5.8 percent of GNP in 1994, which is higher than public spending. The high private spending on education was largely due to after-school tutoring, the purpose of which was to help students enter prestigious universities. The share of students participating in after-school tutoring was the second highest among OECD countries in 2010, and the total cost amounted to 7.9 percent of average household disposable income, accounting for 1.8 percent of GDP in 2010.[9] Since the heavy reliance on private tutoring is highly correlated with family earnings, it is likely to undermine equal educational opportunity with negative impacts on income distribution.

---

[9] OECD (2014a, p. 112).

Table 10.6   Growth of Human Capital and Its Contribution to Economic Growth (Unit: percent)

	GDP	Employment	Human Capital	Physical Capital	TFP
1960–1974	9.07	3.55 (2.13)	1.18 (0.71)	7.19 (2.88)	3.35
1981–1990	8.29	2.79 (1.82)	1.16 (0.76)	10.11 (3.61)	2.10
1991–2000	5.97	1.52 (1.00)	1.33 (0.87)	9.37 (3.24)	0.86
1981–2000	7.13	2.16 (1.41)	1.24 (0.81)	9.91 (3.43)	1.48

Note: Figures in parentheses indicate the contribution to economic growth.

Sources: McGinn *et al.* (1980, p. 123) for 1960–1974; Hahn *et al.* (2002, p. 10) for 1981–2000.

The rapid growth of educational attainment has been an important source of economic growth as it improved the quality of labor. As shown in Table 10.6, the improvement of quality of labor by virtue of education (growth of human capital) increased 1.18 percent per year during 1960–1974, accounting for 7.8 percent of economic growth. As the population's educational attainment continued to rise, its contribution to growth also increased, accounting for 9.2 percent of economic growth in 1981–1990 and 14.6 percent in 1991–2000.[10] It should however be noted that the contribution of education to growth, as shown in Table 10.6, was somewhat underestimated because the qualitative improvement of education arising from the improvement of teacher quality, teaching methods, facilities, and materials were not reflected due to the lack of data availability.

Education also affects growth not only through the direct productivity change of labor but also indirectly through the increase in scientific and technical knowledge, labor mobility, managerial efficiency, responsiveness to economic changes, etc. These indirect effects of education are not captured in the measured labor quality improvement but seemed to appear in unexplained residuals (total factor productivity growth), resulting in a downgrading of education's contribution to growth.[11] As a result, the contribution of

---

[10]For detailed discussion of the estimation procedure, see McGinn *et al.* (1980, pp. 116–126); Hahn *et al.* (2002, pp. 7–10).

[11]For detailed discussion, see McGinn *et al.* (1980, pp. 124–126).

total factor productivity growth to economic growth appears rather high, accounting for 36.9 percent of growth during 1960–1974 and 20.8 percent of growth during 1981–2000. This implies that the genuine contribution of education to growth should be considered higher than the figures shown in Table 10.6.

Chapter 11

Industrialization and Science and Technology Policy

11.1　Evolution of Science and Technology Policy

Korea's successful industrialization process greatly benefited from the active science and technology policy which the Korean government pursued since the early 1960s. From the very beginning, the Korean government realized the importance of science and technology in economic development and made systematic policy efforts to promote it as an essential part of the overall industrial development policy. Therefore, Korea's science and technology policy must be understood in the context of overall industrial development strategy. Broadly speaking, science and technology policy during the last four decades from the 1960s to 1990s can be divided into four distinct phases of evolution, as follows:

- Export Promotion and Skilled Manpower Development (1960s);
- HCI Promotion and Local Technological Capability Building (1970s);
- Technology-oriented Industrial Development and Strengthened R&D Incentives (1980s);
- High-tech Industry Promotion and a Policy Shift from Imitation to Innovation (1990s).

11.1.1 *Export Promotion and Skilled Manpower Development (1960s)*

During the easy import substitution period of the 1950s, no explicit governmental effort was made toward technology development since government policy focused on the rehabilitation of the war-torn economy. Systematic efforts to promote technology development started only after the first five-year development plan was launched in 1962, which placed great emphasis on export-oriented industrial development. In recognition of the importance of science and technology in economic development, the government formulated the five-year technology promotion plan as an integral part of the five-year economic development plan.

The key objectives of the plan were first to set up an administrative and legal framework for science and technology promotion; second, to promote skilled manpower development; third, to facilitate foreign technology imports, and finally to build up the technological infrastructure. Since there was no government agency responsible for technology policy, the government set up the Technology Management Bureau within the Economic Planning Board in 1962 to carry out technology policy planning. The Technology Management Bureau was later reorganized and transformed into the Ministry of Science and Technology (MOST) in 1967.

The second important policy objective during this period was technical manpower development because, given Korea's relatively high literacy rate, manpower development would be the most effective way to enhance the level of science and technology. The five-year manpower development plan was prepared separately to estimate future needs in various skill levels. Manpower demand in terms of craftsmen, technicians, and engineers was estimated, and manpower surveys were conducted every 2 years to supplement the manpower development plan. It is noteworthy that the Korean government realized the importance of technology and manpower development at such an early stage of development and made deliberate efforts to promote it.

The manpower development plan was focused on the adequate supply of skilled workers which would best serve to satisfy the manpower demand during the 1960s in which labor-intensive, export-oriented industrial development policy was pursued. Key policy measures taken to promote manpower development during the 1960s were as follows.[1]

First, measures were taken to integrate the educational plan into the economic development plan to provide an adequate supply of the necessary manpower required for industrial development. The enrollment quotas of technical high schools and engineering colleges, which had been set exclusively by the Ministry of Education, were decided in consultation with the Economic Planning Board, so that the manpower demand arising from economic development could be duly taken into account in educational planning.

Second, technical high schools were greatly expanded and the vocational training system was institutionalized to supplement the supply of skilled workers for which the formal education system was responsible. In 1967, the Vocational Training Act was enacted to meet the rapidly rising demand for skilled workers in the early stage of industrial development. The Act facilitated the establishment of many public as well as private training institutes, including in-plant training programs, which became the major supply sources of skilled workers in the 1960s and 1970s (Table 11.1).

Third, efforts were made to induce foreign investment by enacting the Foreign Capital Inducement Act in 1966 but were not very successful because the Act was highly restrictive imposing various

Table 11.1   Number of Recipients of Vocational Training by Type of Training Institute

	1967–1971	1972–1976	1977–1981
Technical high school	71,749	134,718	257,152
Public vocational training	36,317	81,294	120,117
Private vocational training	62,546	231,442	375,622
(in-plant training)	(48,225)	(117,350)	(337,388)
Total	170,612	447,454	752,891

Source: Kim (1986, p. 44).

---

[1]See Chun (1982, pp. 122–132).

conditions such as local content requirements and mandatory export quotas. Technology licensing was introduced in strategic industries but was strictly controlled in terms of royalty payments and contract periods, etc. Furthermore, all technology licensing was subject to government approval. As a result, FDI and technology licensing did not play an important role during the 1960s.

Fourth, the Korea Institute of Science and Technology (KIST) was established in 1966 to stimulate domestic R&D activities and played a role as the principal agency for industrial research. In short, the thrust of the science and technology policy in the 1960s was focused on skilled manpower development along with the build-up of technological infrastructure for science and technology development.

11.1.2 *HCI Promotion and Local Technological Capability Building (1970s)*

As the thrust of industrial development shifted toward promoting the heavy and chemical industry in the 1970s, science and technology policy was directed toward strengthening technical and engineering education and building local technological capability, because heavy and chemical industries cannot be promoted successfully without the support of technology development. As shown in Table 11.2, various policy measures were taken to promote industrial innovation and technology development.

The government continued to strengthen its efforts in skilled manpower development. Technical high schools were further expanded to meet the increasing demand for skilled workers and technicians. During the 1970s, the number of technical high schools almost doubled with the number of students also quadrupling. Technical high schools were classified into general technical high schools, machinery technical high schools, etc., according to their goals and curriculum in order to enhance the quality of training. The 2-year junior vocational college system was introduced in the late 1970s to meet the increasing demand for technicians in the HCI sector.

Vocational training was largely expanded and strengthened. In 1974, the Special Act on Vocational Training was enacted to facilitate in-plant vocational training. Firms with 500 or more employees were

Table 11.2 Government Policy Measures for Industrial Innovation in the 1960s and 1970s

Policy Measures	Year
1. Tax and Financial Incentives for Innovation	
• Technology Development Promotion Act	December 1972
• Technology Development Reserve Fund (TDRF)	January 1973
• Engineering Service Promotion Act	February 1973
• 8% tax credits for commercialization of new technology	December 1974
• Tax credits for R&D capital expenditure	January 1976
• Preferential loans for technology development	1976 (KDB), 1978 (IBK)
• Tax deduction for local engineering services	December 1977
• Income tax exemption for employee inventions	December 1979
2. Technological Infrastructure	
• Korea Scientific and Technological Information Center	January 1962
• KIST	February 1966
• Establishment of 12 State-funded Research Institutes	December 1975– April 1978
3. Manpower Training	
• Vocational Training Act	January 1967
• KAIS	February 1971
• National Technical Qualifications Act	December 1973
• Special Act on Vocational Training	December 1974
4. Competition Policy	
• Foreign Capital Inducement Act (tax exemption for technology licensing)	August 1966
• Import restrictions for domestically developed new technology products	December 1977
• Automatic approval for technology licensing in strategic industries	April 1978

Source: Kim (1988, p. 250).

obliged to offer a training program for as much as 15 percent of their workforce. This program was extended to firms with 300 or more employees in 1976, while reducing training requirement to 10 percent of workers. Firms that did not offer training programs were penalized through training levies.

The majority of industries including mining, manufacturing, construction, utility, transportation, communication, warehouse, and services were obliged to provide skill training. The Act encouraged many firms to establish their own in-plant vocational training institutes, and large firms established secondary schools for their teenaged workers. As a result, the number of workers who received in-plant training increased dramatically during the 1970s, outnumbering those who received training from technical high schools and public training institutes. Consequently, in-plant vocational training continued to play the major role in skill formation even in the 1970s.

Technology education at the college level was also strengthened to meet the growing demand for engineers and scientists. The government drastically expanded graduate and undergraduate education with a special emphasis on such fields as mechanical engineering, and electrical and electronic engineering.

Since the late 1960s, the government began to bring high-caliber Korean scientists and engineers working abroad back to Korea. However, they were limited in number, which led to the government decision to foster them at home. As a consequence, a new graduate school called the Korea Advanced Institute of Science (KAIS) was established in 1971. It is interesting to note that KAIS was placed not under the jurisdiction of the Ministry of Education but under the MOST to provide special treatment that was not offered to universities. The entire faculty was recruited from abroad and received various incentives including free housing, extremely high salaries, and special research grants. The idea was that the new graduate school would stimulate the advancement of science and engineering education in the Korean university education system.

The National Technical Qualification Act was enacted in 1973 to test various skill levels. Graduates from all types of training institutes were obliged to take qualifying examinations, and different certificate degrees were granted depending on the level of skills. The Act made it possible for workers to enhance their social as well as economic position without formal education.

As the heavy and chemical industry gained growth momentum in the mid-1970s, the need for specialized research institutes was strongly felt in such fields as machinery, electronics, chemicals, energy, telecommunications, etc. Thus, the government established

12 specialized state-funded industrial research institutes in the late 1970s to meet the technological needs of private firms. The core function of state-funded research institutes was to develop industrial technology by pioneering new products and new processes, as well as adapting and assimilating imported technology.

Efforts were also made to promote the innovative activities of private firms by enacting the Technology Development Promotion Act in 1972, which stipulated various tax and financial incentives for technology development. The Technology Development Reserve Fund system was introduced in 1973, whereby firms could set aside reserves for future R&D expenditures which should be spent within 2 years. The reserves, which were exempted from corporate income tax, were not allowed to exceed 5 percent of profit in 1973 and 20 percent of profit in 1977. If the reserves were not used, the firms had to pay a penalty on the reserved amount at an interest rate higher than the prevailing nominal interest rate.

Tax credits for investment in the commercialization of newly developed technology and tax credits for R&D facilities were introduced in 1974 and 1976, respectively, to encourage local technological development. In 1977, tax deductions for earnings from local engineering services were also permitted. Aside from these tax incentives, preferential financing was also provided in the late 1970s.

The government began to liberalize technology imports as the investment in heavy and chemical industries spurred in the mid-1970s. In 1978, technology imports with royalty payments of less than 3 percent of sales were automatically approved in electronics, machinery, shipbuilding, metal, chemicals, and textiles. The restriction was further relaxed in 1979 with respect to royalty payments, contract duration, and coverage of automatically approved industries.

In contrast to technology import, the restrictive policy toward FDI remained virtually unchanged during the 1970s. While joint ventures were preferred, various restrictions were imposed in terms of foreign participation ratio, investment field, investment amount, etc. However, certain exceptions were made for technology-intensive and wholly export-oriented investment or investment by Korean residents living abroad. Thus, we may say that FDI was selectively encouraged, although the overall policy direction remained quite restrictive.

11.1.3   Technology-Oriented Industrial Policy and Strengthened R&D Incentives (1980s)

Entering the 1980s, the industrial incentive system was completely reformed, shifting from industry-specific support to functional support. Thus, renewed efforts were made to stimulate industrial innovation by adopting the technology drive as a major government policy goal. The Industrial Development Fund was created to support industrial rationalization and technology development. Nation-building by technology became the national slogan as the government pursued technology-oriented industrial development.

The technology-oriented industrial policy led the government to intensify its support for industrial innovation of the private sector. Tax and financial incentives that were adopted during the 1970s were strengthened, while a host of new policy instruments were introduced to promote industrial innovation (Table 11.3). In 1981 and 1982, several new tax incentives were introduced: a 10 percent tax credit given to corporate R&D expenditures; local tax exemption for real estate acquisition designated for corporate research institutes; income tax exemption for foreign technicians; a lower special consumption tax for new technology products; tariff cuts for R&D-related commodities, etc.

Tax incentives were further reinforced in 1984 and 1986 with respect to the innovative activities of SMEs and venture capital; income tax exemption for technology-intensive SMEs; tax exemption for capital gains of venture capital; and tax credits for investment reserves of venture capital. In addition to these new tax incentives, the existing incentives were reinforced: the Technology Development Reserve Fund system was extended to cover the service industry, the reserve ratio was raised from 1 percent to 1.5 percent of sales, and the penalty on unused reserves was reduced. An additional 10 percent tax credit for expenditures in R&D and manpower training was provided for expenditures that exceeded the average expenditure in R&D and

Table 11.3   Government Policy Measures for Industrial Innovation in the 1980s

Policy Measures	Year
1. Tax and Financial Incentives for Innovation	
• TDRF system strengthened in terms of coverage, reserve ceiling, etc.	December 1981– December 1986
• Special accelerated depreciation for commercialization of new technology	December 1981
• 10% tax credit for current R&D expenditures with additional 10% tax credit for incremental R&D expenditures	December 1981[a]
• Tax credits for manpower training facilities	December 1986
• Local tax exemption and tariff reduction for private research institutes	December 1981
• Income tax exemption for foreign engineers	December 1981– December 1982[a]
• Income tax deduction for technology export income	December 1981[a]
• Lower special consumption tax for new technology products	December 1981[a]
• Tax exemption for capital gains of venture capital firms	December 1981[a]
• 4-year tax holiday for new technology-based firms (NTBFs)	December 1984[a] December 1986[a]
• Government grants to national NRDPs	1982[1]
• Guarantee for technology development loans by the Korea Credit Guarantee Fund	1983[a]
• Long-term preferential loans from the Oil Reserve Fund	June 1986[a]
• Creation of Industry Development Fund	December 1986[a]
2. Technological Infrastructure	
• Industrial Technology Research Cooperatives Support Act	December 1986[a]
3. Manpower Training	
• Military duty exemption for researchers of private research institutes	1981[a]
• Establishment of the Korea Institute of Technology (KIT)	1985[a]
4. Competition Policy	
• Automatic approval system for technology licensing	July 1980
• Technology licensing approval replaced by report system	July 1984
• Monopoly Regulation and Fair Trade Act	December 1980[a]
• Comprehensive import liberalization program	1983

Note: [a]Indicates newly introduced policy measures.
Source: Kim (1988, p. 256).

manpower training of the past 2 years. Local tax exemption for corporate research institutes was extended to research institutes with 10 researchers or more (previously 30 researchers or more).

Large-scale enterprises were strongly recommended to establish at least one research center per company, while SMEs were encouraged to organize R&D consortia in their related fields. For this purpose, various incentives were provided through tax exemptions, special depreciation allowance, preferential loans, etc. As a result, the number of private research institutes witnessed a massive upsurge from the early 1980s, totaling 1,435 in 1992.

Financial support for technology development was also strengthened during the 1980s. Since commercial banks were very reluctant to finance risky ventures, the government promoted the establishment of venture capital firms through various policy measures to assist the innovative activities of SMEs and to promote the commercialization of new technologies. Prominent among them was the Korea Technology Development Corporation (KTDC), which was established in 1981 as a full-fledged venture capital firm financed jointly by the government and private business firms. By the end of 1986, there were five venture capital firms that were mostly owned by private firms. The Korea Technology Credit Guarantee Fund was created in 1989 to help SMEs engage in technology development.

To develop key industrial technology, the government rolled out the National R&D Program (NRDP) in 1982, specifying R&D projects to be promoted. The program was aimed at promoting R&D projects in high-tech industrial fields and stimulating indigenous technological development. Projects directly related to public interest, such as energy and resource development, were entirely financed by the government and carried out by public research institutes, while projects with commercial value were partly financed by private firms and carried out jointly. The joint research projects covered a wide range of areas including semiconductors, computers, materials engineering, bioengineering, fine chemistry, chemical engineering, systems engineering, etc.

The manpower development policy shifted toward the fostering of high-caliber scientists and engineers. Strong emphasis was placed on the expansion of the graduate school program, particularly that of KAIS. Enrollment quotas of engineering colleges were also expanded in such fields as computer science, telecommunication, electronics, and material science. The Korea Institute of Technology (KIT) was established in 1985 to educate scientifically gifted students selected among high school graduates. University graduate programs were also improved through the provision of research grants and fellowship programs, etc. Thus, the number of graduate students at engineering colleges increased rapidly during the 1980s, rising from 1,427 in 1980 to 6,818 in 1990.

High-caliber Korean scientists and engineers working abroad were continuously brought back to Korea. The program started as early as 1966, when the KIST was set up and largely expanded thereafter. A total of 2,178 scientists and engineers were invited by the government on a permanent or temporary basis during 1968–1994 (Table 11.4). Most of them worked at state-funded research institutes and played a leading role in assimilating and adapting imported technology. The government also initiated overseas study programs in 1982 and dispatched 1,353 scientists and engineers to advanced countries for their postdoctoral studies and research during 1981–1991.

The Foreign Capital Inducement Act was substantially revised in 1984 to encourage FDI. The positive list system was replaced by a negative list system, and the restrictions concerning foreign equity share were also greatly relaxed. While restrictions on foreign

Table 11.4   Korean Scientists and Engineers Recruited by the Government (Unit: person)

	Permanent Basis			Short-Term Basis		
	1968–1980	1981–1990	Total	1968–1980	1981–1994	Total
University	139	355	494	21	203	224
Research institute	130	387	517	182	360	542
Industry and others	7	33	40	74	287	361

Source: MOST (2008, p. 78).

firms were significantly reduced, the various tax incentives provided to foreign investment were abolished to facilitate fair competition between foreign and domestic firms.

Technology licensing was fully liberalized from 1984 as the approval system was replaced by a report system. Firms who want to import foreign technology were merely required to report their intentions to the ministry concerned. If the ministry made no objection within 20 days, the technology import was considered accepted. As a result, technology licensing and FDI witnessed a rapid inflow in the 1980s. Korea relied heavily on turn-key plants and machinery imports in the early years of industrialization as a way to acquire foreign technology but began to rely on technology licensing and FDI in the later years of industrialization.

11.1.4 *High-Tech Industry Promotion and Policy Shift from Imitation to Innovation (1990s)*

Coming into the 1990s, the Korean economy was rapidly exposed to foreign competition so that Korea could no longer rely on the catch-up industrial development strategy taking advantage of low labor costs. It was also increasingly difficult to import advanced technology, since foreign firms were reluctant to provide core technologies. Therefore, the Korean government had to switch its technology policy from imitation to innovation to cope with changing external environments.

In response to these challenges, the NRDP, initiated in 1982, was enlarged and diversified as many ministries began to launch R&D programs of their own, i.e. the Highly Advanced National (HAN) Project of the MOST, the Industrial Generic Technology Development Program of the Ministry of Trade, Industry and Energy (MOTIE), and the Telecommunication Technology Development Program of the Ministry of Information and Communication (MIC), to name a few.

The HAN Project was a large-scale inter-ministerial R&D program launched in 1992 and carried out by investment from both the government and the industry, aimed at the intensive development of strategic industrial technologies to enhance Korea's science and technology level to those of G-7 countries by 2001. Important among the HAN projects were the development of next-generation semiconductor, advanced technology for panel displays, digital HDTV, new energy technology, environmental technology, new materials technology, etc.[2] Some of the projects were very successful including the development of 64M DRAM in 1993, digital HDTV in 1994, the CDMA wireless system in 1996, as well as the production of large TFT-LCDs in 2001. These achievements were made possible by the joint R&D efforts of the government and industry.

The Industrial Generic Technology Development Program covered slightly different technology fields from the HAN Project and placed emphasis on the development of mid-term key technologies with large spillover effects on related industries and core technologies that could be widely applied to the private sector. The Telecommunication Technology Development Program was designed to develop technologies to enhance the competitiveness of the information and communication industry and to build infrastructure for the information society.

Great efforts were also made to enhance the research capability of universities by supporting basic research. Korean universities were primarily oriented toward education with little research activities until the 1980s. Although universities held approximately 80 percent of PhDs in science and engineering, they only spent a small portion of national R&D funds. Therefore, it was imperative to promote university research activities. Accordingly, a new research program was introduced in 1990 in the form of Science Research Centers (SRC) and Engineering Research Centers (ERC). The program introduced by MOST was designed to promote basic research in universities, and 113 centers were established between 1990 and 2006 supported by government assistance of KRW 688.5 billion.

The Ministry of Education also introduced a new program to support research-oriented universities in 1995. Under this program, five universities received KRW five billion for 5 years to upgrade R&D infrastructure and to hire more researchers. To further strengthen

---

[2]For details of HAN projects, see Yang (2001, p. 12).

the research capability of universities, Brain Korea 21 (BK21) was launched in 1998 to enhance the quality of graduate school education by supporting research projects.

Efforts to stimulate private-sector R&D activities continued in the 1990s for the purpose of supporting industrial innovation. Tax and financial incentives were strengthened. For instance, tax credits for technology and manpower development spending were raised from 25 percent to 50 percent. The Science and Technology Promotion Fund and the Information and Telecommunication Promotion Fund were newly established in 1991 to finance private firms' participation in NRDPs and to support private firms involved in information and communication technology development, respectively. Special loan programs with preferential interest rates were provided through the Korea Technology Banking Corporation to support R&D and commercialization projects.

Further efforts were made to strengthen the technological infrastructure of the private sector. The conditions for registering private research institutes and qualifications for research personnel were considerably eased to facilitate the growth of private firms' research laboratories. In order to encourage SMEs to establish research institutes, military service exemption was extended to SME research personnel, and the number of research personnel required for SMEs was reduced from 10 to 5. While large enterprises established their own research institutes, SMEs were encouraged to organize research consortia for collaborative research efforts in specific fields. As a result, SME research institutes witnessed a dramatic expansion, accounting for 93 percent of private-sector research institutes as of the end of 2006.

11.2   R&D Activities and Performance

As mentioned above, the Korean government implemented numerous measures to promote science and technology development, which made a significant contribution to enhancing Korea's technological capability. Various quantitative indicators related to science and technology improved at a remarkable pace during the last half

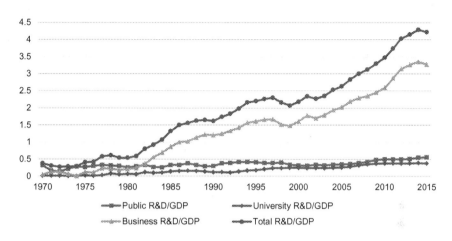

Figure 11.1   R&D/GDP Ratio, 1970–2015 (Unit: percent)

Source: Available at: http://sts.ntis.go.kr/ntisstats.

century, thanks to systematic efforts by the government as well as the private sector to enhance national science and technology capability.

As shown in Fig. 11.1, the R&D expenditure as a ratio of GDP had more than a six-fold increase between 1970 and 2000, rising from 0.37 percent in 1970 to 1.72 percent in 1990 and 2.30 percent in 2000. It is important to note that the R&D/GDP ratio showed a steep climb from the 1980s, largely attributable to the rapid growth of private-sector R&D activities. Private-sector R&D activities appear to have been strongly influenced by two government policy measures.

The first one is the pursuit of comprehensive liberalization policy since the early 1980s. As private firms were increasingly exposed to foreign competition, they were placed under strong pressure to take actions for industrial innovation so as to compete against foreign products. Therefore, it was imperative for them to increase R&D investment for their survival and growth. In the 1970s, no such pressure was felt because the economy was booming with a high inflation rate and the domestic market was protected by the government. There was no pressing reason for them to undertake risky and costly technology development. The result was poor R&D activities of private sector despite some incentives provided by the government.

The second one is the strengthened R&D incentives from the 1980s. While opening the domestic market, the government began to provide various financial and fiscal incentives for industrial innovation. The incentives were strengthened as liberalization accelerated, enabling private firms to undertake investment in technology development, which otherwise would not have been possible. In other words, the liberalization policy coupled with R&D incentives greatly stimulated private firms to increase their investment in R&D. They began to establish in-house R&D facilities, spending an increasing share of their sales on R&D that led to a proliferation of private research institutes since the early 1980s.

The private sector's R&D/sales ratio rose sharply from 0.5 percent to 2 percent during 1980–2000. A particularly sharp increase was observed in the 1980s as it rose from 0.5 to 1.7 percent in 1990, more than a three-fold increase in 10 years. As a result, the private sector share in total R&D funding increased steadily from 48.4 percent in 1980 to 84.1 percent in 1990. After a slight slowdown in the 1990s, it rose again in the 2000s as the private sector continued to lead R&D activities, accounting for 77.5 percent of total R&D spending in 2015, which reached 4.22 percent of GDP, the highest among OECD countries in the same year (see Table 11.5).

The rapid growth of R&D investment made a significant contribution to enhancing Korea's technological capability. As shown in Table 11.5, a remarkable achievement was made in terms of number of patents registered, R&D manpower, corporate research institutes, and technology exports. Certain quantitative indicators such as the R&D/GDP ratio, number of researchers per 10,000 population, and the business R&D/GDP ratio are comparable to or even higher than advanced industrial countries.

Despite the remarkable growth of R&D activities, much remains to be improved because Korea's R&D output appears poor compared to its input, implying low R&D productivity. Although the R&D/GDP ratio is the highest among OECD countries, Korea relies heavily on the import of foreign technology, so that technology exports as a ratio of technology imports was 0.63 in 2015, far below the level of advanced countries. This confirms that Korea has a low

Table 11.5   Major Science & Technology Indicators, Selected Years, 1970–2015

	1970	1980	1990	2000	2010	2015
R&D/GDP (%)	0.38	0.54	1.62	2.18	3.47	4.22
Public R&D/GDP	0.32	0.26	0.30	0.32	0.50	0.56
Business R&D/GDP	0.05	0.21	1.20	1.61	2.59	3.27
University R&D/GDP	0.01	0.07	0.12	0.25	0.38	0.38
R&D Funding (%):						
Government	58.2	49.8	15.9	27.6	28.0	24.7
Private	23.7	48.4	84.1	72.4	71.8	74.5
Foreign	18.1	1.8	—	0.1	0.2	0.8
Business R&D/Sales (%)	0	0.5	1.7	2.0	2.4	3.02
Manufacturing R&D/Sales	—	—	2.14	2.51	2.8	3.74
Service R&D/Sales	—	—	—	—	1.85	2.09
Researcher/10,000 Population	1.8	4.8	16.4	38.0	70.0	89.5
Corporate Research Labs	—	53	966	7,110	21,785	35,288
Tech. Export/Tech. Import	—	—	0.02	0.07	0.33	0.63
Total Patents Registered	266	1,632	7,762	34,956	58,843	101,873
Patents by Koreans	—	186	2,554	22,943	51,404	74,318

Source: Available at: http://sts.ntis.go.kr/ntisstats.

level of technological creativity due to the weak basic research. While universities employ around three-quarters of PhDs, they performed only 9 percent of R&D in 2014, approximately half the OECD average.[3] Although Korea ranked 12th in terms of the number of scientific publications, it ranked 25th in terms of percentage among the world's 10 most cited publications during the period 2003–2012, suggesting that Korea's basic research is low in quality.[4]

Korea is a major exporter of high-tech products, but the value-added content of Korea's manufactured exports is low due to a heavy dependence on the outsourcing of intermediates. For example, the domestic value-added share of manufactured exports was just above 50 percent, the sixth lowest out of 40 countries in 2011, indicating a

---

[3]OECD (2016, p. 98).
[4]OECD (2015a, p. 106).

high import content of exports.[5] It is also noted that despite the higher R&D intensity of business firms, Korea's share of patents registered in the US, Japan, and the European Union was 5.7 percent in 2013, much lower than the shares of the US, Japan, and Germany. What these indicators imply is that the rapid quantitative growth of R&D activities was not matched by corresponding qualitative growth. Therefore, great efforts are needed to improve the innovation system to enhance the efficiency of R&D activities, which will be discussed in Chapter 13.

11.3   Features of Science and Technology Policy

As explained above, Korea made a remarkable achievement in science and technology during the past half century, although much has to be improved to enhance the efficiency of R&D activities. Important features of Korea's science and technology policy and lessons that can be drawn from the Korean experience can be summarized as follows.

First, the Korean government pursued the science and technology policy as an integral part of its overall development plan and linked it closely to industrial development policy. Technology policy changed with different emphasis at different stages of industrial development.

When labor-intensive, export-oriented industrial development was pursued in the 1960s, technology policy was focused on skill formation to meet the rapidly growing demand for skilled workers. In the 1970s, when the heavy and chemical industries were promoted, an emphasis was placed on engineering education along with strengthening vocational training to meet the increasing demand for technicians and engineers. A number of specialized government-funded research institutes were also established to support the adaptation and assimilation of imported technology and to build up local technological capability.

When liberalization was pursued in the 1980s, the emphasis shifted toward stimulating private-sector R&D activities to enhance

---

[5]OECD (2015a, p. 199).

the technological competence of private firms so as to cope with foreign competition. When industrial development based on imported technology was found no longer sustainable in the 1990s, the science and technology policy shifted from imitation to innovation by strengthening basic research and promoting high-tech industries.

Second, the Korean government deliberately promoted local technological capability building in order to facilitate the adaptation and assimilation of imported technology. Emphasis was first placed on the promotion of state-led R&D efforts, followed by the stimulation of private-sector R&D activities. The government set up a number of specialized public-funded research institutes in the late 1970s, which were instrumental in adapting, assimilating and improving imported technology while strengthening local technological capability. Entering the 1980s, the focus shifted toward stimulating industrial innovation by providing the R&D incentives for private firms which were strengthened further in the 1990s and made a major contribution to facilitating industrial technology development.

Third, the technology transfer in Korea mostly took place in the form of capital goods imports rather than technology licensing and FDI. Korea's policy toward FDI and technology licensing was rather restrictive until the 1970s. Korea promoted technology transfers through the procurement of turn-key plants and imports of foreign capital goods, which became a major source for acquiring foreign technology. This policy was very effective in the mature industries because Korea had well-trained human resources.

Fourth, Korea's technology policy placed a strong emphasis on the supply side of technology development. Particular attention was given to manpower development by stressing the supply of skilled workers first, followed by the supply of technicians and engineers. Korean scientists and engineers working in advanced countries were brought back to Korea. They contributed greatly to enhancing the local technological capability, as they worked mostly for public research institutes and constituted the core group of researchers engaged in R&D activities. The Special NRDP was launched in 1982 to promote R&D projects in high-technology fields and to stimulate indigenous technology development. Despite some critics with regard to efficiency of the program, it clearly made a significant contribution to the accumulation of technological capability and the development of Korea's high-tech industries.

Fifth, it should be emphasized that implicit policies such as trade, industrial, and competition policies also played an important role in stimulating industrial innovation. There is no doubt that Korea's progress in technology development owes a great deal to outward-looking, export-oriented industrialization strategy. Exports provided an important means of acquiring, improving, and creating technology by making access to foreign technological information, enlarging the market size, and inducing foreign competition. The increased competition brought by trade liberalization and technology-oriented industrial policy also provided an important motivation for private firms to undertake innovative activities. The increasing importance of implicit policy instruments should not, however, be interpreted to imply that explicit policy instruments such as the provision of financial and fiscal incentives for R&D activities are less important for industrial innovation. Implicit and explicit policies should not be taken as alternative but considered complementary to each other, which means that only well-integrated and combined policy efforts can lead to the effective stimulation of industrial innovation and technology development.

Chapter 12

Social Development and Income Distribution

12.1 Evolution of Social Policy: An Overview

Korea's social policy during the last half century underwent several major changes, reflecting Korea's changing development policy. In the early years, when the growth-first policy was pursued, social policy was not given a high priority and focused on building a legal and institutional basis for the social security, while leaving distribution problem largely to market forces. Social policy received attention in the early 1980s when inequity and imbalance caused by rapid growth began to create social tension. Thus, social welfare became an increasing concern of government policy which was accentuated in the course of political democratization in the late 1980s, shifting the role of public finance from stimulating economic growth to supporting social development.

The financial crisis in 1997 and its aftermath on poverty and income distribution prompted the government to shift development policy from growth to equity so that social welfare became the priority goal of government policy in the 2000s. In short, Korea's social policy over the past five decades from the 1960s to 2000s can be broadly divided into three phases of evolution as follows:

- Building Social Security System (1960s–1970s);
- Policy Shift toward Improving Social Welfare (1980s–1990s);
- Expansion of Social Welfare Programs (2000s).

12.1.1   *Building Social Security System (1960s–1970s)*

Social development policy received less attention during the 1960s and 1970s since the government pursued growth-first policy. "Growth-first, distribution-second" was the basic philosophy underlying the government policy during this period. Distribution was largely left to market forces in the belief that growth would contribute to social development by creating job opportunities and reducing poverty. Thus, fiscal policy during this period was directed toward supporting economic development and raising school enrollment.

As shown in Table 12.1, government expenditures for economic services as a percentage of GDP markedly increased during the 1960s and 1970s, and a similar trend was found in spending for education. The reason for higher educational spending was that education contributes to growth through facilitating human capital formation. In contrast, the welfare expenditure share of GDP was much smaller and remained almost unchanged in the 1960s and 1970s, reflecting the low priority on social welfare policy.

The pursuit of growth-first policy prevented the government from carrying out an active welfare policy due to resource limitation. Therefore, the government had to consider the welfare issue from a long-term development perspective and took a gradual approach focused on building a social security system. The pension program for government employees was first introduced in 1960, followed by pension scheme for military personnel in 1963, industrial accident insurance program in 1964, and pension program for private school teachers in 1975. The voluntary health insurance system that was introduced in 1963 and was revised in 1976 to stipulate the compulsory participation of workers, first for firms with 500 or more employees beginning in 1977 and then for firms with 300 or more employees in 1979.

A number of welfare programs were launched during this period, including the Livelihood Protection Act of 1962 to provide public assistance to the poor, the health care protection system of 1977 to provide low-income households with medical services, and the welfare program for mentally and physically disabled persons of 1978.

Table 12.1   Functional Distribution of General Government Expenditures as
Percentage of GDP, 1960–2015, Selected Years

	1960	1970	1980	1990	2000	2010	2015
Economic Expenditure	3.5	4.3	4.6	4.5	6.1	6.9	6.1
Welfare Expenditure	1.0	1.3	2.1	3.2	4.7	8.8	10.6
Educational Expenditure	2.6	4.0	3.7	3.7	4.0	4.9	5.2
Defense Expenditure	6.0	4.9	5.8	3.8	2.6	2.4	2.5
Other Expenditure[a]	5.5	4.1	4.8	4.3	5.3	8.0	7.9
Total	18.6	18.5	21.0	19.5	22.7	31.0	32.3

Notes: [a]Includes public administration, public order and safety, entertainment, culture, and religion.

Sources: Bahl *et al.* (1986) for 1960; Koh (2008) for 1970–2000; The Bank of Korea for 2010 and 2015.

However, these welfare programs were quite limited in scope and small in size due to limited resources with the result that government spending for welfare was relatively small, reaching a little over 1 percent of GDP in the 1970s (Table 12.1).

Despite the low priority of social development, high economic growth during this period brought about significant progress in social development in a broader sense such as school enrollment, poverty, unemployment, income distribution, infant mortality, life expectancy, health, and nutrition (Table 12.2). The sustained high economic growth not only solved the poverty problem by creating job opportunities but also had a positive impact on income distribution because the unemployed and low-wage workers benefited the most from high growth.

Absolute poverty was drastically reduced as the percentage of people living below the poverty line dropped from 48.3 percent in 1961 to 9.8 percent in 1980 (Table 12.4). As shown in Table 12.2, the unemployment rate which was as high as 8.1 percent in 1963 dropped to 4.1 percent in 1975. Furthermore, the rapid growth of per capita income also contributed to enhancing nutrition and health conditions as demonstrated in life expectancy and infant mortality, reflecting the broad benefits of development. These achievements indicate that during this period social development in the broader sense improved considerably along with growth.

Table 12.2   Major Social Indicators of Korea, 1965–1990

	1965	1975	1985	1990
Population Growth Rate	2.57	1.70	0.99	0.99
Absolute Poverty Rate	40.9	9.8[c]	8.6	7.7
Unemployment Rate	8.1[d]	4.1	4.0	2.4
Average Years of Schooling	5.03[a]	6.62	8.58	9.54
Male	6.19[a]	7.61	9.66	10.55
Female	3.97[a]	5.70	7.58	8.58
Enrollment Rate				
Primary School	91.6	103.2	102.0	100.6
Middle School	39.4	74.2	99.1	99.0
High School	27.0	43.6	86.4	97.2
College and University	6.9	9.5	35.6	38.1
Gini Coefficient	0.344	0.391[b]	0.345	0.323
Infant Mortality Rate	61.8	41.4	13.3	12.8
Av. Life Expectancy at Birth	61.9[e]	65.8[f]	69.0	71.6[g]
Population per Physician	2,645	2,100	1,379	1,007
Daily Calorie Supply (per capita)	2,189	2,390	2,687	2,858

Notes: [a]1966, [b]1976, [c]1980, [d]1963, [e]1966, [f]1979, [g]1991.

Source: Kwon (1993) and Korea Statistical Office.

12.1.2   *Policy Shift toward Improving Social Welfare (1980s–1990s)*

While very successful in terms of growth, the growth-oriented policy began to show undesirable side effects in the late 1970s as the economy overheated due to the ambitious HCI drive policy. Income distribution began to deteriorate owing to soaring inflation and the widening income gap between labor income and property income. This led to an aggravation of income inequality between the rich and poor, creating social tension.

On the other hand, with the rise of income the demand for basic needs such as housing, health, and welfare services grew swiftly, which placed the government under strong pressure to have a proper balance between economic growth and social development. Thus, equity and welfare problems along with macroeconomic stability became an increasingly important policy issue in the early 1980s.

The Chun Doo Hwan government which came into office in 1980 took wide-ranging reform measures including welfare policy. The Constitution was revised in the same year to emphasize equity and welfare aimed at building a welfare society. Public assistance and social welfare services were expanded for the poor, the elderly, and the handicapped, as well as for low-income groups who had mostly been deprived of growth benefits in the past. The Elderly Welfare Act was enacted in 1982 to provide various benefits to people aged 65 or older including free subway transportation in 1982 and free medical diagnosis in 1983. The health insurance program was also extended in 1982 to cover firms with 16 or more employees. As a result, welfare spending began to rise from the early 1980s. However, the government was unable to carry out an aggressive welfare policy until the mid-1980s due to the higher priority accorded to economic stabilization and structural adjustment policy.

The major turning point for welfare policy came in 1987 when the political democratization movement led to birth of new government, stirring strong demand for welfare services and distributive equity. Thus, great efforts were made to strengthen welfare policy leading to rapid growth in welfare spending from the late 1980s. The welfare spending/GDP ratio more than doubled between 1980 and 2000, rising from 2.1 percent in 1980 to 4.7 percent in 2000 (Table 12.1).

The health insurance system, which started as a company-based program in 1977, was extended to a community-based program covering the self-employed and unemployed. The program first began to cover residents in rural areas, and then extended coverage to all urban residents in 1989. The company-based insurance program also further extended its coverage including firms with five or more employees in 1988. Korea was thus able to introduce a universal health insurance system in just 12 years from its inception in 1977, which was not accomplished by any other country including advanced countries.

The minimum wage system was also introduced to improve distributive equity by eliminating excessively low wages. The system was applied first to the manufacturing sector in 1988, to all other industries in 1990, and then to all workplaces in 2000. The National

Pension Scheme was also introduced in 1988, first for firms with 10 or more employees and was gradually extended so that in 1999 firms and businesses of all sizes including farmers, fishermen, and the self-employed were covered by the scheme except for those covered by other pension schemes. With the introduction of the employment insurance system in 1995, Korea came to have four major social insurance programs in the 1990s, namely the national pension, health insurance, employment insurance, and industrial accident insurance.

Social welfare services were also expanded in the 1990s. The Act on Employment Promotion of the Disabled was enacted in 1990 to provide job opportunities for the disabled and to encourage their social integration. Public enterprises and private firms with 300 or more employees were required to employ disabled workers at a rate of at least 2 percent of their entire workforce. The Act on Preschool ChildCare was enacted in 1991 to expand childcare facilities to improve education for children and to support children in low-income families.

In 1988, the government launched a large-scale housing construction project aimed at constructing two million housing units during the period 1988–1992 to solve the housing shortage. The project helped resolve the housing shortage, thereby raising the housing supply ratio considerably from 70.9 percent in 1989 to 79.1 percent in 1993, and this continued to rise in the 2000s, reaching 105.9 percent in 2005.

12.1.3 *Expansion of Social Welfare Programs (2000s)*

The welfare policy prior to the 1997 financial crisis was mostly focused on developing the social insurance system which involves a relatively low fiscal burden. After the financial crisis, however, welfare policy shifted toward strengthening public assistance and welfare services, which incurred a significant burden on public finance.

The Kim Dae Jung government (1998–2003) began to strengthen the social safety net to cope with rapidly rising unemployment and income inequality following the financial crisis in 1997. The government increased wage subsidies to firms that retained redundant workers and expanded vocational training for the unemployed. The public works program was introduced to provide job opportunities for the unemployed. The coverage of the employment insurance system was also extended to firms with 10 or more employees in 1998, and then to firms with one or more employees in 2000.

The most important policy change in this regard was the introduction of the National Basic Livelihood Security Program in 2000, which is designed to guarantee minimum living standards for the entire population. People who live below the poverty line are subsidized by the government and are guaranteed minimum living standards.

The welfare policy was further strengthened under the Roh Moo Hyun government (2003–2008). Various new programs were introduced including the Emergency Relief Program of 2006, and the Long-Term Care Insurance and the Basic Old-Age Pension, both launched in 2008. People aged 65 or older became eligible for old-age pension. In 2008, 60 percent of those aged 65 or older benefited from the pension program.

Faced with a low fertility rate and an aging population, the government launched the Basic Plan for Low Fertility Rates and Aging Population in 2005, and various programs were introduced to boost the fertility rate and encourage women's economic participation. Government support for the care of preschool children was expanded to provide equal educational opportunities for children, to encourage child-bearing, to promote the labor market participation of mothers, and so forth.

The emphasis on welfare policy continued under the Lee Myung Bak (2008–2013) and Park Geun Hye government (2013–2017). A pension program for the disabled was introduced in 2010, and the national basic livelihood security program and basic old age pension program were revised and adjusted to improve their benefits and effectiveness. The Basic Pension was introduced in 2014 to complement the National Pension Scheme. The childcare program was expanded further, so that in 2012 all children up to 2 years old were eligible for government support regardless of household income, and the age limit was extended to children aged three to

Table 12.3   Social Welfare Spending as Percentage of GDP in Major OECD
Countries, 2014

Sweden	Denmark	France	Germany	UK	US	Japan	Korea	OECD Average
28.1	30.1	31.9	25.8	21.7	19.2	22.1	10.4	21.6

Source: Social Expenditure-Aggregate Data, OECD, 2014c.

5 years old in 2013. As a result, government spending for fertility-related programs rose swiftly from 0.22 percent of GDP in 2006 to 1.01 percent of GDP in 2014.[1]

As mentioned above, the welfare program expanded considerably after the financial crisis, which led to a sharp increase in welfare spending. As shown in Table 12.1, social welfare spending as a ratio of GDP showed a dramatic increase, rising from 4.7 percent in 2000 to 10.6 percent in 2015 and became the lion's share of government expenditures, imposing a heavy burden on public finance. Despite its rapid growth, welfare spending was far below the OECD average of 21.6 percent in 2014 (Table 12.3). Therefore, welfare spending is likely to grow further due to the rapid aging of the population.

12.2   Trends of Income Distribution

Income distribution in Korea has been relatively favorable compared to other developing countries and also improved over time until the early 1990s. For this reason, Korea's development was often cited as a model of growth with equity. A number of indicators support this argument, although some of them are subject to debate.

The sustained economic growth over the last four decades brought about a drastic reduction of absolute poverty. Consequently, the population living below the absolute poverty line, which accounted for almost half the population in the early 1960s, dropped to 7.6 percent in 1993, as shown in Table 12.4.

[1]For details, see Kim (2016, p. 320).

Table 12.4   Trends of Income Distribution, 1961–1993

	1961	1965	1970	1980	1988	1993
Absolute Poverty Rate	48.3	40.9	23.4	9.8	9.5	7.6
Gini Coefficient	—	0.344	0.332	0.389	0.337	0.310
Decile Ratio[a]	—	0.463	0.472	0.354	0.466	0.592

Note: [a]Ratio of income of the poorest 40 percent to the richest 20 percent.

Sources: Suh (1985) and Kwon (1993) for absolute poverty; Korea Statistical Office for the Gini coefficient and decile ratio.

The decile distribution of income, defined as a ratio of the bottom 40 percent to the top 20 percent income, increased until 1970, and after a short decline in 1980 continued to rise until 1993, suggesting that income distribution improved in the 1960s and continued to improve further until the mid-1990s. The same trend of improvement was found in the Gini coefficient, which declined until 1970 and continued to decline until the early 1990s except for the rise in the 1970s.

The relatively equal distribution of income in Korea was attributable to a number of historical and socio-economic factors. A series of historical events such as the destruction of physical capital during the Korean War, land reform, and the disposal of Japanese-owned properties to private individuals in the 1950s had the effect of dispersing income-generating assets. In consequence, not many people were wealthy in the 1950s, positively affecting income distribution. In other words, the initial conditions were favorable for income distribution.

The rapid growth of education following independence also had a favorable impact on income distribution. When Korea was liberated in 1945, the literacy rate was as low as 22 percent. Therefore, great efforts were made to enhance school enrollments by introducing the compulsory primary school system in the 1950s, followed by the removal of middle school and high school entrance exams in the 1960s and 1970s, respectively. Since there was little discrimination in terms of sex, social class, and region, this policy greatly contributed to facilitating equal access to education which resulted in a dramatic rise in school enrollments.

From the 1980s onwards, higher education was also greatly liberalized with the tertiary school enrollment ratio rising sharply from 15.8 percent in 1980 to 39.7 percent in 1990, as high as that of developed countries. This implies that tertiary education also became more or less universal in the 1990s. In consequence, Korea enjoyed a fairly equal distribution of educational opportunities, which had a positive impact on income distribution because it contributes to less inequality in income distribution than otherwise.

Development policy also played an important role in income distribution. The rapid growth through labor-intensive industrial development in the 1960s contributed greatly to improving income distribution by creating job opportunities for the unemployed and underemployed, as well as for the growing labor force which increased almost 3 percent per year. The rapid labor-intensive growth led to a high share of labor income relative to property income and non-wage income. It also kept wage differentials low because the educational attainment of workers did not differ so much in the 1960s. As a result, the Gini coefficient in the 1960s was not only low, but also fell slightly, suggesting that growth was the best distribution policy in this period.

Moving into the 1970s, the situation changed because the economy was overheated due to the HCI drive policy, fueling inflation from the mid-1970s. Wages rose sharply, exceeding productivity growth, and real estate speculation became widespread, resulting in a massive increase in land and housing prices. The consequence was the rapid growth of property income relative to wage income, which became a major source of deteriorating income distribution in the 1970s. It should also be noted that the wage gap between skilled and unskilled workers widened, reflecting rapidly growing demand for technicians and engineers in the HCI sector. As a result, the Gini coefficient rose from 0.332 in 1970 to 0.389 in 1980, and the decile ratio as a ratio of the poorest 40 percent to the richest 20 percent of income dropped from 0.472 to 0.354 during the same period (Table 12.4).

Income distribution began to improve in the 1980s, thanks to various policy measures that favorably affected income distribution. As shown in Table 12.4, the Gini coefficient continued to fall while the decile ratio rose until 1993. Most important was the price stabilization policy which significantly dampened opportunities of windfall profits from real estate speculation, an important source of inflation in the past. As the economy picked up in the second half of the 1980s, the wage gap between skilled and unskilled production workers also narrowed due to the shortage of unskilled workers. The introduction of the minimum wage system coupled with the active labor union movement following the 1986 political democratization further pushed the upward trend of wages of low-level skilled workers. The Gini coefficient thus dropped considerably from the mid-1980s until the early 1990s.

The income distribution which improved until the early 1990s stopped improving further from the mid-1990s. The return to a high growth policy under the Kim Young Sam government and the resulting sustained growth refueled inflation which pushed the prices of real estate up, thereby benefiting property owners. Although wages continued to increase fast, they were not likely to have offset the growth of property income arising from the rise in land and housing prices. In consequence, the income distribution tended to deteriorate from the mid-1990s; the relative poverty rate tended to rise slightly from the mid-1990s, and a similar trend is observed in terms of Gini coefficient and decile ratio, as shown in Fig. 12.1. However, as they remained fairly stable until 1997, one can say that the overall distribution of income tended to improve or at least remained very stable until outbreak of financial crisis in 1997.

A similar trend of income distribution was found in terms of the relative change in income class. As shown in Table 12.5, the ratio of the low-income class earning less than 50 percent of the median income, as well as the high-income class earning 150 percent of the median income and above, fell slightly until 1995, while that of the middle-income class earning 70–150 percent of the median income slightly increased during the same period. This implies that the income distribution tended to improve over time until the mid-1990s.

Income distribution rapidly deteriorated following the 1997 financial crisis which had significant economic and social impacts.

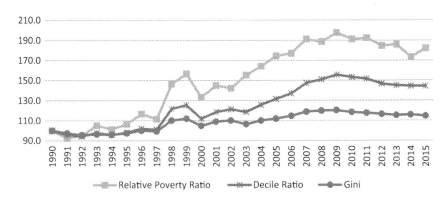

Figure 12.1   Changes in Major Distribution Indicators since the Financial Crisis
(1990 = 100.0)

Notes: Relative Poverty Ratio: Share of income class earning less than 50 percent
of the median income. Decile Ratio: Top 20 percent income as a percentage of
the bottom 20 percent.

Source: Household Survey, Korea Statistical Office.

Table 12.5   Changes in Urban Household Income by Income Class, 1982–2008
(Unit: percent)

	Low-Income Class	Middle-Income Class	Upper-Income Class
1982	11.0	66.7	22.3
1985	11.2	67.4	21.4
1990	7.6	74.2	18.2
1995	9.8	72.0	18.2
2000	10.5	68.5	21.0
2005	13.8	64.7	21.4
2008	14.3	63.3	22.4

Source: Ryu (2009, p. 11).

The decline in employment was dramatic, with the unemployment
rate rising from 2.5 percent in 1997 to 7.4 percent at the end of 1998,
the highest level since 1970. The manufacturing and construction
sectors experienced the largest decline in employment, deteriorating
the labor earnings distribution among production workers. Less educated and unskilled workers suffered the most from wage reduction
and job instability, resulting in the rapid rise of the poverty rate.

On the other hand, people with financial assets benefited greatly from the crisis due to the high interest rate policy which reached nearly 30 percent in early 1998. In consequence, the crisis sharply worsened income distribution, since it severely affected the poor while greatly benefiting financial asset holders.

Income distribution continued to deteriorate as growth remained sluggish after a short recovery in 1999 and 2000, resulting in the rise of the Gini coefficient and the poverty rate (Fig. 12.1). In recent years, however, there were some signs of improvement thanks to government efforts to strengthen the social safety net. Thus, from around 2009, both indicators fell slightly thanks to redistribution through public pensions which played an increasingly important role in poverty reduction. The contribution of public pensions including the Basic Old-Age Pension and Basic Pension to poverty reduction was estimated as high as 76 percent in 2015.[2]

Despite some improvement in recent years, Korea's income distribution cannot be claimed better than the OECD average, because the income gap between the rich and poor is higher than the OECD average. As shown in Fig. 12.2, the income gap between the richest

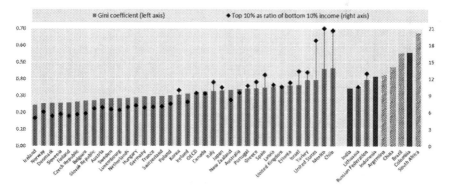

Figure 12.2   International Comparison of the Gini Coefficient and Income Gap between the Richest 10 Percent and Poorest 10 Percent

Source: Society at a Glance, OECD, 2016.

***

[2]Yun (2016, p. 4).

10 percent and the poorest 10 percent in 2014 is higher than the OECD average, although the Gini coefficient is lower.

12.3   Indicator Distribution and Perceived Distribution

We analyzed income distribution in terms of Gini coefficient and decile ratio. However, these indicators have some shortcomings because they do not provide any information on the extent of inequality, which has important implications for distribution. Even if the income of the poor, for example, rose faster than the rich, the absolute income gap between them could be larger due to the big difference in the initial base. Therefore, the poor continue to feel deprived despite higher income growth because of the widening income gap. The crucial problem in income distribution in developing countries is the inequalities in income distribution among different income classes, particularly between the rich and the poor. Therefore, it is worthwhile to examine the income distribution in terms of absolute income change rather than relative income change in order to better understand the implications of inequality and the resulting social consequences.

As shown in Table 12.6, the average income of poverty households, households under the absolute poverty line, increased faster than that of non-poverty households, households above the absolute

Table 12.6   Changes in Poverty Household and Non-Poverty Household Income, 1965–1984 (Unit: KRW 1,000 in 1970 prices)

						Annual Growth Rate (%)				
	1965	1970	1976	1980	1984	1965–1970	1970–1976	1976–1980	1980–1984	1965–1984
Poverty (A)	9.1	15.1	15.3	14.3	16.9	10.8	0.3	−1.8	4.3	3.3
Non-Poverty (B)	22.8	34.1	44.3	55.2	68.5	8.4	4.5	5.7	5.5	6.0
B-A	13.7	19.0	29.0	41.0	51.6	—	—	—	—	—
B/A	2.5	2.3	2.9	3.9	4.1	—	—	—	—	—

Source: Kim (1987, p. 30).

Table 12.7   Changes in Nominal Wages[a] by Income Class, 1976–1985 (Unit: KRW 1,000)

| | 1976 | 1982 | 1985 | Growth Rate (%) | | |
				1976–1982	1982–1985	1976–1985
Upper Class (A)	247	803	1,036	21.7	8.9	17.3
Middle Class (B)	148	436	534	19.7	7.0	15.3
Bottom Class (C)	38	139	175	24.1	8.0	18.5
A-B	99	367	502	—	—	—
B-C	110	297	359	—	—	—
A-C	209	664	861	—	—	—

Note: [a]The weighted average of total monthly salary including bonuses.
Source: Kim (1987, p. 35).

poverty line.[3] The income gap between them has, however, widened instead of narrowing between 1965 and 1970. Thus, poverty households do not feel that distribution has improved despite their higher income growth.

The extent of inequality is also examined in terms of wage income by occupation. All occupations are divided into high-income, middle-income, and low-income classes.[4] As shown in Table 12.7, the nominal wages of low-income occupations rose much faster than those of high- and middle-income occupations during the period 1976–1982. In spite of this, the wage income gap between the low-income class and the two other income classes significantly widened during this period. The wages of low-income occupations continued to grow faster than those of middle-income occupations in the 1980s, but the income gap between them further widened during 1976–1985, in

[3]For an estimation of the absolute poverty line, see Kim (1987, pp. 28–29).

[4]The low-income class comprises blue-collar and simple workers such as miners, traffic guiders, cleaners, harbor workers, simple operators, and assembly workers, while the high-income class covers highly-paid specialists including lawyers, doctors, professors, high-level managers, etc.; meanwhile, technicians, engineers, office workers, managers, pressmen, writers are covered by the middle-income class. This kind of classification is certainly arbitrary, but as the sample accounts for about 40 percent of total employees, it can be said to have representative value. For more details, see Kim (1987, p. 34).

which overall income distribution in terms of the Gini coefficient and decile ratio improved. As a result, there was growing discontent with distribution, despite the sustained high growth of the economy.

The widening income gap between the rich and poor could be tolerated for some time because the poor have the expectation that the disparities would narrow in the near future. However, if such expectations are not realized, people start to complain about distribution, leading to social and political unrest, which became a reality in the 1980s. The radical labor and student movement in the 1980s was, in part, attributable to the growing income gap between the rich and poor, suggesting that the inequality incurred by the growing income gap was far more serious than the Gini coefficient or decile ratio implied. Since the Gini coefficient and decile ratio are no more than simple indicators representing a broad picture of distributional trends, they should be complemented by an income gap analysis in order to better understand the reality of inequality and its social implications.

It should be further noted that the measurement of inequality based on household income data has certain limitations, because the income accruing from speculative investment in real estate is not covered in household income data. This implies that income inequality based on urban household data is underestimated. As a result, there is a widening gap between perceived inequality and statistical inequality. It is well known that in Korea, investment in real estate has been an important means of accumulating wealth due to the soaring prices of real estate. Between 1964 and 1978, the prices of residential land and housing, for example, jumped by more than 30 and 70 times, respectively, whereas wholesale prices rose around five-fold. Thus, those who invested in real estate had enormous windfall gains, resulting in an uneven distribution of wealth which constituted an important source of growing income inequality.

The widening income gap between the rich and poor continued into the 1990s and further aggravated after the 1997 financial crisis, partly due to sluggish growth and partly due to the dual labor market. The labor market is segmented into regular and non-regular workers whose income relative to regular workers dropped from

Table 12.8   Changes in Wages of Regular and Non-Regular Workers, 2005–2014 (Unit: KRW 1,000/month)

	2005	2010	2014	Annual Growth Rate (%)		
				2005–2010	2010–2014	2000–2014
Regular Worker (A)	1,846	2,294	2,604	4.4	3.2	3.9
Non-regular Worker (B)	1,156	1,258	1,453	1.7	3.7	2.6
B/A (%)	62.7	54.8	55.8	—	—	—

Source: Kim (2015, p. 17).

Table 12.9   Changes in Poverty Household and Non-Poverty Household Income, 1996–2003 (Unit: KRW 1,000/month)

	1996	2000	2003	Growth Rate (%)		
				1996–2000	2000–2003	1996–2003
Poverty (A)	324	333	348	0.7	1.5	1.0
Non-Poverty (B)	1,165	1,310	1,464	3.0	3.8	3.3
B-A	841	977	1,116	—	—	—
B/A	3.6	3.9	4.2	—	—	—

Source: Yeo *et al.* (2005, p. 165).

62.7 percent in 2005 to 55.8 percent in 2014 (Table 12.8). Far more striking is the fact that the wages of non-regular workers grew less than that of regular workers, and the same holds true in the case of the income of poverty households against that of non-poverty households, indicating the polarization of income distribution during the post-crisis period (Table 12.9).

Chapter 13

Growth Driving Forces
and Growth Prospects

13.1 The Falling Potential Growth Rate

Since the 1997 financial crisis, economic growth slowed significantly and continued to remain sluggish until very recently. The GDP growth rate, which averaged 4.3 percent during the period 2001–2010, declined to 2.8 percent during the period 2011–2015. As growth continued to remain sluggish, there was increasing apprehension about the growth potential of the Korean economy. According to the Korea Development Institute, as shown in Table 13.1, Korea's potential growth rate has been declining rapidly since the 1990s. It was as high as 8.6 percent in the 1980s and then sharply declined thereafter, falling to approximately 3 percent in the mid-2010s. It is likely to decline further due to rapid population aging and related structural problems.

Korea is one of the most rapidly aging societies with the lowest birth rate in the world. The growth rate of the overall population has been declining steadily and is expected to start contracting from 2030. As a result, the working-age population, defined as a share of the population aged 15–64 years old to the total population, is projected to peak in 2016 and fall rapidly thereafter. Furthermore, working hours have also continued to fall and thus, as shown in Table 13.2, the growth of effective labor supply declined steadily since the early 1990s. Even if the labor force participation rate were to increase slightly, it is very likely that effective labor supply will

Table 13.1   Prospects of Potential Growth Rate, 1981–2050 (Unit: percent)

	GDP	Physical Capital	Employment	TPF
1981–1990	8.6	4.3	1.7	2.5
1991–2000	6.4	3.4	1.2	1.9
2001–2010	4.5	1.9	0.8	1.8
2011–2020	3.6	1.5	0.5	1.6
2021–2030	2.7	1.2	0.0	1.5
2031–2040	1.9	0.8	−0.4	1.5
2041–2050	1.4	0.5	−0.5	1.4

Source: Kim *et al.* (2013, p. 69).

Table 13.2   Growth of Major Labor-Related Factors (Unit: percent)

	1980–1989	1990–1997	1998–2008	2009–2015
Working Age Population	2.44	1.78	1.17	1.19
Economically Active Population	2.47	2.40	1.01	1.44
Employment	2.60	2.39	1.00	1.37
Average Weekly Working Hours	54.86	52.61	48.93	44.29
Employees × Working Hours Growth	2.76	1.65	0.03	1.32

Sources: Samsung Economic Research Institute for 1980–2008; The Bank of Korea for 2009–2015.

record negative growth in the near future, thereby constituting a major factor constraining potential growth. As shown in Table 13.1, the growth of labor input, which has been declining rapidly since the 1990s, is projected to make no contribution to growth from the 2020s.

As a result of rapid aging, the proportion of the population aged 65 and older is expected to increase rapidly, resulting in the rise of the old-age dependency ratio. The old-age dependency ratio, defined as the population aged 65 and older per population aged 15–64 years old, is estimated to rise faster than Japan from 15 percent in 2010 to 38 percent in 2030, with far-reaching impacts on investment, consumption, fiscal balance, and real estate prices, among others.

Capital accumulation, the major contributing factor to growth in the past, also slowed significantly since the early 1990s. Gross fixed capital formation, which increased 5.6 percent per year in the 1990s, dropped to 3.2 percent growth in the 2000s and 2.2 percent growth during 2011–2015 due to the global trade slowdown and increasing outward FDI, which was far greater than inward FDI.

Korean industries are facing strong competition from China, which is rapidly catching up with Korea in capital and technology-intensive industries, while Korea is gradually losing competitiveness owing to high labor costs and slow productivity growth. Some heavy industries such as shipbuilding, steel, and petrochemicals are placed under strong pressure for restructuring. Although the overall corporate leverage remains relatively low, profitability has fallen significantly since the global financial crisis. As a result, the share of vulnerable firms with an interest-coverage ratio below 1.5 rose beyond 35 percent in 2015, with serious implications for corporate investment and economic growth (IMF, 2016, p. 10).

Population aging and the demographic structural change are also expected to depress investment by reducing demand for housing, education, infrastructure, etc. Thus, weak investment is expected to continue in the future with negative impact on growth. According to KDI, as shown in Table 13.1, the contribution of capital input to growth has markedly declined since the early 2000s and is projected to decline further until the 2020s.

In view of the diminishing role of factor inputs, productivity growth is expected to play an increasingly important role in growth, but the prospects are not so encouraging. The Korean economy has enjoyed relatively high total factor productivity growth of over 2 percent until the 1990s. This high productivity growth benefited greatly from the rapid growth of productivity-enhancing factors such as high school enrollment, the market opening of the economy, the expansion of the productive manufacturing sector, and high R&D expenditures. As noted in earlier chapters, the school enrollment ratio is as high as advanced industrial countries, trade is fully liberalized, the manufacturing share of GDP is as high as nearly 30 percent, and the R&D/GDP ratio is among the highest in the

Table 13.3   Potential Growth Rate of Korea, 2001–2018 (Unit: percent)

	Potential Growth Rate	TFP	Capital Input	Labor Input
2001–2006	5.2	2.0	2.2	0.9
2006–2010	3.8	1.4	1.8	0.6
2011–2014	3.4	0.8	1.7	0.9
2015–2018	3.1	0.8	1.4	0.9

Source: Kim *et al.* (2001, p. 30).

world. This implies that these factors have more or less peaked, so that productivity growth based on the quantitative growth of these factors no longer seems sustainable, as evidenced in recent productivity growth.

According to the Bank of Korea, as shown in Table 13.3, total factor productivity growth began to decline sharply from the early 2000s, falling from 2 percent in the 2001–2005 to 0.8 percent in the 2011–2014 and is expected to remain unchanged during 2015–2018. Slowing productivity growth is also projected by KDI, although the degree of the slowdown is much lower than that estimated by the Bank of Korea, as shown in Table 13.1.[1] As the sources that drove high productivity growth in the past are almost exhausted, substantial productivity growth is unlikely unless great efforts are made to improve the quality of productivity-enhancing factors, which require a series of structural as well as institutional reforms.

In this regard, Korea's current situation of rapid aging, slowing growth, and sluggish productivity growth is often compared to that of Japan 20 years ago. As shown in Fig. 13.1, Korea displays a very similar demographic trend and structure, with a lag of around 20 years. Japan's population started to contract in 2010, while in Korea the decline is expected to begin in 2030. Japan's potential

---

[1]Total factor productivity growth as shown in Table 13.1 is not directly comparable with the one in Table 13.3, due to the difference in coverage of period. For the declining productivity growth since the early 2000s, see also IMF Country Report No. 16/278 (2016, p. 39); Chandra and Zhang (2014, p. 7).

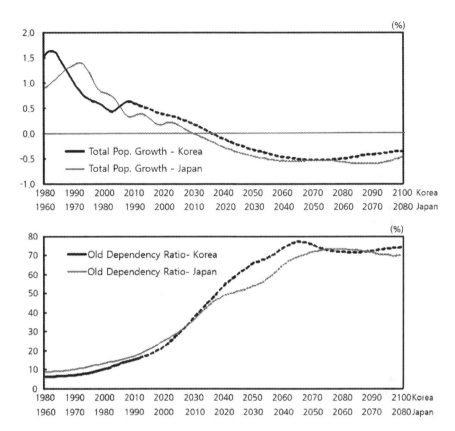

Figure 13.1 Population Growth and Old-Age Dependency Ratio of Korea and Japan

Source: Cho (2015, p. 15).

growth rate plunged from 4 percent in the 1980s to less than 1 percent in the 2000s. In the early 1990s, the decline was primarily the result of decelerating capital formation and total factor productivity growth (Fig. 13.2). Both sluggish investment and productivity growth were to a large extent considered the consequences of delayed restructuring and balance sheet repair.[2]

---

[2]IMF (2016, p. 38).

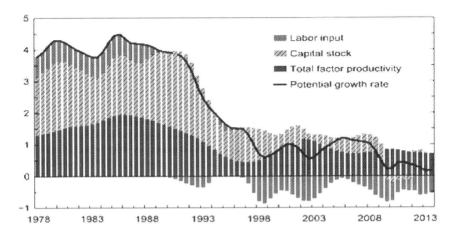

Figure 13.2   Japan's Potential Growth Rate, 1978–2013 (Unit: percent)
Sources: Bank of Japan (2014), quoted from Danninger and Steinberg (2015).

Korea's potential growth rate also dropped rapidly from 5.3 percent in the early 2000s to the 3 percent level in the mid-2010s, which, like Japan, was primarily due to the rapid decline of capital formation and productivity growth. According to the Bank of Korea, the potential growth rate has been on a downward trend since the early 2000s, falling to 3.4 percent in the 2011–2014 period and projected to fall further to 3.1 percent from 2015 to 2018 (Table 13.3). This downward trend is also projected by KDI (Table 13.1).

As shown in Fig. 13.2, Japan's extremely low potential growth remained almost unchanged until the mid-2010s after a short recovery, suggesting that Korea might also face such low potential growth in the near future due to similar structural problems, such as rapid population aging, delayed corporate restructuring, and sluggish productivity growth. Korea also faces other structural challenges such as rising household debt and a rigid labor market, which are all expected to have an adverse effect on potential growth. This suggests that comprehensive structural reforms are required to boost potential growth in order to avoid a protracted period of economic stagnation as experienced by Japan.

13.2 Policy Directions for Raising Potential Growth

As mentioned above, Korea is facing a number of structural problems that exert a downward drag on potential growth. To raise potential growth, comprehensive structural reforms are required aimed at raising labor supply, stimulating private investment, facilitating industrial restructuring, promoting new growth industries, and enhancing productivity growth. Key policy measures directed toward raising potential growth are summarized in the following.

13.2.1 *Increasing Labor Supply and Stimulating Investment*

To cope with the shrinking working-age population and declining working hours, efforts are needed to raise the labor supply by boosting labor force participation, particularly that of women, who are underrepresented in the workforce. The labor force participation rate for women was around 59.6 percent in 2012, lower than the OECD average of around 65 percent. The labor market segmentation into regular and non-regular markets is also detrimental to labor participation and is an important source of income inequality due to the sharp difference in earnings between regular and non-regular workers. Therefore, labor market dualism should be reformed to increase employment and reduce income inequality. Active immigration policies are also called for to raise the level of foreign labor whose share in total labor force is the second-lowest next to Japan among OECD countries.

Weak investment trends are expected to continue due to population aging and related structural problems. Therefore, great efforts are needed to stimulate private investment by reducing barriers to trade and investment. Korea's product market regulation (PMR) indicator was the fourth most stringent in the OECD in 2013 and centered on services, reflecting regulations in network industries such as telecommunications, air transport, retail, professional services, and banking (OECD, 2016, p. 31). Since then, the government made efforts to lower regulatory burdens but was largely unsuccessful due to resistance from the vested interest groups. Regulatory reform has to be accelerated to relax the regulation of key services and network industries, which would not only boost investment but also yield significant productivity gains.

13.2.2 *Upgrading Human Capital Formation*

Along with raising labor force participation and relaxing regulations, efforts should be made to stimulate total factor productivity growth, which has been very sluggish since the early 2000s. Although factors affecting total factor productivity are numerous, there is no doubt that education and R&D play a key role in productivity growth. This seems particularly important in Korea where much remains to be done to enhance the efficiency of education and R&D activities.

With regard to education, it seems imperative to improve the quality of higher education. The excessive expansion of higher education brought about too many universities accompanied by rapid growth in educational spending. Total spending at the tertiary level in 2012 was 2.3 percent of GDP, one of the highest in the OECD. The result was the proliferation of poorly performing tertiary institutions, producing low-quality graduates who failed to meet skill and knowledge levels demanded by the industry, and this led to creating a huge mismatch in the labor market. In 2011, for example, 44.9 percent of university graduates were employed in fields that did not match their field of study, and 23.4 percent of engineering and natural science graduates were also working in mismatched jobs.

Far more serious is the labor market mismatch of advanced degree holders, caused by the overexpansion of graduate schools. The number of local PhDs increased rapidly since the 1980s, with PhDs per 10,000 reaching 2.4 in 2011, which is lower than Switzerland (4.5), Sweden (3.6), and Germany (3.3) but higher than the US (2.3), the Netherlands (2.2), and Japan (1.4).[3] Particularly striking is the rapid growth of PhDs in the area of natural science and engineering, the share of which rose from 39.7 percent in 1991 to 45.1 percent in 2012.[4] As a result, 65 percent of these PhD holders are working

---

[3]Hong (2013, p. 290).
[4]Hong (2013, p. 282).

Table 13.4 Social Rate of Return on Higher Education, 1980–2010 (Unit: percent)

	Junior College		University	
	Men	Women	Men	Women
1980	0.113	0.172	0.153	0.138
1985	0.107	0.179	0.179	0.195
1990	0.088	0.132	0.142	0.150
1995	0.054	0.106	0.098	0.109
2000	0.060	0.103	0.108	0.116
2005	0.051	0.078	0.112	0.106
2010	0.069	0.058	0.114	0.092

Source: Kim *et al.* (2012, p. 42).

in areas that do not require a doctoral degree. This implies that a considerable amount of educational spending has failed to translate into corresponding human capital formation, thereby holding back productivity growth.

Graduates of higher education are also often paid less than the average wage of high school graduates, indicating the low rate of return on higher education. As shown in Table 13.4, the social rate of return on higher education has steadily declined in both junior college and university since the mid-1980s, and in the case of junior college it dropped to 5-6 percent in 2010 which is much lower than 8.5 percent of OECD average. The rate of return in junior college was not only lower than that of university, but also its decline was much steeper pushing high school graduates to enter the university, which in turn led to its excessive expansion. This is, however, unlikely in the future as the number of high school graduates is expected to fall rapidly due to falling birth rate. Therefore, there is an urgent need to close poorly performing tertiary institutions through restructuring while raising their qualities by enhancing competitiveness.

In addition to improving the quality of higher education, vocational education must be strengthened to raise productivity. During the last several decades, educational policy has placed too much emphasis on higher education, hampering vocational education and training. The share of vocational school students relative to academic high school students, which was higher than 50 percent in the 1970s, declined sharply thereafter and fell to 23 percent in 2012, creating great shortages in the skilled labor force. The adult education and lifelong learning systems are also underdeveloped. As a result, only about 50 percent of workers participate in lifelong learning, which is lower than the OECD average, and the proportion of adults with weak skills who participate in adult education is also below the OECD average. Therefore, efforts are needed to strengthen vocational education and training while promoting adult education and lifelong learning programs to improve labor productivity.

13.2.3   *Enhancing the Efficiency of R&D Activities*

As mentioned earlier, Korea has witnessed remarkable growth in R&D spending over the past four decades and became the most R&D-intensive country in the world, investing 4.2 percent of GDP in R&D in 2015. Moreover, the business sector accounts for more than three-quarters of total R&D spending, which is also one of the highest among OECD countries. As mentioned earlier, the problem is that the rapid quantitative growth of R&D was not accompanied by corresponding qualitative growth, indicating low R&D productivity. Therefore, the return on R&D investment must be increased by strengthening basic research; tightening links between universities, public research institutes, and business firms; enhancing the efficiency of government-funded research institutes (GRIs); and supporting the innovation of the service sector and SMEs.

A major cause of low R&D productivity is the weak link between universities, GRIs, and enterprises. For example, 97.9 percent of the R&D financed by enterprises was performed in the business sector in 2014, compared to only 1.3 percent at universities and 0.8 percent at GRIs, indicating the weak linkage across the R&D system. As a result, technology transfer from universities to the business sector is very low, accounting for only 5 percent of company patents compared to around 9 percent in Canada and the US (OECD, 2016, p. 98). Thus, great efforts are required to stimulate R&D cooperation between these institutions to improve technology transfer and commercialization.

In addition to upgrading the quality of universities, the role of universities in R&D should also be reinforced, particularly in basic research, which serves as the key to breakthrough innovations. While universities employ around three-quarters of PhDs, they performed only 9 percent of R&D in 2015, about half the OECD average, and only approximately 20 percent of basic research is carried out by universities compared to 50–75 percent in other OECD countries (OECD, 2016, p. 97). Therefore, the R&D activities of universities must be strengthened to enhance basic research.

Since the early 1960s, Korea pursued state-led technology development relying heavily on GRIs. Accordingly, GRIs have grown rapidly covering a wide area of industrial technology and made significant contributions to enhancing Korea's technological capabilities. However, as they grew bigger and became the main recipient of government-funded R&D projects, the role and efficiency of GRIs encountered a number of problems.

R&D projects carried out by GRIs often overlap with those of private firms and universities. Their R&D activities are increasingly criticized for weak cooperation with universities and private firms. While their R&D activities are mostly oriented toward applied and development research, they have failed to meet the expectations of the private sector, which has significantly expanded its R&D capabilities. In recent years, the R&D performance of GRIs is considered poor, even compared to those of their earlier years in terms of patents, technology exports, technology transfer, and SCI publications, implying their growing inefficiency.[5]

Therefore, it seems necessary to redefine the role of GRIs and strengthen their cooperation with universities and private firms, particularly with SMEs where R&D is low. Firms with less than 250 workers accounted for only 24 percent of total business R&D, compared to the OECD average of 33 percent. GRIs may also play a role in assisting the service sector, which accounted for only 9 percent of business R&D in 2011, well below the OECD average of 38 percent (OECD, 2014a, p. 76).

---

[5]Lee *et al.* (2013, p. 73).

13.2.4 *Promoting New Growth Industries*

Korea relied heavily on the industrial targeting strategy that enabled Korea to catch up with Japan in heavy and chemical industries, which became Korea's leading export sector. As mentioned earlier, these traditional export industries excluding the ICT sector are gradually losing their competitiveness and at the same time face strong competition from China. Confronted with such changing economic environment, the Korean government began to search for future growth industries since the early 2000s. Unlike the previous one, the new industrial policy became more technology-focused, placing an emphasis on promoting R&D and innovation. In other words, the nature of industrial policy changed from industrial targeting to technology targeting focused on the promotion of high-technology industries and venture firms.

In 2001, the Kim Dae Jung government attempted to promote high-technology industries such as information technology, nanotechnology, biotechnology, environmental technology, etc. As the Kim government was primarily concerned with recovery from the financial crisis, no substantial progress was made in promoting high-tech industries except some high-tech venture firms. In 2003, the Roh Moo Hyun government launched a similar program designating ten fields as the engine of next-generation growth and pursued a comprehensive plan for technological development in these future growth engines.[6] In 2008, the Lee Myung Bak government launched the ambitious five-year plan for a green economy, and classified 17 sectors of the economy as new growth engines focused on green technology, such as new and renewable energy, low carbon energy, LEDs, green transportation systems, etc.

These efforts to transform the Korean economy into an innovation-driven economy were continued in 2013 by the Park Geun Hye government under the slogan of "Creative Economy Initiative." The major objective of the initiative was to develop strategic technologies to generate new jobs and revitalize the economy through

---

[6]For details, see Dynamic Korea: A Nation on the Move (2004, pp. 55–59).

innovation, thereby raising the potential growth rate to 4 percent. The Five-Year Basic Plan for Science and Technology (2013–2017) was launched, aimed at enhancing R&D investment and its efficiency, developing strategic technologies, and strengthening support for SMEs and venture firms. The plan was very ambitious, comprising 30 priority and 120 strategic technologies that covered energy, environment, ICT, and healthcare. More specifically, the priorities included smart grids, carbon capture and storage, big data applications, and personalized pharmaceuticals, among others.[7]

However, as the economy continued to remain sluggish, the government policy shifted to structural reforms to bring the economy back to a normal growth path and attempted to carry out reforms in the regulatory system, the public sector, as well as the labor market, which were considered a prerequisite for economic revitalization. The government failed, however, to implement structural reforms due to resistance from the vested interest groups and an associated political crisis, which in the end led to the fall of the Park government in March 2017. In consequence, no substantial progress was made except for the establishment of 17 creative economy innovation centers in major cities to support start-ups.

As mentioned above, many efforts were made to promote new growth industries since the early 2000s, but the results were not satisfactory except for the ICT sector. A number of factors were responsible for this less successful performance. The most important among them seems to be the lack of policy continuity, attributable to the single five-year term of presidency. The five-year period often proves too short to carry out reform programs, particularly technology programs which require a longer period for their proper implementation. As a result, many programs remained unfinished and were usually discarded by the next government irrespective of their economic justification, because the new government wants to have its own policy and programs implemented. This created

---

[7]For details, see OECD (2014b, pp. 198–199), and also see the press releases of Ministry of Science, ICT, and Future Planning (2014) and Ministry of Trade, Industry, and Energy (2015) of the Korean government.

serious policy instability, disrupting the investment decisions of private businesses. To ensure policy consistency, it is imperative to carry out institutional reforms including the revision of the Constitution.

Another related issue is the role of government in pursuing the technology approach to industrial development. Despite the increasing role of the private sector in R&D and innovation, the government continues to retain the dominant role in the decision-making process, so that the selection of programs and projects are usually managed by the government with little room left for private initiatives. Such a strong government-led strategy no longer seems appropriate at the present development stage of the Korean economy, because it could hamper the development of a diffusion-oriented innovation policy, which is crucial for market-oriented industrial development.

Therefore, the role of government should change from manager to fair coordinator and facilitator, leaving much more room for private initiatives in the decision-making process. Thus, an emphasis should be placed on improving the innovation system by creating an ecosystem that promotes start-ups and venture firms, strengthening innovation capacity through more funding for basic research, as well as enhancing the efficiency of R&D and innovation by strengthening links between universities, research institutes, and the business sector.

It was pointed out that the nature of industrial policy since the early 2000s shifted from industrial targeting toward technology targeting. However, this should not be interpreted to imply the complete abolition of the sectoral approach in industrial policy. Sectoral targeting is necessary for various reasons, such as externalities and market failure, or the strategic importance of the sector. For example, when the promotion of knowledge-intensive business services is considered critical for new sources of growth, they need to be promoted. In this case, the technology approach alone may be insufficient, because it requires other types of supports such as investment promotion, skill and training, and design of regulation. Therefore, technology targeting and sectoral targeting should not be considered mutually exclusive.

13.2.5 *Promotion of Service Sector*

Korea's rapid growth in the past was largely driven by the manufacturing sector which came to account for nearly 30 percent of GDP, the highest among OECD countries. Manufacturing-driven growth seems to have reached its limit, since the manufacturing sector is gradually losing its comparative advantage due to rising labor costs and severe competition from the emerging economies, notably China. As shown in Table 13.5, the labor productivity of the Korean manufacturing industry was about 40 percent of US productivity in 2010, and also much lower than those of Japan, Germany, and the UK. The role of the manufacturing sector as an important source of job creation has also significantly diminished due to growing overseas production and labor-saving technical progress, resulting in growth without employment.

Declining manufacturing competitiveness prompted Korean policymakers to consider the service sector as the next stage of development in the light of its increasingly important role in the economy. Although service sector growth lagged behind manufacturing growth, it has been growing fairly steadily, accounting for 57.5 percent of GDP and 68.9 percent of employment in 2011, and is likely to grow further as evidenced in advanced industrial countries where the service economy plays a central role in the growth process. Service sector exports are also growing fairly fast, although their share in total exports is low, accounting for only 16.8 percent in 2009. Over

Table 13.5   Labor Productivity[a] in the Manufacturing and Service Sectors, 2010 (Unit: percent)

	Korea	US	UK	Germany	Japan
Manufacturing (US = 100.0)	38.2	100.0	54.9	62.9	63.0
Services (US = 100.0)	29.7[b]	100.0	64.4	72.8	84.2[c]
Services/Manufacturing (Manufacturing = 100.0)	51.0	65.6	76.9	75.8	87.7

Notes: [a]Value Added per Employee, USD; [b]Korea = 2009; [c]Japan = 2008.
Source: OECD (2014b, p. 168).

2004–2012, service exports grew at an annual rate of 11.8 percent, faster than that of manufactured goods of 10.7 percent.

A fundamental problem faced by the Korean service sector is its extremely low productivity associated with structural weaknesses. Due to the pursuit of manufacturing-led growth strategy, the service sector was given less attention until the 1990s and highly regulated and protected for a long time. The regulatory burdens and lack of competition led to the less efficient use of resources, resulting in low productivity. Korea's service sector labor productivity is one of the lowest among OECD countries (OECD, 2016, p. 75).

As shown in Table 13.5, value added per employee in the service sector was less than a third, and a little over a third, of levels in the US and Japan in 2010, respectively. Service sector productivity as a ratio of manufacturing productivity was also below that of major OECD countries and dropped to 0.51 in 2010, indicating the growing productivity gap between the service sector and manufacturing.

Structural weaknesses and low R&D investment also contributed to low service sector productivity. The service sector is dominated by SMEs with less than 250 employees which accounted for 99.9 percent in 2010, and 98.4 percent were micro-firms with no more than 10 employees and largely engaged in traditional wholesale and retail trade including restaurants with extremely low productivity. On the other hand, knowledge-intensive services such as finance, real estate, and business services were less developed due to entry barriers and restrictive competition, and accounted for only 18.3 percent of service sector value added in 2013, which is far lower than that of the US (33.5 percent), the UK (29.8 percent), and Germany (27.4 percent).[8] Over the period of 2011–2013, only 28 percent of service firms in Korea introduced some type of innovation, which was the lowest in the OECD, and only 6.4 percent of service sector firms were engaged in R&D activity in 2014, compared to 22.3 percent of manufacturing firms.[9]

---

[8] OECD Factbook 2013, quoted from Cho and Kim (2015, p. 181).
[9] OECD Economic Surveys Korea (2016, p. 96).

The government has rolled out a series of policy measures to promote the service sector since the early 2000s. The Roh Moo Hyun government launched a comprehensive promotional program in 2005, selecting 27 priority subsectors covering knowledge-based services, social services, and traditional life-related services. No substantial progress was made, however, because the government failed to carry out regulatory reform and market opening, which were essential framework conditions to promote competition. As mentioned earlier, Korea's PMR was the fourth most stringent among OECD countries in 2013. The service sector was particularly regulated intensely and was subject to 4,336 regulations by 2013, four times higher than the manufacturing sector; this led government policy to focus on regulatory reform in the service sector.[10]

Regulatory reform efforts were continued under the Lee Myung Bak government and strengthened further under the Park Geun Hye government, since it was conceived as an essential part of creative economy initiatives. The regulatory reform was focused on promising service industries which could help strengthen competitiveness, create jobs, and improve quality of life. A number of initiatives were newly introduced, along with the expansion of existing ones including the "cost-in, cost-out (CICO)" system whereby the net cost incurred by a new regulation is offset by the same amount of savings, the adoption of the negative system, the expansion of the Thorn under the Nail and sunset rules, and the Sinmungo system which allows citizens to directly propose regulatory reform. Seven service industries, namely medical care, tourism, culture, education, finance, logistics, and software, were selected as promising industries, and regulatory reform was directed at promoting market competition and pioneering new export markets in these industries.[11]

Considerable progress has been made in regulatory reform, as reflected in the number of service sector regulations which fell from 4,336 in 2013 to 3,443 as of June 2015. Nonetheless, the service sector still seemed heavily regulated, since the number of service

---

[10]OECD (2016, p. 84).
[11]For details see, OECD (2016, pp. 87–89).

sector regulations accounted for more than half of the regulations registered on the portal site as of June 2015, which totaled 6,378. The regulations were concentrated in finance, logistics, education, medical care, media and information, and real estate (Park, 2015, p. 106). Therefore, further efforts are needed to accelerate regulatory reform, particularly in such high value-added fields as medical care, tourism and culture, and business services so as to enhance their competitiveness.

The promotion of the service sector certainly requires more than regulatory reform. It has to be supported by other policy measures including fiscal and financial incentives for investment and R&D. The incentive system favoring the manufacturing has to be ended by ensuring equal treatment between services and manufacturing in order to facilitate the balanced development of the two sectors. Human capital in the service sector should also be fostered, and barriers to international trade and investment liberalized so as to promote competition.

Chapter 14

The Korean Development Model: Characteristics and Lessons

Korea's outstanding economic and social performance is attributable to the interaction of various factors whose relative importance cannot be easily gauged. Political stability and strong leadership commitment to development were prerequisites for economic development. The labor force in the 1960s was cheap, but educated and industrious. This backlog of human capital combined with the formulation of an outward-oriented development strategy laid the foundation for remarkable economic achievement.

The essence of Korea's success story lies in its successful industrialization policy, which enabled Korea to enjoy sustained high growth over the past half century, emerging as a new industrial power within a relatively short span of time. What were the underlying factors behind this remarkable achievement? It seems, therefore, worthwhile to highlight the important features of Korea's development process in terms of development strategy, role of government, incentive system, and related issues to draw lessons from the Korean development experience. The most important features and lessons from the Korean experience can be summarized as follows.

First, the government played a key role in initiating as well as promoting economic development, particularly in the early stage of development. In the early 1960s, Korea was caught in a state of low-level equilibrium trap characterized by low savings and investment rates, low growth, and high population growth. In order to break the vicious circle of poverty, the government pursued a state-led development strategy, intervening directly in resource allocation and setting industrialization as the primary goal of development policy. It actively engaged in steering the development process in terms of reforming the administration, coordinating investment activities, targeting certain industries for promotion, and undertaking direct investment in key industries and infrastructure development. In other words, the government played the role of a prime mover in the development process until the 1970s.

Second, the strong leadership commitment to development, supported by an efficient bureaucracy, played a crucial role in the successful implementation of development plans. President Park led the development policy in the 1960s and 1970s by launching the construction of the Seoul–Busan Highway, the HCI drive, and the New Village (Saemaul) Movement. It is further noteworthy that President Park constantly monitored the performance of development policies by presiding over various meetings such as the Monthly Export Promotion Meeting and the Monthly Economic Review Meeting.

The strong leadership commitment to development also placed the bureaucracy under strong pressure to formulate realistic policy measures. Elite bureaucrats were rewarded with various incentives such as promotions and overseas training, which strongly motivated them to work hard. They became the leading force in decision-making processes and policy formulation, and were able to design development strategies and policies based on rational economic reasoning, as they were completely shielded from political pressure groups.

Third, the importance of the role of market in Korea's development process should not be overlooked. Although the government intervened extensively in resource allocation, it also attempted to nurture the functioning of the market mechanism by gradually liberalizing the economy. In the 1960s, the government began to liberalize trade, first in exports, followed by import liberalization. The import liberalization policy was suspended in the 1970s due to worsening balance of payments difficulties and the industrial policy shift toward promoting the heavy and chemical industry.

Moving into the 1980s, the government made renewed efforts for liberalization, because policymakers realized that given the growing complexity of the economy, resource allocation should be gradually left to market forces. Thus, the liberalization policy went far beyond the trade regime, extending to financial, industrial, technology, and competition policies. The liberalization policy accelerated in the 1990s, as the Korean economy was rapidly integrated into the world economy. Although the liberalization policy was hit by the 1997 financial crisis due to policy failures, there is no doubt that it made a significant contribution to Korea's rapid growth and development until the mid-1990s.

Fourth, the government adopted different policies at different stages of development to cope with changing economic environments. In the 1950s, the government, while rehabilitating the war-torn economy, made efforts to lay the groundwork for development by undertaking land reform, expanding education, and facilitating private ownership of properties, which greatly contributed to building the institutional basis for capitalistic market-oriented development in Korea.

In the 1960s, an outward-oriented industrial development policy was pursued to facilitate growth through the exports of light man-ufactured products, in which Korea had a comparative advantage. In the 1970s, the heavy and chemical industries were promoted to cope with rising protectionism for labor-intensive industries in developed countries. When serious structural problems were caused by the heavy and chemical industry drive, the government quickly responded in the early 1980s by undertaking a series of market-friendly policy reforms to enhance industrial competitiveness while stabilizing the economy. This greatly contributed to regaining industrial competitiveness and sustaining growth. In other words, the strong policy adaptability to changing economic environments enabled the Korean economy to enjoy sustained high growth without serious disruptions until the mid-1990s.

Fifth, different incentive schemes were applied at different stages of industrial development. Tariff and non-tariff measures were primarily used to promote industries in the early stage of industrial development, followed by fiscal and financial measures to stimulate investment for their growth. As the industries reached a certain stage of development, the policy shifted toward enhancing their competitiveness by providing incentives for innovation and R&D activities, while opening up the market. It should also be noted that the incentive system was not industry or market neutral but selective, supporting priority industries through trade restrictions, subsidies, and credit allocation. It was gradually replaced by a functional system to support industrial innovation and technology development.

In this regard, it is important to note that incentives were provided in exchange for concrete performance criteria to ensure effective policy implementation. For example, preferential export credit was provided in exchange for export performance; tax and financial assistance for HCIs was provided based on investment activity. The industrial rationalization program was implemented by providing assistance in exchange for capacity reduction and the production of certain designated vehicles, etc. The matching fund system was used for technology development, obliging participating firms to contribute a certain proportion of R&D investment. This kind of performance- or reciprocity-based assistance made the government support more effective and productive.

Sixth, the Korean experience suggests that the import substitution policy needs to be complemented by manpower and technology policy. Korea is one of a handful of countries that succeeded in infant industry protection. The HCIs in the 1970s were heavily protected and supported by the government, which led to overinvestment and inefficiency. Korea was able to overcome these problems by introducing a series of policy measures for structural adjustment and industrial innovation, while opening up the market. In other words, the carrot and stick policy was implemented by exposing private firms to foreign competition while offering them various incentives for R&D and manpower development. These combined policy efforts played a decisive role in enhancing the industrial competitiveness of HCIs, indicating that trade and financial policy alone is insufficient and should be complemented by manpower and technology policy for the successful implementation of import substitution policy.

Seventh, science and technology policy played a critical role in Korea's successful industrialization. The Korean government placed a strong emphasis on science and technology development as early as 1962, when the first five-year development plan was launched. Policymakers knew that given Korea's poor natural resource endowment, manpower and technology development would be the most effective way to facilitate the industrialization process. The five-year science and technology promotion plan was formulated as an integral part of the overall development plan. More importantly, the five-year manpower development plan was prepared separately to estimate future needs in various skill levels, and a manpower survey was conducted every 2 years to support the manpower development plan. It is remarkable and perhaps unique in developing countries that the government realized the importance of manpower and technology development at such an early development stage and made deliberate policy efforts to promote it.

In the 1960s, when the export drive policy was pursued, emphasis was placed on skill formation through reinforcing vocational education and training. In the 1970s, science and technology policy was directed to support the HCI drive by strengthening engineering education and indigenous technological capability building. The government set up a number of specialized state-funded research institutes, invited Korean scientists from abroad, and continued to strengthen the supply of technicians and engineers to meet the increasing demand for them.

In the 1980s, when trade liberalization was pursued, the government intensified its support toward private R&D and industrial innovation in order to enhance industrial competitiveness. Moving into the 1990s, the science and technology policy shifted from imitation to innovation, because the catch-up industrial development strategy was no longer sustainable due to rising labor costs and growing technology protectionism in developed countries. Thus, an emphasis was placed on the promotion of venture firms and high-tech industries accompanied by support toward basic research.

Eighth, the Korean experience suggests the importance of social and political stability in the development process. The rapid growth of the Korean economy, which began in the early 1960s, would not have been possible without social and political stability. The social environment was conducive to economic development since Korea had a homogenous society with no serious regional or religious conflicts. Korea's political environment was also, in general, favorable to economic development until the 1990s. There was some political crisis in the late 1970s and the late 1980s, but it did not last long enough for the economy to suffer severely.

Finally, it should be mentioned that Korea's outstanding economic performance has not been without costs, as evidenced by the financial crisis in 1997 which had a far-reaching impact on the Korean economy. If the crisis had been avoided, the income distribution, poverty, and growth problems would not be as serious as we face today. Three fundamental factors seem to have been responsible for the crisis, which can be summarized as follows.

First, the fundamental underlying cause of the crisis is closely related to the high growth policy, which the Korean government pursued over four decades from the 1960s through the 1990s, except under the Chun Doo Hwan government. Since the economy grew beyond its potential growth rate, it suffered from chronic inflation and balance of payment difficulties for decades, which resulted in growing external debt. The Chun Doo Hwan government was aware of these problems and implemented wide-ranging reform measures focused on growth with stability. This policy was highly successful in combating inflation and improving balance of payments difficulties, so that the external debt was considerably reduced by the end of the 1980s (Table 14.1).

Unfortunately, the stability-oriented policy was discontinued as the Roh Tae Woo government returned to a growth-oriented policy in 1989. President Roh initially tried to maintain the stability-oriented policy, but soon faced strong resistance from the large conglomerates that became increasingly powerful after the government lifted

Table 14.1   Growth, Inflation, Wages, Balance of Payments, and External Debt, 1985–1997, Selected Years (Unit: percent)

	GDP Growth	CPI Increase	Wage Increase	Current Account (USD million)	Total External Debt (USD million)
1985	7.5	2.5	9.2	−795	57,255
1987	12.3	3.1	10.1	10,058	49,601
1989	6.8	5.7	21.1	5,344	43,375
1991	9.7	9.3	17.5	−8,417	55,657
1993	6.3	4.8	12.2	821	67,330
1995	8.9	4.5	11.2	−8,665	119,799
1996	7.2	4.9	11.9	−23,120	157,363
1997	5.8	4.4	7.0	−8,287	174,231

Sources: National Accounts 2009, The Bank of Korea; The 60-Year History of the Korean Economy-1 (2010, appendix tables 2-6, 2-7, 2-9, 2-10).

controls on them. On the other hand, wage hikes associated with the democratization movement weakened the competitiveness of Korean industries, resulting in the considerable slowdown of exports and growth in 1989. This prompted the Roh Tae Woo government to return to a growth-oriented policy, which continued further under the Kim Young Sam government to stimulate the economy.

Although the policy was successful in terms of growth, it led to inflation and balance of payments deterioration cumulating foreign debt. As shown in Table 14.1, external debt, which declined from the mid-1980s, began to rise rapidly from the early 1990s. This implies that if the stability-oriented policy did continue under the Roh Tae Woo and Kim Young Sam governments, it would have been possible for the government to maintain external debt at a manageable level, thereby avoiding the financial crisis. The Korean government and business people were accustomed to high economic growth for so long that it was not easy for them to get rid of it, and in the end they paid a very high price for it.

The second fundamental factor related to the first was the policy failure to control chaebols. Chaebols were effectively controlled by the government until the Chun Doo Hwan government by means of carrot and stick policy. After political democratization in 1987, however, state control over chaebols weakened considerably, resulting in the increasing concentration of their economic power. Efforts were made to regulate chaebols under the Roh Tae Woo government and the Kim Young Sam government through various policy measures, such as cross-shareholding regulations and the basket control of credit, etc., but they were ineffective because the government feared that the bankruptcy of chaebols would potentially have a negative impact on the economy, and this led to the over-investment and over-diversification of chaebols. The collusive relation built up between businessmen and politicians also dampened the effectiveness of government policy, illustrated by Samsung's entry into the already overcrowded automobile market in 1994.

As a result, chaebols continued to grow fast, occupying an increasing share of production and employment. As shown in Fig. 7.1, the shipment share of the 100 largest companies in mining and manufacturing, which decreased during the 1980s, began to rise in the 1990s. Chaebols became even more powerful as they helped politicians through campaign contributions and exerted a strong influence on public policy. The government was forced to heed the voices of chaebols when formulating policies because of their dominant position in the economy. In the early 1990s, for example, the government knew that the Korean won was considerably overvalued, but did not take any corrective action influenced by pressure from business groups. The reason was that the depreciation of the exchange rate would trigger inflation and increase the debt service burden of big corporations, which were heavily leveraged. Thus, the overvalued exchange rate remained unchanged, which led to encouragement of excessive foreign borrowings.

Third, institutional factors also played an important role in the eruption of the crisis. A series of deregulation and liberalization measures were implemented in the early 1990s in trade, finance, and corporate sectors to facilitate market-led development. Influenced by the global movement toward liberalization, policymakers believed that liberalization and deregulation would lead to efficient resource allocation, thereby sustaining high growth while resolving much of the structural problems that plagued the Korean economy. However, this government policy largely failed because of institutional deficiencies. Financial liberalization failed to improve the efficiency of the financial sector due to the pervasive moral hazard of "too big to fail," and the lack of a strong regulatory and supervisory framework. Instead, it aggravated the situation as it led to huge corporate debt and non-performing loans.

The government also dismantled the selective industrial policy which, among others, monitored the investment activities of chaebols. There was no longer an effective control and coordination mechanism that could keep a check on the excessive competition among chaebols. The liberalization and deregulation policy was originally conceived to promote competition in order to activate a self-regulating market mechanism. However, the policy failed to change the management behavior and business patterns of chaebols, because government control over them had grown considerably weak following the financial liberalization. No longer controlled by the government, chaebols expanded their investment through debt financing and cross-debt guarantee practices among their affiliates, which led to overinvestment and overdiversification.

In consequence, the government's liberalization and deregulation policy ended up aggravating the structural problems of the Korean economy, as reflected in the rise of the current account deficit and the rapid increase of non-performing loans from late 1996. In response, the Kim Young Sam government attempted to reform labor laws to enable layoffs for structural adjustment, as well as to reform the financial sector to strengthen the prudential regulation of financial institutions. However, the Kim government failed due to the lame-duck phenomenon, which is inevitable in a single-term presidency. Politicians, labor unions, and even bureaucrats did not support the president because they knew he was set to lose his power very soon, indicating that the institutional weakness inherent in Korea's political system also contributed to the failed reform attempts.

References

Ahn, Chong Jik, *The Future Directions for the Korean Economy*, Dong A Publishing Company, Seoul, 1962 (in Korean).

Amsden, A. H., *Asia's Next Giant*, Oxford University Press, New York, 1989.

Amsden, A. H., "Diffusion of Development: The Late-Industrializing Model and Greater East Asia", *The American Economic Review*, Vol. 81, No. 2, pp. 282–286, May, 1991.

Bahl, R., Kim, Chuk Kyo, and Park, Chong Kee, *Public Finances During the Korean Modernization Process*, Harvard University Press, Cambridge, Massachusetts, 1986.

Balassa, B., "The Process of Industrial Development and Alternative Development Strategies", in B. Balassa (ed.), *The Newly Industrializing Countries in the World Economy*, Pergamon Press, New York, 1981.

Balassa, B., "Korea's Development Strategy", in Jene K. Kwon (ed.), *Korean Economic Development*, Greenwood Press, New York, 1990.

Ban, Sung Hwan, Moon, Pal Yong, and Perkins, D. H., Rural Development, Harvard University Press, Cambridge, Massachusetts, 1980.

Bank of Korea, National Accounts 2009, 2010.

Bank of Korea, National Accounts 2014, 2015.

Baygan, G., Venture Capital Policy Review: Korea, OECD, 2003.

Chandra, S. J. and Zhang, Longmei, "How can Korea Boost Potential Output to Ensure Continued Income Convergence?" IMF Working Paper, International Monetary Fund, Washington, D.C., 2014.

Chang, Ha-Joon, *The Political Economy of Industrial Policy*, St. Martin's Press, New York, 1994.

Chang, Ha-Joon, Park, Hong-jae, and Yoo, Chul Gyue, "Interpreting the Korean Crisis: Financial Liberalization, Industrial Policy and Corporate Governance", *Cambridge Journal of Economics*, Vol. 22, No. 6. pp. 735–746, 1998.

Chang, Soo Myung, Kong, Eun Bae, and Lee, Han Il, "Role of Education in Enhancing Industrial Competitiveness", Korea Educational Development Institute, 2004 (in Korean).

Chun, Sang Keun, *Science and Technology Policy in Korea: A Testimony by a Former Policy Maker*, Jung Woo Publishing Company, Seoul, 1982 (in Korean).

Cho, Dong Chul, "Will Korean Economy Repeat 20 Years Stagnation of Japanese Economy", Paper presented at KDI Policy Seminar, August 27, 2015 (in Korean).

Cho, Byoung Kyu and Kim, Ju Hoon, "Institutional Reform for Creating Labor Demand", Paper presented at KDI Policy Seminar, July 7, 2015 (in Korean).

Cho, Soon, "The Dynamics of Korean Economic Development", Institute for International Economics, Washington, D.C. 1994.

Choi, Sung No, "Thirty Largest Business Groups", Korea Economic Research Institute, 2000 (in Korean).

Choi, Sung No, "Large-scale Business Groups in Korea", Korea Economic Research Institute, 2001 (in Korean).

Chosun, Ilbo, "Korea's University Advancement Rate 82%, Highest in the OECD", May 24, 2011 (in Korean).

Committee for Sixty Year History of the Korean Economy, "Sixty Year History of the Korean Economy-I", 2010 (in Korean).

Committee for Sixty Year History of the Korean Economy, "Sixty Year History of the Korean Economy-II", 2010 (in Korean).

Committee for Sixty Year History of the Korean Economy, "Sixty Year History of the Korean Economy-III", 2010 (in Korean).

Committee for Sixty Year History of the Korean Economy, "Sixty Year History of the Korean Economy-Summary", 2011 (in Korean).

Danninger, S. and Steinberg, C., "Japan's Growth Challenge: Needs and Potential", in D. Botman, S. Danninger, and J. Schiff (eds.), *Can Abenomics Succeed?* International Monetary Fund, Washington D.C., 2015.

Frank, Jr., C. R., Kim, Kwang Suk, and Westphal, L., Foreign Trade Regimes and Economic Development: South Korea, National Bureau of Economic Research, New York, 1975.

Haggard, S., *Pathways from the Periphery: The Politics of Growth in the Newly Industrializing Countries*, Cornell University Press, Ithaca and London, 1990.

Hahm, Joon-Ho and Mishkin, F. S., "Causes of the Korean Financial Crisis: Lessons for Policy", Korea Development Institute, Mimeo. 1999.

Hahn, Chin Hee, Choi, Kyung Soo, Kim, Dong Suk, and Lim, Kyung Mook, *Prospects of Potential Growth Rate of the Korean Economy: 2003–2012*, Korea Development Institute, 2002 (in Korean).

Hahn, Chin Hee and Shin, Sukha, "Understanding the Post-crisis Growth of the Korean Economy: Growth Accounting and Cross-country Regressions", in Takatoshi Ito and Chin Hee Hahn (eds.), *The Rise of China and Structural Changes in Korea and Asia*, Edward Elgar, Northampton, Massachusetts, 2010.

Hirschman, A. O., "The Changing Tolerance for Income Inequality in the Course of Economic Development", *Quarterly Journal of Economics*, pp. 544–65, 1973.

Hong, Sung Chan, "Expansion and Limitation of Research-Oriented Universities in Korea", in Ki Wan Kim and Ju Ho Lee (eds.), *Studies on Innovation for National R&D System*, Korea Development Institute, 2013 (in Korean).

Hwang, In Hak, "Economic Concentration: Looking from Korean Perspective", Korea Economic Research Institute, 1997 (in Korean).

Hwang, In Hak and Choi, Won Rak, "Regulation of Economic Concentration: What are the Issues?", *Regulation Research*, Vol. 22, 2013 (in Korean).

International Monetary Fund, "Republic of Korea", IMF Country Report No. 16/278, 2016.

Joh, Sung Wook, "The Korean Corporate Sector: Crisis and Reform", Korea Development Institute, November 1999.

Johnson, C., "What is the Best System of National Economic Management for Korea", Institute of Public Policy Studies, Seoul, October 11, 1991.

Jones, L. P. and Sakong, Il, *Government, Business, and Entrepreneurship in Economic Development: The Korean Case"*, Harvard University Press, Cambridge, Massachusetts, 1980.

Kang, Kwang Ha, Lee, Yung Hoon, and Choi, Sang Oh, "Policymaking System during Korea's High Growth Period", Korea Development Institute, 2008 (in Korean).

Kang, Seung Kook, Lee, Kwang Hyun, Park, Hyun Jung, and Kim, Ki Suk, Educational Indicator Analysis of 60 Years Educational Development of Korea, Korea Educational Development Institute, 2005 (in Korean).

Kang, Hwan Koo, Kim, Do Wan, Park, Jae Hyun, and Han, Jin Hyun, "Estimation of Potential Growth Rate of the Korean Economy", The Bank of Korea, 2011 (in Korean).

Kim, Bok Soon, "Wages in 2014 and Wages Prospects in 2015", Korea Labor Institute, 2015 (in Korean).

Kim, Chuk Kyo, "Productivity Analysis of Korean Export Industries", Working Paper 7203, Korea Development Institute, June 1972.

Kim, Chuk Kyo, "Industrial Growth and Productivity Change", in Toshio Watanabe and Woo Hee Park (eds.), *Economic Development of Korea*, Bunshindo, Tokyo, 1983 (in Japanese).

Kim, Chuk Kyo and Lee, Chul Heui, "Ancillary Firm Development in the Korean Automotive Industry", in Konoske Odaka (ed.), *The Motor Vehicle Industry in Asia*, Singapore University Press, 1983.

Kim, Chuk Kyo, Ryu, Ji Sung, and Hwang, Kyu Ho, "Productivity Analysis of Manufacturing Industry in Korea, Taiwan and Japan", Insititute of Economic Research, Hanyang University, 1984 (in Korean).

Kim, Chuk Kyo, "Industrial Policy of Taiwan", Korea Economic Research Institute, 1984 (in Korean).

Kim, Chuk Kyo, Income Distribution between Poverty and Non-Poverty Income Group, *Hanyang Journal of Economic Studies*, Vol. 8. No. 2, Institute of Economic Research, Hanyang University, 1987 (in Korean).

Kim, Chuk Kyo, "Government Policy and Industrial Innovation in Korea", Paper Presented at International Symposium on Technological Competition in the 21st Century, August 1987, Duisburg, Germany, Revised Version to appear in *Hanyang Journal of Economic Studies*, Vol. 9. No. 1, 1988.

Kim, Chuk Kyo, "On the Origins of the Korean Financial Crisis: An Institutional Approach", Duisburg Working Paper, N0.55/2000, Duisburg, Germany, 2000.

Kim, Chuk Kyo, "Development Planning and Policy-Making Process in Korea", in Chuk Kyo Kim (ed.), *Korea's Development Policy Experience and Implications for Developing Countries*, Korea Institute for International Economic Policy, 2008a.

Kim, Chuk Kyo, "Liberalization Policy in Korea's Development Process", in Chuk Kyo Kim (ed.), *Korea's Development Policy Experience and Implications for Developing Countries*, Korea Institute for International Economic Policy, 2008b.

Kim, Chuk Kyo, "Korea's SMEs Development Policy and Its Implications for Indonesia", in Chuk Kyo Kim (ed.), *Korea's Development Policy Experience and Implications for Developing Countries*, Korea Institute for International Economic Policy, 2008c.

Kim, Chuk Kyo, *Economic Development of Korea*, Pak Young Publishing Company, Seoul, 2012 (in Korean).

Kim, Chuk Kyo, *Economic Development of Korea*, 2nd edition, Pak Young Publishing Company, Seoul, 2016 (in Korean).

Kim, Chung Kon, Choi, Bo Yung, Lee, Bo Ram, and Lee, Min Yung, "SME Support Strategy for Overseas Investment in Major Countries", Korea Institute for International Economic Policy, 2014 (in Korean).

Kim, Chung Yum, Thirty Year History of Korean Economic Policy, *Chung Ang Daily News*, Seoul, 1990 (in Korean).

Kim, Dong Suk, Kim, Jin Myun, and Kim, Min Soo, "Analysis of Sources of Korea's Economic Growth: 1963–2000", Korea Development Institute, 2002 (in Korean).

Kim, Eun Mee, "Contradictions and Limits of a Developmental State: with Illustrations from the South Korean Case", University of Southern California, January 1992, Mimeo.

Kim, Jae Won, "Initial and Further Vocational Training in Korea", Paper presented in Korean–German–Japanese Symposium on Technological Development and Vocational Education and Training, Kyung Hee University, November 1986.

Kim, Hwan Koo, Kim, Do Wan, Park, Jae Hyun, and Han, Jin Hyun, Estimation of Potential Growth Rate of the Korean Economy, The Bank of Korea, 2001 (in Korean).

Kim, Namdoo, "Measuring the Costs of Visible Protection in Korea", Institute for International Economics, Washington, D.C., 1996.

Kim, Kwang Suk, "Evolution of Korea's Industrial and Trade Policies", Institute for Global Economics, Seoul, 2001 (in Korean).

Kim, Kwang Suk, "Korea" in D. Papageorgiu, M. Michaely, and A. M. Choksi (eds.), *Liberalizing Foreign Trade: Korea, Philippines, and Singapore*, Cambridge: Basil Blackwell, 1991.

Kim, Mi Ran, Kim, Kyung Jong, Choi, Soo Jung, and Nam, Ki Kon, "Analysis of Social Economic Effects of Vocational Education Investment", Korea Research Institute for Vocational Education and Training, 2012 (in Korean).

Kim, Seung Tae, Hwang, Soo Kyung, Lee, Jun Sang, and Shin, Suk Ha, "Long-term Macroeconomic Prospects of Korean Economy", Korea Development Institute, 2013 (in Korean).

Kim, Young Hwa, Park, Yong Hyun, and Han, Sung Hi, "Education and National Development in Korea (1945–1995)", Korea Educational Development Institute, 1997 (in Korean).

Kim, Won Kyu, "Total Factor Productivity Analysis by Size of Firms", Issue Paper 2012-279, Korea Institute for Industrial Economics and Trade, June 2012 (in Korean).

Koh, Young Sun, "Korea's Economic Growth and Role of Government", Korea Development Institute, 2008 (in Korean).

Korea Development Institute, "Comprehensive Study of Korea's Industrial Competitiveness — Statistical Data", 2003 (in Korean).

Korea Educational Development Institute, "Korea's Educational Indicators", 1997 (in Korean).

Korea Development Bank, "Long-Term Prospects of Capital Goods Industry", 1989 (in Korean).

Korea Development Bank, Fifty Year History of Korea Development Bank, 2004 (in Korean).

Korea Federation of SMEs, "SMEs Status Indicators", 2014 (in Korean).

Krueger, A. O., *The Developmental Role of the Foreign Sector and Aid*, Harvard University Press, Cambridge, Massachusetts, 1979.

Krueger, A. O., "Industrial Development and Liberalization", in L. B. Krause and Kim Kihwan (eds.), *Liberalization in the Process of Economic Development*, University of California Press, Berkeley, 1991.

Krueger, A. O., "Korean Industry and Trade over Fifty Years", in Dong-Se Cha, Kwang Suk Kim, D. H. Perkins (eds.), *The Korean Economy 1945–1995: Performance and Vision for the 21st Century*, Korea Development Institute, 1997.

Krueger, A. O. and Yoo, Jungho, "Falling Profitability, Higher Borrowing Costs, and Caebol Finances During the Korean Crisis", in D. T. Coe and Se Jik Kim (eds.), *Korean Crisis and Recovery*, IMF and KIEP, Seoul, 2002.

Krugman, P., "What happened to Asia", MIT, Mimeo, 1998.

Kwon, Soonwon, "Social Policy in Korea: Challenges and Responses", Korea Development Institute, 1993.

Lee, Chung Hoon, "Preparing Korea for Global Competition in the 21st century: An Agenda for Institutional Reform", East-West Center, Mimeo, 1999a.

Lee, Dae Gun, "Korean Economy: 1945–1950s", Samsung Research Institute, Seoul, 2002 (in Korean).

Lee, Hahn-Been, "Korean Development from the Socio-Cultural Perspective", Paper presented at International Forum on Trade and Development Policies, Korea Development Institute, June 11–20, 1985.

Lee, Jae Hyung, "Analysis of Competition Structure and Industrial Concentration of Korean Mining, Manufacturing and Service Sector", Korea Development Institute, 2007 (in Korean).

Lee, Jae Hyung, "Korea's Industrial Organization and Market Structure", Korea Development Institute, 2013 (in Korean).

Lee, Jaemin, "East Asian NIEs' Model of Development: Miracles, Crisis and Beyond", *The Pacific Review*, Vol. 12, No. 2, pp. 141–162, 1999b.

Lee, Ju Ho, Kim, Ki Wan, and Hong, Seong Chang, "Diagnosis of National R&D System", in Ki-Wan Kim and Ju-Ho Lee (eds.) *Innovation in National R&D Mechanism: Recommendations for Creative Economy*, Korea Development Institute, 2013 (in Korean).

Lee, Ju Ho, Chung, Hyuk, and Hong, Seung Chang, "Is the Korea First Class Human Capital Country?", in Yong Sung Kim and Ju Ho Lee (eds.) *Comprehensive Study on New Directions for Human Capital Policy*, Korea Development Institute, 2014 (in Korean).

Lee, Hong Jik and Chang, Jun Hyuk, "Analysis of Slowing Service Sector Growth", Research Paper 2007-20, The Bank of Korea, 2007 (in Korean).

Lee, Kye-Sik and Moon, Hyung-Pyo, "Public Management Reform in Korea: Progress to Date and Future Directions", in Lee-Jay Cho, Yoon Hyung Kim, and Chung H. Lee (eds.), *Restructuring the National Economy*, Korea Development Institute, 2001.

Lee, Kyu Uck, "Market Structure and Monopoly Regulation, Korea Development Institute", 1977 (in Korean).

Lee, Kyu Uck and Yoon, Chang Ho, "Theory of Industrial Organization", Bupmoon Publishing Company, Seoul, 1993 (in Korean).

Lee, Suk-Chae, "The Heavy and Chemical Industries Promotion Plan", in Lee-Jay Cho and Yoon Hyung Kim (eds.), *Economic Development in the Republic of Korea*, University of Hawaii Press, Honolulu, Hawaii, 1991.

Lewis, W. A., *The Theory of Economic Growth*, Richard D. Irwin, Inc. Homewood, Illinois, 1955.

Lim, Wonhyuk, "Public Enterprise Reform and Privatization in Korea: Lessons for Developing Countries", Korea Development Institute, 2003.

Lim, Wonhyuk, "Reflections on Korea's Development" in *From Despair to Hope: A Memoir by Kim Chung-yum*, Korea Development Institute, 2011.

Mason, Edward S., Kim, Mahn Je, Perkins, D. H., Kim, Kwang Suk, and Cole, D. C., *The Economic and Social Modernization of the Republic of Korea*, Harvard University Press, Cambridge, Massachusetts, 1980.

Mathews, J. A., "Fashioning a new Korean Model out of the Crisis: The rebuilding of institutional capabilities", *Cambridge Journal of Economics*, Vol. 22. No. 6. pp. 747–759, 1998.

McGinn, N. F., Snodgrass, D. R., Kim, Yung Bong, Kim, Shin-Bok, and Kim, Quee-Young, *Education and Development in Korea*, Harvard University Press, Cambridge, Massachusetts, 1980.

Ministry of Education, Science and Technology, *2009 Science and Technology Annual*, Seoul, 2010.

Ministry of Science, ICT, and Future Planning, Press Release, March 7, 2014.

Ministry of Trade, Industry, and Energy, Press Release, January 7, 2015.

Moon, Pal Yong, "Evolution of Agricultural Products Pricing Policy", in *Modernization Process of Korean Agriculture*, Korea Agricultural Development Institute, 1980 (in Korean).

Moreira, M. M., *Industrialization, Trade and Market Failures*, St. Martins's Press, New York, 1995.

Nam, Sang-Woo and Kim, Jun-Il, "Macroeconomic Policies and Evolution", in Dong-Se Cha, Kwang Suk Kim, Dwight H. Perkins (eds.), *The Korean Economy* 1945–1995, Performance and Vision for the 21st Century, Korea Development Institute, 1997.

OECD, OECD Science, Technology and Industry Scoreboard 2007.

OECD, Economic Surveys Korea, 2014a.

OECD, Industry and Technology Policies in Korea, 2014b.

OECD, Social Expenditure-Aggregate Data, 2014c.

OECD, In It Together (Why Less Inequality Benefit All), 2015b.

OECD, Main Science and Technology Indicators, OECD, Vol. 2015a.

OECD, Society at a Glance, 2016.

Office of Presidential Secretariat, "Past and Present of Korean Economy: Implementation and Performance of Five-Year Development Plans", 1975 (in Korean).

Park, Chung Soo, "Performance of Service Sector Regulation and Future Policy Issues", *Regulation Research*, Vol. 24, 2015 (in Korean).

Park, Ki-Hong, "Information Technology Industries in Korea: Success and Challenge", in Workshop on Industrial Development and Restructuring, Korea Institute for Industrial Economics and Trade, 2003.

Radelet, S. C. and Sachs, J. D., The Onset of the East Asian Currency Crisis, Harvard Institute for International Development, Mimeo, 1998.

Rodrik, D., Grossman, G. and Norman, V., Getting Interventions Right: How South Korea and Taiwan grew rich, *Economic Policy*, Vol. 10, No. 20, 1995.

Ryu, Kyung Jun, "Analysis of Trends and Causes of Korea's Poverty Changes", KDI Policy Forum, July 13, 2009 (in Korean).

Sakong, Il, "Korea in the World Economy", Institute for International Economics, Washington, D.C., 1993.

Sakong, Il and Koh, Youngsun, "The Korean Economy: Six Decades of Growth and Development", The Committee for the Sixty-Year History of the Korean Economy, 2010.

Samsung Economic Research Institute, "SERI Economic Focus" Augus 4, 2009 (in Korean).

Shin, Kwang Sik, "Policy Issues and Directions for Chaebol Reform", Korea Development Institute, 2000 (in Korean).

Song, In Sang, *Rehabilitation and Growth*, 21st Century Books, Seoul, 1994 (in Korean).

Stern, J. J., Kim, Ji-hong, Perkins, D. H., and Yoo, Jung-ho, "Industrialization and the State: The Korean Heavy and Chemical Industry Drive", Harvard Institute for International Development, 1995.

Suh, Sang-Mok and Yeon, Ha-Cheong, Social Welfare during the Structural Adjustment Period in Korea, Working Paper 8604, Korea Development Institute, 1986.

Suh, Sang Mok, "Economic Growth and Change in Income Distribution: The Korean Case", Working Paper 8508, Korea Development Institute, 1985.

Suh, Suk Tai, "Import Substitution and Economic Development in Korea", Working Paper 7519, Korea Development Institute, 1975.

The Government of the Republic of Korea, Dynamic Korea — A Nation on the Move, 2004.

The World Bank, *The East Asian Miracle*, Oxford University Press, New York, 1993.

Wang, Yunjong and Zang, Hyoungsoo, "Adjustment reforms in Korea since the Financial Crisis", Policy Paper 98-02, Korea Institute for International Economic Policy, 1998.

Westphal, L. E. and Kim, Kwang Suk, "Korea", in B. Balassa (ed.), *Development Strategies in Semi-industrial Economies*, Johns Hopkins University Press, Baltimore, 1982.

Yang, Heeseung, "Industrial Technology Policy and R&D Practice in Korea", Korea Institue of S&T Evaluation and Planning, November, 2001.

Yang, Junsok, "Liberalization Measures in the Process of Korea's Corporate Restructuring", Korea Institute for International Economic Policy, 2002.

Yeo, Yoo Jin, Kim, Mi Kon, Kim, Tae Wan, Yang, Shi Hyun, and Choi, Hyun Soo, "Analysis of Trends and Sources of Poverty and Inequality", Korea Institute of Health and Social Welfare, 2005 (in Korean).

Yoo, Seong Min, "Evolution of Government-Business Interface in Korea: Progress to Date and Reform Agenda Ahead", Working Paper 9711, Korea Development Institute, November 1997.

Yoo, Seong Min and Lee, Sung Soon, "Evolution of Industrial Organization and Policy Response in Korea: 1945–1995", in Dong-Se Cha, Kwang Suk Kim, D. H. Perkins (eds.), *The Korean Economy 1945–1995: Performance and Vision for the 21st Century*, Korea Development Institute, 1997.

Yun, Heesuk, "Implications of Recent Income Distribution Trends on National Pension Reform Discussions, KDI Focus", Korea Development Institute, 2016.

Index

Odaka, K., 115
Off-Farm Household Income, 14
Office of Investment Ombudsman, 164
Office of Tax Administration, 9
Old-Age Dependency Ratio, 249
Operating Profit-to-Sales Ratio, 48
Outward direct investment, 165
Outward FDI, 165
outward-looking development strategy, 75, 152
outward-oriented development policy, 25, 54
outward-oriented industrialization policy, 7, 55
outward-oriented policy, 27
overall liberalization ratio, 158
overvalued exchange rate, 44

Park administration, 33
Park Chung Hee, 7
Park Chung Hee government, 198
Park, Chung Soo, 257, 262
Park Geun Hye government, 147, 233, 256
Park, Ki-Hong, 114
Park Kuen Hye government, 23
Paul Krugman, 174
per capita GNP, 7
performance- or reciprocity-based assistance, 77, 266
Plaza Accord, 96, 118, 121, 137, 139
Plaza Accord in 1985, 49
Pohang integrated steel mill (POSCO), 73, 111, 189
polarization of income distribution, 243
policy loans, 16, 20, 160
political democratization movement, 17, 64
Pony, 118
Post-War Reconstruction, 1
potential growth rate, 250
preferential policy loan, 33
President Chun Doo Hwan, 35, 156

President Kim, 161
President Kim Dae Jung, 22
President Kim Young Sam, 181
President Park, 10, 11, 72–74, 89, 91, 93, 102, 155, 264
President Park Chung Hee, 71
President Rhee Syngman, 31
Price Stabilization and Fair Trade Act, 144
private savings rate, 45
private spending on education, 203, 204
pro-market ideology, 19
product market regulation (PMR), 251, 261
profit-to-sales ratio, 47, 48
Project assistance, 3
protectionist policy, 76
Public and Private Spending on Education, 204
Public Enterprise Sector, 33
Public Law 480, 2
Public Offering Promotion Act, 52
public savings rate, 45
public spending on education, 203, 204

Radelet, S. C., 173
rate of return on assets and equity, 56
rate of return on capital, 46–48, 55
rationalization program, 95, 158
real effective exchange rate, 18, 20, 21, 175
reciprocity, 77
relative poverty rate, 237
Relative Poverty Ratio, 238
return on assets, 49, 57, 178
return on equity, 57, 178
revisionist, 26, 27
revisionist view, 25, 27
Rhee Syngman government, 7, 32, 198
rising technology protectionism, 96
Rodrik, D. 54, 61, 62
Roh Moo Hyun government, 23, 147, 233, 256, 261

Printed in the United States
By Bookmasters